JUNIOR CE

# KEY SKILLS IN

# ENGLISH

## Higher Level
### Third Edition
**Pat O'Shea**

Published in 2013 by Mentor Books

43 Furze Road
Sandyford Industrial Estate
Dublin 18
Tel: 01 – 2952112  Fax: 01 – 2952114

Website: www.mentorbooks.ie
Email: admin@mentorbooks.ie

Edited by: Treasa O'Mahony
Design & Layout: Mary Byrne

ISBN: 978-1-909417-06-9

© Pat O'Shea 2013

1 3 5 7 9 10 8 6 4 2

Printed in Ireland by W&G Baird Ltd

**MENTOR BOOKS**

# Contents
## Paper One

# Paper Two

## ACKNOWLEDGEMENTS

The publishers would like to thank the following for kind permission to reproduce material:

Anouska Christy, *Empire*; Bloomsbury Publishing for an extract from *Alphabetical Order* by Michael Frayn; Bob Englehart, Political Cartoons; Caitriona Giblin, *Irish Daily Star*; Colm O'Shea; HarperCollins UK for an extract from *Open: An Autobiography* by Andre Agassi; Karl Byrne, *Irish Daily Mail*; Lucas Alexander Whitely for an extract from *No Place Like* by Gene Kemp; Marie Glancy; Martyn Turner; Melissa Merciez from Universal Uclick for *Calvin & Hobbes*; Orion Publishing Group for an extract from *The Maeve Binchy Writers' Club* by Maeve Binchy; Penguin for an extract from *Slam* by Nick Hornby; Roísín Ingle, *The Irish Times*; Simon Community.

The Publishers have made every effort to trace and acknowledge the holders of copyright for material used in the book. In the event of a copyright holder having been omitted, the Publishers will come to a suitable arrangement at the first opportunity.

## DEDICATION
For Suvi: *'In summer, the song sings itself'*
(William Carlos Williams)

**Glossary (in yellow and bold):** Explanations of words highlighted in yellow throughout this book can be found in the glossary at the end of each chapter.

# Paper One

This paper is worth **180 marks**.
There are **four sections** in Paper One:

**Section One:**   Reading (**40 marks**)

**Section Two:**   Personal Writing (**70 marks**)

**Section Three:** Functional Writing (**30 marks**)

**Section Four:**   Media (**40 marks**)

### Section One: Reading
**In the exam:** Read the extract provided and
answer the 3 or 4 questions that follow.

### Section Two: Personal Writing
**In the exam:** From the list of titles provided,
choose one and write a prose composition on it.

### Section Three: Functional Writing
**In the exam:** From a choice of two options, select one
and write a composition in the style specified.

### Section Four: Media
**In the exam:** From a choice of two questions,
select one to answer.

# 1. Reading

## Contents

## Key Exam Skills: *Reading*

**1** **Find specific information in the text.**
All the required information to answer the questions will be found in the text provided.

**2** **Offer your opinions.**
Form an opinion based on information given in the text and share it with the reader.

**3** **Form impressions based on the text.**
Interpret ideas or feelings that are implied rather than stated by the text.

**4** **Comment on the style of the writer.**
You need to be able to comment on the style of a writer or the style of the writing used in the text.

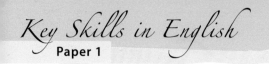

# 👓 SECTION 1: READING

It is recommended that you spend approximately **30 minutes** on this section of Paper One. It is worth **40 marks**. You will be asked to **read** an extract from a text which you will not have seen before and **answer** three to four questions based on it. You will not have time to write very long answers.

Pay attention to the marks allocated to each question as this will guide your length of answer. It is very important that you do not exceed the time limit. If you do exceed it, you may not have enough time to complete the entire paper. The questions are specifically designed to allow you to complete the section within the given time frame.

## (a) Types of Questions

There are usually four types of questions you could be asked to answer.

### 1. Find specific information in the text.

This is quite a straightforward task. The answer will be in the text and you must identify where it is and comment on this information if you are told to do so.

For example, in a past exam paper a question asked the candidate to seek specific information from the text:

> In the passage you have just read the writer mentions a number of elements that enable him to write.
> (a) Identify two of these elements that the writer says contribute to his writing. **(5)**
> (b) Basing your answer on the passage, explain how one of these elements contributes to the writing of his stories. **(10)**      **JC Exam Question**

In order to answer this question, you will need to find the specific elements mentioned by the writer and select two of them. Again basing your answer on what is said in the passage, you will have to explain how one of these elements contributes to the writing. **All** of the information you need can be found in the passage.

In another exam paper, two questions were directly related to finding specific information in the text, which was about keeping a goldfish as a pet:

> (a) Why does the writer recommend a goldfish as a pet? Support your answer with evidence from the first paragraph of the passage. **(10)**
> (b) What historical facts about goldfish do you learn from reading this passage? **(10)**
>      **JC Exam Question**

You need to read the questions very carefully to ensure that you are looking for the correct information. **All** of the required answers will be found in the information provided in the passage.

## 2. Offer your opinions.

Remember that you cannot *give* an opinion, you can only *form* an opinion or *share* your opinion with others. So when you are asked to offer your opinion, you are being asked to move beyond the information presented in the passage, form an opinion based on that information and share it with the reader (in this case, an examiner).

A recent exam paper had a question which required you to form and share your opinions:

> From your reading of the above extract, what do you think is the most significant challenge facing news journalists today? Explain your answer. **(15)**
>
> **JC Exam Question**

Notice that the wording of the question is different from the questions seeking specific information. The focus is now on what you *think* having read the passage carefully. However, while you are quite free to form your own opinions, it is not enough to just say what you think. You must give reasons or explanations for your opinions based on the passage.

A very careful reading of the question is required here. Notice that you are asked to base your opinion on your reading of the extract. The words 'most significant' are also very important in this question. You cannot ramble on about the different challenges. You must identify one and explain why you think it is the most important/significant one. An unsupported opinion will not achieve a high grade in the Junior Cert exam, so be very careful in your reading of each part of any question.

Another exam paper had a question requiring you to give a supported opinion:

> (a) In paragraph six Morpurgo says "the story will be written when the moment is right". From your reading of the passage what do you think he means by this comment? **(10)**
>
> (b) From what you have read above do you think that Morpurgo enjoys being a writer? Give reasons for your answer. **(15)**

As you can see, the ability to form and share an opinion – which you can justify from your reading of a passage – is a **KEY SKILL** in the Reading section of the exam. Read the passages and questions in exam papers from at least the last ten years and you will see how often this type of question appears. Therefore, it is important to practise this **KEY SKILL**.

You might find the following phrases useful when offering your opinion:

In my opinion... .
Having considered the evidence of the above passage, I think that...
Based on my reading of the passage, I believe that...
I think... because (give some factual basis for your opinion from the passage)

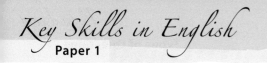

You can get a sharp focus in your answer by using the actual wording of the question to open your answer:

> From what I have read in the above passage, I do think that Morpurgo enjoys being a writer. One reason why I think this is because he says...
> (quote from passage) etc.

### 1. You Try It

Which of these sentences are facts and which are opinions? Explain your responses.

  (a)   My father came from Belfast but lived most of his life in Dublin.
  (b)   Dublin is not a nice city to live in nowadays.
  (c)   Mary Freeley is a very kind, considerate person.
  (d)   The first musical instrument I ever played was a concert flute.
  (e)   Levi Strauss was born in Germany in 1829.
  (f)   Modern parents do not train their children to behave properly in public.

Now take the sentences which you marked as opinions and develop each one into a paragraph which offers some factual evidence to support the opinion.

### 3. Form impressions based on the text.

Forming an impression is not quite the same thing as identifying information or forming an opinion. Writers can give you the impression of someone or something in order to influence the way you form your opinion. You can also form your own impression of the writer from the content of the passage.

In this type of question the **KEY SKILL** being examined is more **subtle.** You need to be aware of the connotations (suggestions or associations) of words. A simple example will make the differences clear:

**(a)** John Smith is a cruel person. This is being stated as a fact by the writer. It is specific information.

**(b)** In my opinion, John Smith is a cruel person. You would need to select the information that made you form such an opinion. You would not say that The writer gives me the opinion that John Smith is a cruel person because nobody can *give* you your own opinion.

However, you can say, The writer tries to give me the impression that John Smith is a cruel person. You would then need to identify the words, phrases, techniques etc. employed by the writer which influenced you in forming such an impression.

This kind of question asks you for ideas or feelings that are implied rather than stated by the text. You have to demonstrate the **KEY SKILL** of being able to infer meaning, which means reading between the lines. Therefore, you need to decide what someone thinks from *how* they express themselves, not just from *what* they say. Look very carefully at details and imagery used to work out what the writer feels about the subject and whether they are being serious, sarcastic or funny etc.

The Reading Section of a recent exam paper had a question which asked you to form an impression of the writer from your reading of what she had written:

> From reading this extract, what impression do you form of the writer, Maeve Binchy? **(10)**                                                                    **JC Exam Question**

As the passage was written by Maeve Binchy herself, you were obviously not *told* what to think of her! There is no specific information given about the writer's character. Your task here is to work out what kind of person you believe the writer to be based on what she says in the passage, the way she says it, the attitudes she displays etc. In the sample answer to this question on page 22, you can examine the way this is done.

The important thing to remember when offering an opinion or forming an impression is that you **must** give reasons from the text to justify your opinion or your impression.

---

## 2. You Try It

> *Her skin was a rich black that would have peeled like a plum if snagged, but then no one would have thought of getting close enough to Mrs. Flowers to ruffle her dress, let alone snag her skin. She didn't encourage familiarity. She wore gloves too.*
>
> **From:** *I Know Why the Caged Bird Sings* by Maya Angelou

Paying close attention to details and word choice, explain the impression you form of Mrs. Flowers from this short extract.

---

### 4. Comment on the style of the writer.

You need to be able to comment on the style of a writer or the style of writing used in a passage. Style refers to *how* something is written rather than what it is about (although these two things are linked). One of the **KEY SKILLS** you need to develop is being able to identify points of style and understand why a writer uses specific techniques in different types of writing. You also need to be able to comment on the effect on the reader of various points of style.

Questions on style occur frequently in the Junior Cert exam. The following have appeared in recent exam papers.

(a) This passage is written in an autobiographical style. Identify two aspects of this style evident in the passage and comment on their effect on you as a reader.

(b) Darwin had an eye for detail. Briefly discuss this view with reference to the passage.

(c) Did you find this passage entertaining? Give reasons for your answer.

(d) Basing your answer on the way the passage is written, how serious do you think the writer is in his criticism of the behaviour of cinema audiences?   **JC Exam Questions**

A good way to approach questions on style is to think of the word **RAFT**.

R = **Reason** for the writing. Is it to argue? persuade? describe? inform? advise? narrate? etc.

A = **Audience.** Who is going to read it? The language used should be appropriate for the readership.

F = **Format.** The format of writing is connected to the reason for the writing. An informative piece (e.g. a newspaper article) would not be organised in the same way as a descriptive passage of writing (e.g. an extract from a novel). Also look at such features as sentence length, syntax (word order) and any specific presentational devices such as headings, sub-headings, illustrations, bullets, boxed text etc.

T = **Tone.** The tone or atmosphere created by the writer should be appropriate. Tone is conveyed through the language used. The tone of a passage could be serious, disturbing, funny, light-hearted, mock-serious, entertaining, poignant, nostalgic, cynical etc.

Each of these aspects affects the style of a passage and the techniques chosen by the writer to maximise the effect on the readers. Keep **RAFT** in mind when discussing style.

## (b) Style Features
**The following is a list of the most common features of style to look for in different types of writing:**

- **Word choice:** Are the words used in the passage simple, complex, archaic (old words and expressions not often used in modern writing) or jargonistic (using terms specific to a certain subject, e.g. data, spreadsheet, gigabytes etc. in passages on computer or technology subjects)?

- **Descriptive style:** Examine any words or phrases which appeal to the senses. Look closely at details to see how they build a picture in the mind of the reader. Writers often use details to harness the power of words. Descriptive writing **stimulates** and captures the reader's attention and can create a lasting impact.

- **Formal or colloquial:** The writer's decision to use a chatty, casual style (colloquial) or a more formal, serious style will depend on the reason for the writing and the potential readership.

- **Sentence length and paragraphs:** Does the writer vary the length of sentences or does he/she prefer long or short sentences? Good writing usually has a variety of sentence lengths which creates different effects. Are paragraphs varied or similar in length? Are any paragraphs remarkable for being short or unusually long?

- **Personal or Impersonal:** This will be obvious from the use or absence of personal pronouns such as **I** and **We** when addressing the reader. A personal style gives a sense of intimacy between the writer and reader. This encourages more engagement with the subject matter. Impersonal writing is more suited to arguing a point or giving information.

● **Argumentative:** Good argumentative writing uses points based on facts to logically develop an argument and reach a **rational** conclusion. Personal opinion is absent in order to avoid **bias**. Emotional turns of phrase or exaggerated statements are also avoided. The **counter-argument** or opposite viewpoint is treated with respect and not dismissed as nonsense; however, it is **refuted** by the writer. Look for the following: evidence of research; specific, factual information; the inclusion of quotes from experts; appeals to the reader's intellect rather than their feelings.

● **Persuasive techniques:** Language of persuasion tends to be **emotive** and often uses hyperbole (exaggeration), e.g. 1. It is completely ridiculous to have a landline in your house – everybody has a mobile phone nowadays. 2. Letters take forever to arrive in the post.

Persuasive arguments often use exclamations or orders to persuade the reader, e.g. This cannot be tolerated any longer or We need to address this issue as a matter of extreme urgency.

In order to persuade the reader to adopt a point of view on a subject, the writer may use **rhetorical questions** for effect, e.g. Do you think money grows on trees? or triadic patterns (grouping three words for effect), e.g. The young, the rich and the famous; The good, the bad and the ugly. Unlike argument, persuasion attempts to manipulate the reader emotionally to accept the beliefs or opinions of the writer.

● **Reflective:** This style of writing lacks the highly emotive language often used in persuasion. Phrases which encourage thought and consideration are commonly found in this style. Words and phrases such as perhaps, probably, on the other hand, it seems are used instead.

● **Autobiographical:** This type of writing is always written in the first person and is therefore **subjective** in nature. It is based on personal recollection and narrative. Watch out for personal **insights** and **anecdotes** and examine how the writer adds detail and colour to make events more interesting and **compelling** for the reader.

● **Imagery: Metaphors**, **similes** and other forms of imagery enhance autobiographical writing. Ask yourself if the writing sounds like an authentic voice (does it sound real?). An informal approach is usual in this style of writing. The tone created can be **nostalgic**, disillusioned, positive or negative etc.

● **Informative:** This type of style is used to **convey** information in a clear, factual manner. In the Reading section of Paper One, you might find this style used in articles and reports taken from newspapers or news websites. Although this style deals with factual information, there is often a persuasive element which can influence the reader to adopt a particular attitude/stance. For example, information in a report which discusses poverty or hunger can be organised in such a way as to provoke a strong emotional response in the reader – not because the writer has used emotive or persuasive techniques, but because the facts are presented in a blunt manner and are shocking in themselves.

13

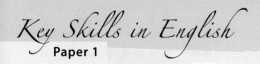

## 3. You Try It

Identify any of the points of style listed on pages 12 - 13 in the following extracts. Some sentences may have more than one feature.

(a) *I was a lonely child, growing up in a small village in the West of Ireland, at a time when poverty was the norm. I often felt hunger gnawing my insides like a greedy beast, while the chill of winter invaded my very bones.*

(b) *Now is the time to stop talking and to start acting! We must stand up for what we know is right and not allow the plague of greed and intolerance to spread in our land.*

(c) *A recent survey conducted by the Irish Independent newspaper found that 48% of children under the age of fourteen had consumed alcohol.*

(d) *Do you want to live in a society which denies freedom of choice and demands conformity to outdated, meaningless, stubborn beliefs?*

(e) *Many of us can reflect on what would have happened if we had made a different decision at important points in our lives. I have been considering this question in identifying two turning points in my life.*

(f) *As a youngster I was always against hunting in any form, but when I became a farmer and saw the horrific injuries inflicted on lambs by foxes, I quickly changed my mind.*

(g) *I had my bike nicked, and when I saw the scum who did it I thought I'd scare them, so I went into my house, opened a kitchen drawer and got a knife.*

(h) *As the words left my mouth I knew it was bad. The jury sat saucer-eyed staring at me in disbelief.*

## (c) Exam Focus

In every section of the Junior Cert exam you will be rewarded for:

**Relevant answers:** This means that you must show that you have read the question properly, understand the task in each question and can make relevant points and support them from the text in your answer.

**Well-structured answers:** This means that you have a clear, logical method for answering questions. Another way of saying **well-structured** is **well-organised**. You should aim to have (1) a brief introduction; (2) one developed, relevant point per paragraph; (3) smooth movement or linking from one paragraph to the next; and (4) a brief conclusion. The length of your answers will be related to the marks being awarded for the answer and the type of question being asked. Not all answers need to be the same length.

**Clarity of expression:** This means that you use language which is clear. You will lose marks for repeating words or phrases, using fussy and artificial language and including boring, overused **clichés**. You will gain marks for using variation in your word choice, choosing apt and interesting ways of expressing yourself and displaying a capacity to come across as a unique voice. The most important point to remember is that what you write must make complete sense to the reader. You can avoid many pitfalls by keeping control over the length of your sentences. Long, rambling sentences often lose clarity.

**An appropriate tone:** This means that you must choose the correct tone to suit your readership. For example, if you were asked to write an article for your school magazine on the subject of school uniforms, you would use a different tone to the one you would use if asked to make a speech to the Board of Management on the same topic. The article would be informal and chatty, while the speech would be more formal and serious.

**Good grammar, spelling and punctuation:** You cannot afford to be careless about correct grammar, spelling and punctuation. You need to practise proofreading your work. Make lists of errors which occur frequently in your writing and revise the appropriate rules thoroughly. For example, if you repeatedly forget how and when to use the apostrophe, you need to sort it out before you sit your exam. Look up the rule, make sure you understand it and then re-read all your work, carefully checking for that one error. A list of common errors and how to avoid them can be found at the back of this book on pages 237-248.

## (d) Step-by-Step Approach to Answering Questions

1. Always begin by reading the **introduction** to the passage, as it will contain essential information to help you understand the **context** of the passage.

2. Next, read the questions **before** you read the passage itself. This will help you to focus your reading and save time. Notice the differences in the questions in order to avoid any overlap or repetition in your answers.

3. Note how many marks are being awarded for each question. Even if all questions get the same marks, it is not essential, or even advisable, to write the same length of response for each question. The length of your answer will be related to the question and the time at your disposal. Just make sure that you do not exceed 30 minutes for this section.

4. Highlight the **key words** or **task** in each question. This is where having a few coloured highlighter pens may come in useful. You could use one colour to highlight the important words/tasks in the first question and use the same colour to highlight the parts of the text which you are going to use to provide support or evidence for that answer. You can do the same with the other questions, using a different colour each time. This will help you save time by making your evidence or support stand out clearly when organising your answers.

5. Beginning with the first question, carefully re-read it and then read the passage. Have your highlighter or pen ready to mark the words, phrases or sentences that you will be quoting as support for your answer. Keep the focus on the first question only and make sure that you are not straying into parts of the other questions.

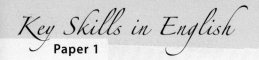

6. Now you are ready to organise your answer. Try to think of three or four relevant points, which are a direct response to the question asked. Make sure that you can quote from or refer to the passage to support your answer.

7. You are now ready to write your answer. Open with a brief summary of your points. Write one paragraph for each point, supporting with relevant quotation. Conclude with a brief reference back to the question.

8. Repeat this pattern for each question asked.

9. Make sure that you include a personal approach in your answers where possible. For example: I think this because..., In my opinion..., Personally, I dislike this character because... . Such personal comments are essential when you are asked for your impression or your opinion in the question.

## (e) Putting It Into Practice

Bearing in mind all of the points listed on page 15 and above, let us see how they can be put into practice on the Reading Section of an exam paper.

Remember: Always begin by reading the **introduction** to the extract. We need this information to help us to understand the context (background) of the passage.

Remember: Read the questions **before** you read the passage itself to sharpen focus and save time. Take note of the differences in the questions in order to avoid any overlap or repetition in your answers.

Remember: Highlight the **key words** or **task** in each question. The text will now be colour-coded/underlined/circled/ticked. Colour coding is used in this example, but you can use any system you prefer. Keep the focus on the first question only and make sure that you are not straying into parts of the other questions. Repeat this procedure for each question.

Read the following passage and then answer the questions that follow.

**Introduction**
The following edited extract is adapted from *The Maeve Binchy Writers' Club*. The book arose from a writing course, which aimed to help aspiring writers start and finish a book. Each week successful writer Maeve Binchy wrote a letter to the students on the course sharing her thoughts on a different aspect of writing. In the adapted extract, Maeve gives advice on telling a story.

**Note:** In the example on pages 17-18, the questions appear <u>before</u> the extract. In the Junior Cert exam, the questions appear <u>after</u> the extract.

**Answer the following four questions:**

1. **What elements** of story writing does Maeve Binchy **offer advice** on in this extract? **(10)**

2. As a regular reader of books, **which element of story writing,** identified by Maeve Binchy, **do you consider to be the most important?** Explain your choice. **(10)**

3. **Explain in your own words,** what **you think** the writer means when she says in paragraph 4, '...writing was not a matter of painting by numbers.' **(10)**

4. From reading this extract, **what impression do you form of the writer,** Maeve Binchy? **(10)**                                                                    **JC Exam Questions**

*Dear Writers' Club members,*

*I can't tell you what story to write. Nobody can do that except you. There is no point in telling anyone else what to write about. But I can share with you some of the advice I got along the way from wise editors, men and women whose job it is to know what people like and to keep us writers somehow on the rails.*

*They say that when beginning a story you should always try to catch people at some interesting juncture of their lives, like when they have to make a choice or decision, or when someone has betrayed them, or at the start of love or the end of love. It's better to come across them at some kind of crisis than in the middle of a long, lazy summer where nothing happens.*

*The notion of change is important in a story. It would be a dull tale indeed if the hero took no notice of the disintegration of his family, if he was the same unaltered dullard after four hundred pages. The reader would feel fairly short changed.*

*They told me that we must be interested in the hero or heroine – that doesn't mean making the person into a walking saint or goody-goody, but it does mean giving them a strong and memorable personality. There is no point whatsoever in spending pages and pages describing someone who is a dithering, dull kind of person without purpose, views or motivation. We have to care enough about the people to follow them through to the last page. When I heard this I began to panic a bit and asked humbly what kind of person might be interesting enough to hold the reader's attention. I wouldn't be able to create Captain Ahab, the man who pursued Moby Dick, or Rhett Butler who didn't give a damn in Gone with the Wind. But I was told that writing wasn't a matter of painting by numbers. They couldn't just create some formula leaving me to join up the dots. I had to think, and work out the kind of people whose lives and adventures I would be interested in myself. This way I might be on the way to make others interested in them too.*

*In my case I was interested in people who were told that if they were good they would be happy, and therefore disappointed when it didn't always turn out like that. So I worked out that, in a way, people*

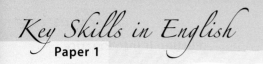

create their own happiness not just by being good, whatever that is, but by seeking opportunities, taking chances, taking charge of their own destiny. It interested me for a start, and then kept me going. It could work for you too, if you found a theory around which to base a story.

Another good piece of advice I got was to think of the story as a journey. Something happens to the main character at the start, and we follow him or her dealing with it, or not dealing with it, or ignoring it, or making it worse. Whatever. Now I don't mean a literal journey, they don't even have to leave home. But they have to progress, be different people for better or worse at the end. The man who thinks his son is on hard drugs, his colleagues in the office on the take or his own gambling out of control, has to do something. You can't leave him static in the same plight at the end of chapter fourteen as he was at the outset. The woman who has had a bad medical diagnosis, a faithless friend, an unjust accusation of shoplifting or proof that her brother is a murderer must have taken steps of some sort over whatever it is. She can't just sit there page after page letting it all wash over her.

They also say that pace is important when you are telling a story. Again, nobody can hold your hand over this, but I have found that at the beginning it helps to make a kind of chart of the book chapter by chapter, giving myself orders like, 'By the end of chapter two we must know that she cannot afford to pay the rent and will be evicted', and then, 'By the end of chapter three we must know that her rent will be paid for her, but at a price.' If you do this in advance it stops you dawdling about till you're ready and generally dragging the thing out and making it endless. There is no right or wrong pace, it's up to you. A gentle lyrical story will call for one kind of speed, a fast moving action thriller another. But there's no harm being aware of it.

I hope it's all going well for you and that you are getting your ten pages a week done.

Maeve.

---

**Answer Plan**

### Question 1

As I have identified my support for the first question (highlighted in red), I am now in a position to organise my answer. The elements I am going to refer to are:

- characters at interesting time in their lives; must be strong and memorable
- importance of change in character
- story is a journey for main character which we follow – it has a theme
- pace is important to maintain interest and to ensure your story makes sense

You can briefly jot down a rough plan, like this one, for each of the four questions, but do not write a detailed plan. You will not have time to do that. Instead, let your highlighting of key words and phrases guide your short plan for each answer.

## Sample Answer

**Question 1:** What elements of story writing does Maeve Binchy offer advice on in this extract?

| ANSWER | COMMENTARY |
|---|---|
| In this extract Maeve Binchy offers very practical advice to writers. She emphasises the importance of the elements of characterisation, plot, theme, pace and planning. | *Opening paragraph sums up main points concerning elements of story writing.* |
| It is clear that characterisation is an element of great importance. Binchy advises writers to 'try to catch people at some interesting juncture of their lives' when they are experiencing some kind of 'crisis'. She insists that 'we must be interested in the hero or heroine' and remember him/her as having a 'strong, memorable personality'. | *First point is now dealt with in a single paragraph. Notice how the wording of the question is used and the way the relevant quotation is 'knit-in' to the sentences and not just tacked on to the end of the point.* |
| Good characterisation is linked by Binchy to the element of plot. If we 'think of the story as a journey' which the main characters undertake, we can follow and see how they deal with the challenges and obstacles which they encounter and how they change as a result of their experiences. She advises writers to remember that the 'notion of change is important in a story' and creates an interesting plot. | *The next point is now introduced and linked to the previous point. Again, the key words **element** and **advice** are used in the paragraph to show clear focus on the task.* |
| Finally, the writer refers to the element of pace and its importance for good narrative writing – 'pace is important when you are telling a story'. There is no point in 'dragging the thing out and making it endless'. In order to control pace, the writer suggests that her fellow writers could 'make some kind of chart' and know by advance planning what is going to happen in each chapter. | *The final point is now introduced and developed with ample quotation from the text.* |
| Maeve Binchy offers advice to writers on each of these important elements of good story writing | *The concluding paragraph briefly sums up. Notice again how the wording of the question is incorporated to give a sharp focus.* |

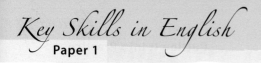
## Sample Answer

**Question 2:** As a regular reader of books, which element of story writing, identified by Maeve Binchy, do you consider to be the most important?   Explain your choice. **(10)**

### ANSWER

As a regular reader of books I consider that Binchy's point concerning the changes which are brought about in a character as a result of experience is the most important element of story writing.

In practically every one of my favourite books  something does 'happen' to the main character 'at the start' and I have often been **enthralled** by the way they deal with the situation. I enjoy following them on their 'journey' of self-discovery and learning how they become 'different people for better or worse at the end'. For example, in the novel 'The Adventures of Huckleberry Finn' by Mark Twain, the main character  goes on a 'journey' which the reader follows and he makes 'progress'.  At the end, Huck is not the same character as he was at the outset.  He has matured and learnt something from his experiences. He does not remain 'static'.

Although Huckleberry Finn goes on an actual journey, I can understand what Maeve Binchy means when she says that the journey need not be a 'literal journey'. It can be a journey of the mind or spirit. The important thing is that a character faced with a **dilemma** must take 'steps of some sort' to resolve the dilemma. These 'steps' are what maintains my interest. I want to know what is going to happen next. I do not think that anybody would be very interested in a story where the main character just lets everything 'wash' over them! How boring would that be?

In conclusion, I consider character development to be the most important aspect of story writing as it is so central to theme and plot. No other technique could compensate for poor characterisation in my opinion, as **credibility** would be seriously **compromised.**

### COMMENTARY

*Notice how the opening uses the actual wording of the question. An element of story writing is clearly identified and it is linked to a point made by Maeve Binchy.*

*In the previous paragraph, the writer implied that he/she is a 'regular reader of books'. This is strengthened by the reference to a classic novel to clarify the point. Notice the use of direct quotation and close reference to the text. Also notice the appropriate, very personal tone of the response.*

*Notice the smooth link to the next paragraph and the close reference to the text to support the argument.*

*The short conclusion restates the opening point, again identifying and explaining why it is the 'most important' element in the opinion of the writer.*

## Sample Answer

**Question 3:** Explain in your own words, what you think the writer means when she says in paragraph 4, '...writing was not a matter of painting by numbers.' **(10)**

**ANSWER**

When the writer says that '...writing was not a matter of painting by numbers', she is referring to the fact that good writers do not stick to a strict formula when creating characters or plots.

Painting by numbers is a system where painters follow a numbered pattern. Each number represents a colour and all the painter has to do is fill it in and the painting just **materialises** automatically. However, there is very little creativity or skill required to follow such a formula. The writer is making the same point about the craft of writing – there is no single formula for success.

Given the other aspects of good story writing which Binchy describes in the rest of the passage, I think it is true to say that by using this phrase she is highlighting the need to have an imaginative and individual approach to writing.

**COMMENTARY**

*The opening refers directly to the phrase which needs to be explained and gives a brief summary of the meaning.*

*This paragraph explains the phrase in more detail and is consistent with what has been said in the opening. The writer is using his/her own words and not relying on the wording of the passage.*

*The conclusion refers back to the phrase which has been explained, sums up the explanation and again places it in the context of the entire passage.*

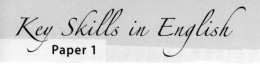
## Sample Answer

**Question 4:** From reading this extract, what impression do you form of the writer, **Maeve Binchy?** (10)

**ANSWER**

**COMMENTARY**

From my reading of the extract, I get the impression that Maeve Binchy is an experienced writer who is not only generous, practical and helpful in the advice she gives to aspiring writers but who is also honest and humble.

*This opening paragraph sums up the character **traits** of Maeve Binchy. Several descriptions are included – experienced, generous, practical, helpful, honest and lacking in **condescension.***

There is no doubt that Binchy is an experienced writer, given that she is a 'successful writer' who advises other aspiring writers and has directed writing courses on which a book has been based. All these details suggest that she is experienced.

*This paragraph develops the first point with close reference to the introduction and other information from the body of the text.*

I also get the impression that Binchy is a generous, helpful person who understands the need for practical guidance. She is willing to 'share ... some of the advice' that her editors have given her in the past and hopes that 'it could work' for the aspiring writers also. Her practicality is obvious when she suggests that writers could make 'a kind of chart of the book chapter by chapter'.

*This paragraph combines three related traits of Maeve Binchy and uses the text to provide a basis for forming the impression. Note how the quotations are inserted into the sentences and not just 'tacked on' at the end. This is the best way to use quotation in this type of answer.*

Particularly impressive is the fact that Binchy is such an honest individual who does not address new writers in a condescending manner. She is quite open about the fact that she had to learn the craft of writing 'along the way' and was, at times, inclined to 'panic a bit' and needed to 'humbly ask' for advice. She does not pretend that she can create good writers: 'I can't tell you what story to write' and 'nobody can hold your hand over this'. But she is eager to offer help and relevant advice. Her lack of condescension is apparent when she addresses the new writers as 'us writers' which suggests that she sees them as her equals, despite the vast differences in experience and success which exist between them.

*A particularly impressive trait is identified in this paragraph and is developed in some detail from the evidence of the text.*

In conclusion, my impression of Maeve Binchy is extremely positive due to the character traits revealed in the passage.

*The conclusion is short but sums up the impression formed.*

## OVER TO YOU

1. Now that you have seen the **Step-by Step Approach** in action, get as much practice as you can with past exam papers, examples from textbooks and as many different types of writing as you can find in newspapers, magazines, internet sites etc.

2. The passage below is a piece of autobiographical writing. Read it carefully and answer the questions which follow.

The following edited extract is taken from *Open: An Autobiography* written by the famous tennis player, Andre Agassi. Agassi is about to play in the US Open while suffering from a painful congenital back problem.

# pen An Autobiography

*One thing I've learned in twenty-nine years of playing tennis: Life will throw everything but the kitchen sink in your path, and then it will throw the kitchen sink. It's your job to avoid the obstacles. If you let them stop you or distract you, you're not doing your job, and failing to do your job will cause regrets that paralyze you more than a bad back.*

*I lie on the bed with a glass of water and read. When my eyes get tired I click on the TV. Tonight, Round Two of the U.S. Open! Will this be Andre Agassi's farewell? My face flashes on the screen. A different face than the one in the mirror. My game face. I study this new reflection of me in the distorted mirror that is TV and my anxiety rises another click or two. Was that the final commercial? The final time CBS will ever promote one of my matches?*

*I can't escape the feeling that I'm about to die.*

*It's no accident, I think, that tennis uses the language of life. Advantage, service, fault, break, love, the basic elements of tennis are those of everyday existence, because every match is a life in miniature. Even the structure of tennis, the way the pieces fit inside one another like Russian nesting dolls, mimics the structure of our days. Points become games become sets become tournaments, and it's all so tightly connected that any point can become the turning point. It reminds me of the way seconds become minutes become hours, and any hour can be our finest. Or darkest. It's our choice.*

*But if tennis is life, then what follows tennis must be the unknowable void. The thought makes me cold.*

*Now I can take a nap. At thirty-six, the only way I can play a late match, which could go past midnight, is if I get a nap beforehand. Also, now that I know roughly who I am, I want to close my eyes and hide from it. When I open my eyes, one hour has passed. I say aloud, It's time. No more hiding. I step into the shower again, but this shower is different from the morning shower. The afternoon shower is always longer — twenty-two minutes, give or take — and it's not for waking up or getting clean. The afternoon shower is for encouraging myself, coaching myself.*

*Tennis is the sport in which you talk to yourself. No athletes talk to themselves like tennis players. Pitchers, golfers, goalkeepers, they mutter to themselves, of course, but tennis players talk to themselves — and answer. In the heat of a match, tennis players look like lunatics in a public square, ranting and swearing and conducting Lincoln-Douglas debates with their alter egos. Why? Because tennis is so damned lonely. Only boxers can understand the loneliness of tennis players — and yet boxers have their corner men and managers. Even a boxer's opponent provides a kind of companionship, someone he can grapple with and grunt at. In tennis you stand face-to-face with the enemy, trade blows with him, but never touch him or talk to him, or anyone else. The rules forbid a tennis player from even talking to his coach while on the court. People sometimes mention the track-and-field runner as a comparably lonely figure, but I have to laugh. At least the runner can feel and smell his opponents. They're inches away. In tennis you're on an island. Of all the games men and women play, tennis is the closest to solitary confinement, which inevitably leads to self-talk, and for me the self-talk starts here in the afternoon shower. This is when I begin to say things to myself, crazy things, over and over, until I believe them. For instance, that a quasi-cripple can compete at the U.S. Open. That a thirty-six-year-old man can beat an opponent just entering his prime. I've won 869 matches in my career, fifth on the all-time list, and many were won during the afternoon shower.*

*With the water roaring in my ears — a sound not unlike twenty thousand fans — I recall particular wins. Not wins the fans would remember, but wins that still wake me at night. Squillari in Paris. Blake in New York. Pete in Australia. Then I recall a few losses. I shake my head at the disappointments. I tell myself that tonight will be an exam for which I've been studying twenty-nine years. Whatever happens tonight, I've already been through it at least once before. If it's a physical test, if it's mental, it's nothing new.*

*Please let this be over.*

*I don't want it to be over.*

*I start to cry. I lean against the wall of the shower and let go.*

Answer the following **three** questions:

1. What, according to Andre Agassi, are the negative aspects of being a tennis player? **(10)**

2. What impression do you form of the writer from reading the above extract? **(15)**

3. Comment on three features of style evident in the extract and their impact on the reader. **(15)**

# Glossary

**anecdotes:** short stories used to illustrate a point

**bias:** taking sides, prejudice

**clichés:** worn-out over-used phrases or sayings

**compelling:** persuading or almost forcing the reader to agree

**compromised:** weakened or harmed

**condescension:** to act in a way that suggests you believe you are superior to or better than others

**context:** background

**convey:** make known

**counter-argument:** the opposing argument

**credibility:** capable of being believed

**dilemma:** having to make a choice while being uncertain

**emotive:** expressing or generating emotion

**enthralled:** to be spellbound by something

**insights:** being able to understand somethings in a deeper way

**materialises:** becomes real

**metaphors:** images which compare two things without using 'like' or 'as'

**nostalgic:** feeling a longing for the past

**rational:** reasonable

**refuted:** proved wrong

**rhetorical questions:** asking questions simply for effect, no answer expected.

**similes:** images which compare two things using 'like' or 'as'

**static:** showing little or no change

**stimulates:** encourages interest or activity

**subjective:** from a personal point of view

**subtle:** not immediately obvious

**traits:** distinguishing features, characteristics

# 2. Personal Writing

## Contents

## Key Exam Skills: *Personal Writing*

**1 Choose a title from the list provided.**
Remember: if a format is specified (e.g. Write a speech), you must stick to that format.

**2 Create a plan for your composition.**
This can be a quick spider diagram, a mind map or even a question & answer plan.
Examples of these plans are provided in this section.

**3 Write an introduction.**
You want your opening paragraph to make a strong impression on the reader and to 'hook' them into reading more.

**4 Develop the essay.**
Your plan will help to keep you on track when writing the body of your essay.
The genre (type of writing) will also have a big influence on how you develop your piece of writing.

**5 Write a conclusion.**
Your conclusion is just as important as your opening paragraph. If possible, try to create some kind of link to the opening to give a sense of unity to your piece.

# SECTION 2: PERSONAL WRITING

It is recommended that you spend approximately **60** minutes on this section of Paper One. This section offers you your best opportunity to write a creative and personal response. It is also worth the highest marks of any section in the Junior Cert exam: **70 marks**. You will be given a wide choice of titles and you must write a piece on one of them.

To ensure you choose the right option for you on the day of the exam, you should experiment with different types of writing and read as many examples as you can. You can then select the format or style which most appeals to you.

Except where a style is clearly stated (e.g. *Write a **short story*** or *Write a **speech** etc*), you may choose the **genre** of writing you would like to use for your essay, e.g. persuasive, descriptive, narrative/short story, etc.

**Note:** *The words* **composition, essay** *and* **personal writing** *are generally interchangeable in this section.*

The examiner will mark your essay by impression. He/she will decide which grade the essay is worth and will award marks accordingly. Examiners are also instructed to cross-check their results by using a Marking Breakdown system. This system divides the marks in the following manner:

| | |
|---|---|
| Content | 20 |
| Structure | 15 |
| Expression | 30 |
| Mechanics | 5 |
| Total | 70 |

In order to do well in this section, you need to pay close attention to each of the above divisions of marks. Notice how expression is worth the highest marks, followed by content, structure and mechanics (spelling, punctuation etc).

**Content:** This refers to **what** you write. The content should be **relevant** to the title or the task, create interest and demonstrate originality of approach.

**Structure:** This refers to the way you **organise** your sentences and paragraphs and whether you present your ideas in a logical, orderly way or not. The opening, body and conclusion of the essay should demonstrate your control over your writing. Planning is very important in order to do well in this area.

**Expression:** This refers to **how** you express yourself or communicate your ideas. Your **clarity** of expression, variety of word choice, original use of imagery or clever turns of phrase are all important in order to achieve a high mark here.

**Mechanics:** This refers to accuracy of spelling, punctuation and grammar. Although this may seem unimportant because it only receives 5 marks, you must remember that the clarity of your expression can be badly affected by poor mechanics.

# (a) Step-By-Step Approach

Read carefully through the list of options below. These options were available in the Personal Writing section of a recent Junior Cert exam paper. A step-by-step approach to choosing and answering one of these options is provided in this section.

*1. Music in my life*

This title allows for a variety of responses. You could discuss the role music plays in your life, write a short story in the first person (i.e. use **I** as the narrator of the story) keeping the importance of music central to the plot, write a letter to your parents or music teacher thanking them for making music such an important part of your life, create a series of diary entries which clearly show the role music plays in your life, imagine giving an interview on the subject etc.

**2. Write a composition beginning with the lines** *'I was a very cute toddler; I've seen the photographs.'*

Again, this allows for a variety of responses including a narrative (story) essay, descriptive composition etc. The given sentence should be used as the opening of the essay, as instructed.

*3. The beauty of quiet places*

This option also allows for a variety of responses inspired by the title, but you need strong descriptive skills to write effectively on this subject.

*4. My most useful possessions*

This allows for a variety of responses inspired by the title. An important word here is *useful*. It must be addressed in the essay. However, a broad interpretation of the word *useful* is allowed. For example, what you consider to be useful might seem totally useless to most people. Don't be afraid to be original!

*5. You and some friends enter a major talent competition. Write a series of diary entries recording your experiences.*

Here you must use a diary format and style. You need to stick with this format for the entire essay. (An example of this style is provided on pages 59-62.)

*6. Write a speech for OR against the motion: 'All teenagers should have to participate in sport'.*

Your composition will need to show awareness of a style appropriate to the delivery of a speech. You cannot decide to write this as a short story or in any other format because the wording specifically requires a speech.

*7. A talent I would like to have*

This allows for a variety of responses inspired by the title. The word *talent* is a key word which allows for a broad interpretation but which must be addressed clearly in the essay.

*8. Write a story which includes the words, 'I wish I had listened'.*

While you may choose from a variety of ways to tell a story, it must be a narrative (i.e. a story) inspired by the title. The given sentence must be included, but it can be used anywhere in the story (unlike in Option 2).

From an examination of the titles listed on page 29, you can see that options 5, 6 and 8 tell you which format to use, while the other titles allow you to choose a format which appeals to you. Notice how the word *Write* usually precedes the more specific titles.

If you look at past exam essay titles, you will see that every year a wide variety of options are offered. There is certain to be a title that you will be able to write about. You might even enjoy it!

## 1. You Try It

Read the following titles and explain how each one could be written using a different format.

**(a)** The importance of friends in my life

**(b)** Write a story involving a case of mistaken identity.

**(c)** An undiscovered paradise

**(d)** I could hardly sleep with excitement. Only three more days to go...

**(e)** Everyone deserves a second chance.

So, let's put the step-by-step approach into action.

### Step One: Choose Title

The first step is to choose the title which most interests and appeals to you. Read each option before you decide. Many of the titles allow you to adopt the format with which you feel most comfortable (e.g. speech, diary entry). Make sure that you look at each key word in the title and in the stated task.

Let us take Option 6 from the options listed on page 29.

*Write a speech for OR against the motion: 'All teenagers should have to participate in sport'.*

### Step Two: Plan

Planning means that you think about the title, choose how you will approach it and organise your response. The examiner will expect you to present your ideas in a logical manner. Doing this will ensure a higher grade.

Think very carefully about the wording of the question and break it up, if necessary, to make sure that you have not left out any important element.

#### (i) Thinking and Organising

(a)   The task is to write **a speech.** You cannot use any other type of format.

(b)   It must be either **for** or **against.** You cannot write a discussion showing all the pros and cons while avoiding a clear position on the topic. In other words, this is a debate, not a discussion. You must clearly agree or disagree with the motion (the proposal). However, you must acknowledge that there is another viewpoint but show why your position is more rational.

(c)   It is a good idea to break down the wording of the motion into smaller phrases so that you are really clear about what the motion means.

- **All teenagers:** It isn't teenagers, most teenagers or the majority of teenagers: what do you think about the word *All*?
- **should have to:** This suggests compulsion, i.e. not giving people a choice. Is that right or fair?
- **participate in sport:** The word *participate* could mean different things. Can people participate without actually having to play the sport? How could they do this? Suppose the wording was *compete in sport*?

As you can see, by breaking up the wording of the task and thinking about each aspect, the writer has actually already started to explore their ideas.

### (ii) Brainstorming

Brainstorming means writing down every idea that comes into your head very quickly after you have analysed the title. You can use different methods in your brainstorm.

(a) **A spider diagram:** You put the title in the middle and create 'legs' which represent your ideas (this spider can have as many legs as you like!). When you finish your diagram, you choose the ideas you plan to use and arrange them in a logical order. Your final plan might look something like this:

**Spider diagram**

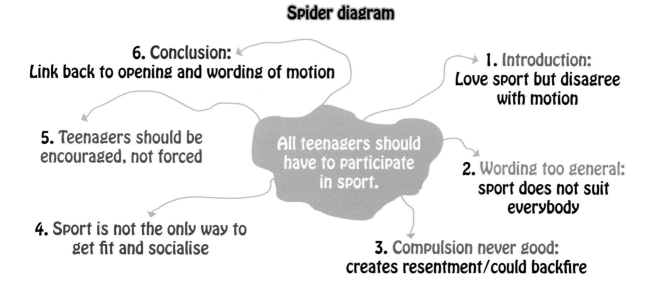

6. Conclusion:
Link back to opening and wording of motion

1. Introduction:
Love sport but disagree with motion

5. Teenagers should be encouraged, not forced

All teenagers should have to participate in sport.

2. Wording too general:
sport does not suit everybody

4. Sport is not the only way to get fit and socialise

3. Compulsion never good:
creates resentment/could backfire

You need to develop each point well and create links between the different ideas when you write the essay. This plan is closely based on the wording of the motion and shows that you have carefully read and analysed it. You are showing that the motion is not simply *Sport is good for teenagers*. Remember that you will be writing a speech – this is just your plan.

(b) **A flow chart:** In this plan, you can draw circles or boxes on your rough work page and jot down an idea in each one, making sure that your ideas are linked and follow a logical structure. The ideas here are similar to the spider diagram but arranged slightly differently.

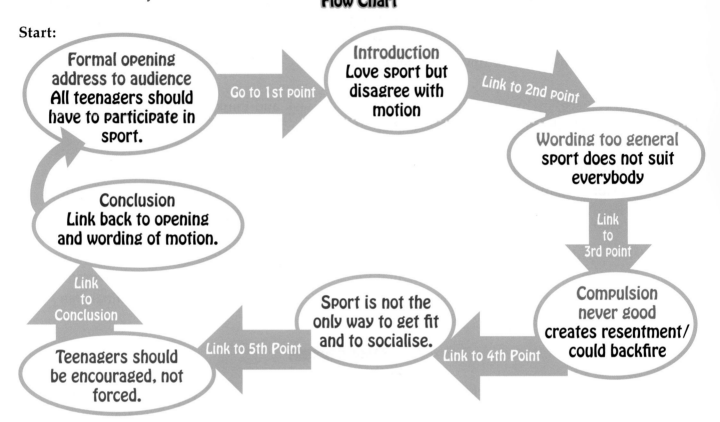

In the example above, each point is clearly identified. If you get into the habit of planning every essay you write, you will develop a habit of thinking and planning quite quickly. Writing the essay in the Junior Cert exam will be far quicker when you know exactly what you are going to say.

In the exam, be very sure that you know what you are going to say before you begin to write.

(c) **A question & answer list:** With this type of plan, you write down ideas that come into your head, in any order. You ask yourself questions and decide how you would answer them. You follow this by selecting and de-selecting, until you know which ideas you are going to use and which ones you are going to ignore. Sometimes ideas can be combined into one if they are closely related. You might find this type of plan the quickest one to write if you have not been practising with the spider or flow chart diagrams. See the example of this type of plan on the next page.

**Note:** You do not need to write in as much detail for the question & answer plan. You could summarise more. The important thing is to know clearly what you want to say and organise your response.

# Question & Answer Plan

| | |
|---|---|
| **Introduction: Do I agree or disagree?** | I decide to disagree. |
| **Why?** | The motion is too general and sounds like bullying. |
| **Why is it too general?** | Use of word 'all' is too general – bullying – explain – give examples. |
| **How is it bullying?** | Does not respect personal choice. Explain. Include **anecdote**? |
| **What would opposition say?** | Value of sport for health and team work etc. |
| **How would I answer that?** | There are lots of other ways to keep fit and healthy. Taking part in sport is not the only way to engage in team work. People can join teams for other sorts of activities – explain – give examples. |
| **Opposition might say that most teenagers are lazy and making sport compulsory would force them to get away from computers or TV.** | That is not the truth. Explain and give examples. |
| **Am I saying that teenagers should avoid sports?** | No! I'm arguing that teenagers should have a choice in the matter. There are lots of ways to engage in physical activity besides sport. |
| **So what is my major objection to motion?** | I disagree with the wording. It's the way to kill any interest a person could have because teenagers are notoriously rebellious. |
| **What would be a better wording for the motion?** | Teenagers should be <u>encouraged</u> to participate in sport and <u>other physical activities</u>. This allows choice, avoids compulsion and respects the rights of teenagers. |

**Remember:** Don't just write the argument, it must be a speech!

**(d) A mind map:** This is a bit like a spider diagram but you can keep adding on to each leg and creating extensions which enlarge on the idea. Let's look at another title from the list of options on page 29 and see how a mind map could help with planning.

### Option 4: My most useful possessions

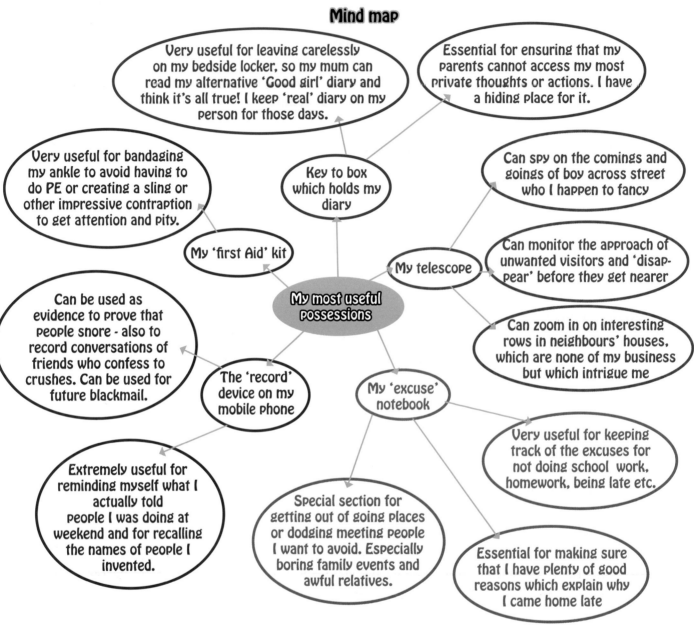

The title is at the centre of this diagram. The main ideas are individually identified and a rough idea of how they will be developed is shown in the extension circles. The student (female in this case) has chosen a mock-serious approach which is witty and original. Before writing, however, she will have to decide how to introduce and conclude the essay.

The plans you have just seen are quite detailed. You will not get enough time to plan in such detail in the exam, but this is a good way to plan your essays when you are doing them as homework. Then, in the exam, you will be able to think quickly and use short notes when planning.

**TIP** Writing the essay in the exam will be far quicker when you know how to plan, know exactly what you are going to say and know exactly how you will conclude.

Although you might find the planning part slow at first, keep going until you can manage a reasonably detailed plan in approximately 15 minutes. You will be given an hour to write your essay, so that still leaves 45 minutes to actually write it. This is plenty of time because examiners are not looking at how much you write but at the relevance of your writing to the title and your structure, style, originality and accuracy. You will find that a planned essay almost writes itself. You do not have to stop to think what you will say next or fall into the trap of repeating the same points or rambling off the subject.

The whole purpose of a good plan is to allow you to think, stimulate your imagination and provide time to organise your paragraphs in a logical way. It is time well spent. You can, of course, make some adjustments to your plan if some new idea emerges as you write. Be flexible, but be wary of abandoning your plan and just trusting to chance.

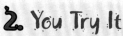

## 2. You Try It

Make plans for each of the following titles. Use a different type of plan for each.
  **(a)** My pet hates
  **(b)** Write a speech for or against the motion, *'Transition Year should be made compulsory'*.
  **(c)** *'The day started the same as any other, nobody could have known that by evening ...'* Continue the story.
  **(d)** What the world needs now

### Step Three: Write Introduction
Because you have chosen your title carefully and planned your answer, you are now ready to write your composition.

Keep the opening paragraph short. Use it to hook your reader and make them want to read on. Avoid unnecessary boring details such as 'My mum told me it was time to get up. I got out of bed and went downstairs to eat my breakfast.' Who cares about that? Make a BIG impression with your opening. Try some of the following opening techniques:

✴ **A startling comment:** This surprises the reader and functions as a 'hook' to keep reading. For example, comments like *My ego is so small it could fit in a matchbox* or *Umbrellas should be banned* or *It was a man's body alright. The men dragged it slowly back from the water's edge* immediately capture the imagination and encourage us to keep on reading. If you use a startling opening, make sure that you expand on it and relate it to the essay in general.

✴ **A rhetorical question:** This encourages the reader to focus and engage with your subject. *Have you ever had the feeling that you're invisible?* or *Are you watching television but enjoying it less? If so, have you asked yourself why?* or *Are you scared to go to school every day?* These questions also give emphasis to a point.

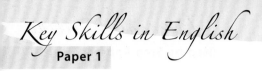

* **A suitable quotation:** You may remember some lines from a poem which you studied as part of your course, or something somebody said in one of your novels, short stories or plays. It must, however, be **apt** and related to the topic. *It's so much easier to suggest solutions when you don't know much about the problem* (**Malcolm Forbes**); *It is never too late to give up our prejudices* (**Henry Thoreau**). Quotations like these could be used in an essay which attempts to argue a point.

* **An anecdote:** This is a very short story which illustrates some point relevant to your topic. Keep it short, to the point and relevant to your topic, as you are only using it for introductory purposes. This can be a very effective opening for your essay, but use it carefully. For example, an essay about racism in Irish society could open with a short narration of a racist incident. This could then be commented on as you introduce your first point.

* **A description of a place or person:** This can be effective in introducing a short story. *Mrs Grey sat on a hard chair in the corner looking – but at what? Apparently at nothing. She did not change the focus of her eyes when visitors came in. Her eyes had ceased to focus themselves; it may be that they had lost the power. (Old Mrs Grey* by Virginia Woolf). Here you see an example from an experienced writer but notice that she does not use big words or complicated sentences. The words are simple and the details are well-chosen to grab our attention and make us want to know more.

* **A piece of short dialogue:** You need to make sure that this dialogue is relevant to the story or topic and keep it very short. *'Where's John going with that torch?' said Michael to his mother, as they closed the front door of the house for the last time. 'I have no idea,' his mother replied, 'but I hope he is not going to do anything foolish.'* The reader may want to continue reading to find out the answer to the question, to discover why the family are leaving their home and to know why the mother thinks John might be about to act foolishly. Sometimes, you are given a piece of dialogue with which to open your essay, as in Option 2 on page 29, *'I was a very cute toddler; I've seen the photographs.'* A well-chosen piece of dialogue could also be used to open an opinion piece.

* There are other ways to open your essay in addition to those listed above. A good idea is to read the opening few sentences of novels and short stories; articles in newspapers or magazines; reports and informative passages; personal opinion pieces and autobiographies. You can learn excellent techniques by examining how professional writers manage to grab their readers' attention. **Never** plagiarise (copy) and pretend it is your own work. However, you can analyse other people's writing and see how different techniques work and try them out in your own writing.

### 🦎 You Try It

Write the opening paragraphs for each of the essays you planned on page 35. Vary your technique each time.

**Step Four: Write and Develop the Essay**

Once you have opened your essay effectively, you now need to develop it before you write your conclusion. Your plan is crucial in helping you make sure that you avoid a disorganised, repetitive and vague piece of writing.

The way you develop your writing depends very much on the genre (type of writing) that suits the title.

Remember the mnemonic **RAFT**, which we used in the Reading Section:

R = **Reason for the writing.** Is it to argue? persuade? describe? inform? advise? narrate? etc.

A = **Audience.** Who is going to read it? The language used should be appropriate for the readership.

F = **Format.** The format of writing is connected to the reason for the writing. An autobiographical piece would not use the same format as an argument. An informative piece would not be organised in the same way as a descriptive passage of writing.

T = **Tone.** The tone or atmosphere created by the writer should be appropriate. Tone is **conveyed** through the language used. The tone of a passage could be serious, disturbing, funny, light-hearted, mock-serious, entertaining, poignant, nostalgic, cynical etc.

Each of these aspects affects the style of a passage. Keep them in mind when writing your own essay.

**Here are some points which apply to developing all types of writing:**

✤ Each paragraph should make one distinct point, if it is an argument, persuasive or opinion piece. The point should be clearly stated and developed in the paragraph. Make your point, give evidence or an explanation and then move on to the next point or stage of your essay. Take for example the following:

*I disagree with people who say that young people should not have a job during the school year.* **[Point]**. *Both of my brothers worked in the local filling station every weekend during their last three years at school. The experience taught them valuable lessons about money, the need to be responsible and how to balance work with leisure. This paid off. They realised that different jobs attract different wages or salaries, so they wanted to get good points in their Leaving Cert. They took responsibility for their own study and handled time well to ensure they had some quality free time. Working helped them to mature and become more independent. Some of their friends, who never had a job, wasted time hanging around town, updating their Facebook pages or playing video games. They missed the chance to gain independence and to grow up a bit. I won't listen to people who say having a job is a bad idea. I have already applied for one!* **[Evidence for point]**

✤ If it is a short story or descriptive piece of writing, change paragraph for each new character introduced and for each change that occurs in the plot.

37

❖ Link your paragraphs. You should move smoothly, not jump from one idea to the next.

❖ Vary sentence length and vocabulary as much as you can, but do not try to impress the reader with fancy words! Good English is Clear English. Clever combinations of ordinary words are most effective.

❖ Keep looking back at the title or task to ensure that the development of the essay is relevant. Every paragraph should be a step on the path to your conclusion.

**4. You Try It**

From the opening paragraphs you wrote on page 36, choose one and develop the essay in full, making sure you link ideas carefully.

### Step Five: Conclude the Essay

■ The way you end your essay is just as important as the way you open it. You should try to create some kind of a link with your opening paragraph in order to give a sense of unity to the essay, a sense of having come full circle. Essays must conclude in a way that makes it clear that the discussion, argument, story etc. is now over.

■ If you began your essay with a quotation, anecdote, question etc., you might return to this and comment on it again in a different way. For example, you could show how the words of the quotation applied to your discussion; you could give an ending to the anecdote you began with, or refer back to it in some way; or you could suggest an answer to your rhetorical question. **The important thing is to try to create a link back to the opening.**

■ You could restate your position on the motion of your debate or the stance you have taken. Try to avoid a simple repetition of the title or what sounds like a 'get-out' tactic, e.g. *So, as you can see, I do not think that teenagers should have to participate in sport.* This is stating the obvious and does not demonstrate any creativity or effort to end in a satisfying manner. You could instead say something like *Teenagers should not be treated as some kind of sub-species, who need to be compelled by adults to make sensible choices. We have minds and plenty of common sense of our own!* **or** *In conclusion, I believe that teenagers deserve to be treated with respect and allowed to choose what is best, given their own situation and circumstances. Why should they tolerate being forced to participate in sports or anything else when they are on the verge of adulthood and capable of making their own choices?*

■ You could briefly summarise the main points of an argument or discussion. However, this can be a bit bland unless you add a strong, concluding sentence.

■ A short story could end with a resolution of some conflict for the main character. This does not necessarily have to be a 'happy ending', but there should be some sense of closure. Avoid boring and lazy endings, e.g. **I woke up and it was all a dream.**

■ A piece of autobiographical writing or a personal opinion piece could end with a thoughtful reflection on what has been shared in the course of the writing.

■ As in openings, a composition could end with a question, a quotation, a startling comment or a brief piece of relevant dialogue.

The conclusion of your essay is very important and you should give it some thought in the planning stage. It should be kept brief but it should not read as if you were bringing the writing to a sudden halt, rather than a satisfying ending. Read plenty of examples from all the resources at your disposal, which will give you ideas for this very important paragraph.

## 5. You Try It

Using the essay which you planned, opened and developed in this section, write a short, effective conclusion.

## (b) Genres

Four genres (types) of writing are considered in this section. These are:
   (i) Writing to Argue, Persuade or Offer an Opinion
   (ii) Writing a Narrative or Short Story
   (iii) Writing a Personal Essay
   (iv) Writing a Descriptive Essay
Guidelines are provided for each genre.

## (i) Writing to Argue, Persuade or Offer an Opinion
### I. Argument: Key Skills

♦ Show that you have thought about both sides of the argument. This will show that you are fair and have a balanced viewpoint. However, make sure that your own position is clear, e.g. *It is true to say that wearing school uniforms gives students a sense of identity with their school community. What about their sense of personal identity though? Isn't that just as, if not more, important?*

♦ Each paragraph should contain **one point only** which is explained and supported.

♦ Be respectful. Never say *The members of the opposition are talking a load of rubbish* or *It is ridiculous to suggest ...* This weakens your own argument because you sound biased and unable to see any viewpoint other than your own.

♦ Lists can be useful to build up to a point. For example: *People can enjoy dancing, walking, cycling, working out in the gym and many other activities to remain fit.*

♦ Use words and phrases that will help the reader follow your argument: *However, but, therefore, and so, moreover, as a result, it follows that, in spite of this, nevertheless, sometimes, of course* etc. Using such connective phrases helps your writing to flow smoothly and links your ideas. You can also use connective words to make your opponents' ideas sound less **credible** than your own, e.g. *whereas the truth seems to be, but my research suggests, studies demonstrate that* etc.

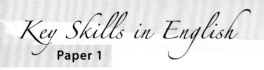

♦ Be precise in choosing your words. Because argument is based on reason, you need to avoid using emotional language or exaggeration in order to make your point. Phrases like *in fact* and *indeed* can help to strengthen a point. Vary your vocabulary and avoid **cliché** or needless repetition.

♦ Rhetorical questions can help give a sharp focus to your point and can encourage your reader to see things from your point of view, e.g. *Would you like to be forced to do something against your will?* **or** *What is the point of having rules if people can ignore them without suffering any consequences?*

♦ **Allusion** to experts or other authorities can give an added boost to an opinion and make it appear more credible and rational, e.g. *This point has been explored extensively in the work of ... the acknowledged expert in ... who agrees that ...*

♦ Vary sentence structure. Short, punchy sentences create variety and can be used for dramatic effect and for emphasis. Make sure longer sentences are controlled.

## 2. Persuasion: Key Skills

Persuasive argument is a form of argumentative writing. Because both styles have a similar purpose, most of the above points are applicable to this style also. The main points of difference are:

❀ Persuasion is less objective in its approach to a subject than argumentative writing.

❀ You can persuade by using emotional language and exaggeration for effect, e.g. *Holiday resorts milk cash from people like us and then moan and groan about our supposedly foul mouths and bad behaviour. They like our money though! There's nothing foul about that!*

❀ Personal language directly addresses the reader using such words as *us, we, you, our.* This makes the reader feel like a member of a group who shares similar ideas. It is convincing, e.g. *Surely we are not going to allow ourselves to be fooled into believing that ... ; I think you can all agree with me when I say that ...* etc.

❀ Persuasive writers make use of techniques such as:
**Irony:** *What bright spark suggested that ...*
**Repetition:** *Never, never, never will we compromise our freedom or surrender our beliefs.*
**Lists of three:** *Our battle for justice will take courage, determination and willpower*
**Humour:** *Was it Einstein who said that 'Everybody is a genius. But if you judge a fish on its ability to climb a tree, it will forever believe that it is stupid?'* Witty comments and sayings engage the reader and win them over to your way of thinking.

❀ Conversational tone can be used in persuasion. It can make you seem to be 'one of the crowd' and, therefore, appealing to the reader. You may also use language in a sarcastic way to attack an opponent or mock their argument, e.g. *You would need to be a lunatic to believe that politicians are working for the people* **or** *It must be glaringly obvious to even the most dim-witted individual that...* Be very careful not to overdo sarcasm or irony as it can backfire and weaken your argument.

✿ Persuasive writers sometimes use alliteration to make their points memorable, e.g. *The point just made by the member of the proposition is irrelevant, irritating and irresponsible; You need glamour, guts and greed to do well in showbusiness.*

✿ Personal anecdotes can be used to back up your claims, e.g. *I can tell you that I have to work extremely hard to get a good education. The supposedly 'free' education system does not give me enough support to buy the books and other equipment I need for school. I don't want to burden my parents with the bills, so I work in a supermarket for most of my summer holidays. Can people, therefore, honestly claim that all teenagers are lazy, spoilt little parasites?*

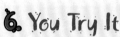 You Try It

1. Using some of the above techniques write a short speech where you try to persuade your listeners that umbrellas should be banned.
2. Write an essay in which you persuade your reader that all blood sports should be banned.

## 3. Offering an opinion: Key Skills

Opinion essays have many of the same features as argument and persuasive essays, but they are not written to influence the opinions of readers in the same way.

◎ In order to write a convincing essay, you need to think about the subject and ensure that you have a strong enough opinion about it, which you can discuss and support.

◎ Avoid changing your opinion in the course of your writing.

**TIP** It is always a good idea to write your opinion in one or two sentences at the planning stage and refer back to it throughout the essay.

◎ It is not enough to simply present facts, information or other evidence when writing this type of discursive essay. You need to give your own view on the subject. The reader wants to know what *your* opinion is!

◎ Feelings and emotions play a major role in this type of essay.

◎ A substantial part of the essay may be descriptive.

◎ The ideas, thoughts or feelings expressed should reveal sincerity and personal involvement.

◎ You must aim for a clear, logical pattern, so that your opinions appear to be sensible and well thought out.

◎ Avoid broad, general statements, e.g. *Older people do not understand modern technology* or *Nobody cares about the world's poor.* Phrases like *Many people believe* or *Most people think* are also too general. Be specific in what you claim.

◎ Don't lecture your reader!

◎ As you will only have one hour to write your essay, concentrate on three or four major points. (You will also have introductory and concluding paragraphs.)

◎ Arguments, persuasive essays and opinion pieces can be written in the format of:
   • a speech • a debate • a letter • a radio broadcast • a magazine article etc.

## ✎ You Try It

Write an essay on each of the following titles:
   **(a)** What the world needs now
   **(b)** My recipe for happiness
   **(c)** Everyone deserves a second chance.

**Remember:** Reason for writing? Audience? Format? Tone?

**Sample Question**
**Write a speech for OR against the motion:** *All teenagers should have to participate in sport.*

# Sample 1: Argumentative Essay

**ANSWER**

**COMMENTARY**

Chairperson, adjudicators, members of the proposition and fellow students, I wish to oppose the motion that *All teenagers should have to participate in sport.*

*As this essay is a debate, it begins with the standard formal opening address to the audience.*

Should teenagers, or anyone for that matter, be forced to participate in any physical activity against their will? As individuals we all have our own likes and dislikes, beliefs, abilities, talents, fears and insecurities. The combination of all of these things influences what we choose to do and not to do. For anybody to suggest that 'all' teenagers should 'have' to take part in sports, whether within school hours or as an extra-curricular activity, amounts to nothing less than bullying!

*Rhetorical question gives sharp focus to first point – uses wording of motion.*

*Use of list aids conciseness.*

*Word 'bullying' is strong and effective.*

Let me start by looking closely at the word 'all'. I notice that the first speaker for the proposition conveniently ignored that key word. Not everybody is physically or mentally able for the pressures which sport can place on an individual. Yes, I know that the proposing team has made the point that people can participate at their own level of ability. To my mind, this is a **condescending** attitude. Who wants to be the person who looks the most foolish or awkward on the playing field? Who would like to be regarded as the 'dud' because they do not have perfect co-ordination, perfect sight, perfect bodies? I think it would be wise to acknowledge that many people feel vulnerable when forced to engage in sports. I have seen and heard the hisses of derision and the name-calling that goes on when a player cannot think quickly enough or run fast enough when it really counts. It can quickly become more like a blood-sport, with the poor victim trying to avoid the vicious glares and the lash of sarcasm. Is this really beneficial for any teenager?

*Next sentence links to wording of motion.*
*Point is clearly stated.*

*Point is being developed.*
**Refutation.**
*Rhetorical questions being used for emphasis.*

*Nice use of grouping in threes.*

*Good use of personal anecdote.*

*Emotive language to influence listeners.*
*Use of imagery.*

The second speaker made an excellent job of pointing out the wonderful benefits associated with taking part in sports. I cannot disagree with one word. But, again, rather conveniently, there was no mention of the **compulsion** element. Compulsion has been shown to breed resentment. Nobody likes to feel that they are being compelled to do anything – even if it is meant to be for their own good. Teenagers, especially, hate being ordered to do things against their will. Surely it would be far better to encourage people to engage in sporting or other healthy pursuits rather than saying that they 'have to' and have no choice in the matter. From my own experience as a teenager, I can get pretty stubborn when I feel I'm being bullied by adults who think they always know what is best for me. They don't! They haven't a clue what goes on in a teenager's mind and they have forgotten what it is like to be in that odd space where you are neither a child nor an adult. They forget how important independence is to a young person.

*Smooth move to next point and **counter-argument** is being acknowledged.*

*Point is clearly stated.*

*Point is being developed.*

*Another personal illustration of the point.*
*Use of colloquial language.*
*Variation in sentence length.*

*Effort to appeal to emotion of listeners.*
*Point consolidated in last sentence*

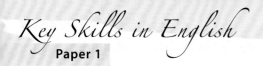

| ANSWER | COMMENTARY |
|---|---|
| Not only is compulsion counter-productive, it is damaging because sport does have many health and social benefits. Nobody in their right mind is going to argue that sitting in front of the TV or computer all day guzzling junk food and getting no exercise is good for mind or body. However, I know people who loathe sport and PE classes in school but who are extremely fit and active. They enjoy dancing, walking, cycling, working out in the gym and many other activities that keep them fit without the stresses which many sporting activities can impose. | *Good link to next point which is clearly stated. Counter-argument acknowledged again.* *Illustration from personal experience.* *Good use of listing which builds to the point.* |
| Any activity which involves teenagers getting together can present opportunities for making friends and becoming confident. What about all the clubs and activities which people are allowed to choose for themselves and which are not imposed on them? Music, drama, art – even debating! Many non-compulsory activities can promote self-esteem, self-discipline, dedication, motivation and leadership. The important thing is that teenagers are allowed to choose. | *Rhetorical questions effectively used.* *Final sentence of paragraph consolidates point.* |
| It must be clear to all of you listening to this debate that the proposition cannot put forward a reasonable argument which maintains that all teenagers should have to participate in sport. | *Smooth movement to conclusion. Argument has been solidly based on the actual wording of the motion from the opening.* |
| There is no doubt that sport is one of the great pleasures of life. I know. I am a sportsperson. But the notion of being compelled to participate, coupled with the **implication** that there cannot be any exceptions for any reasons, is not a motion which any reasonable person could uphold. I beg to oppose. | *Brief summary of argument.* *Final sentence is standard for a debate.* |

(**Note:** This sample answer was based on Option 6 from the list of titles on page 29.)

### Worth Noting

■ Notice how the writer has decided to maintain a serious approach to the subject and does not engage in any humorous writing.

■ The writer has decided to concentrate on the actual wording of the motion in order to undermine the possible advantages the proposition might be able to gain. Most people do not agree that people should be compelled or forced into playing sport. It is a rational argument.

■ There is a clear sense of structure. The normal formalities for opening a debate are used and the writer begins the actual argument with a rhetorical question which will form the basis for the entire argument. A **consistent**, logical conclusion is reached.

■ Persuasive techniques are used but the writer does not go overboard in appealing to emotion. The style is a mix of logical, factual comments which are based on personal experience and some persuasive elements.

■ Several features of an argumentative style are present: rhetorical questions, illustration by examples, anecdotes, lists building to a point, use of images, **colloquial language** etc. Objective facts, **statistics**, allusions etc. are not used as this writer is basing the argument on the way the motion is phrased. This is acceptable.

■ The counter-argument is acknowledged and respected, but the writer keeps the focus on the key words of the motion in order to undermine and oppose it.

**Apply the RAFT criteria to this essay. How does it measure up?**

**Reason** for writing = To write a speech for a debate. Is that successfully done in this essay?

**Audience =** Fellow students, members of opposition and perhaps teachers and other adults acting as judges or as chairperson. Is the language appropriate for a debate?

**Format =** Has the writer used the correct format and style for a debate speech? Clarity of expression? Use of a variety of sentence lengths? Proper linking of paragraphs? Clear opening and concluding paragraphs?

**Tone =** Has the writer adopted an appropriate tone or attitude to the subject? Could some extra variation in tone have helped? How could this be done?

So how would this essay do in the Junior Cert exam according to the current marking scheme?

| | | |
|---|---|---|
| **Content** | 17 / 20 | All of the content was relevant to the title. Slightly repetitive. |
| **Structure** | 15 / 15 | The structure was appropriate. **Coherent** argument. |
| **Expression** | 28 / 30 | Excellent clarity. There could have been a little more creativity. |
| **Mechanics** | 5 / 5 | Spelling, punctuation and grammar are accurate. |

**Total =**   65 / 70 = 93% = Grade A

**Sample Question**
Modern technology - A good or bad thing?

## Sample 2: Opinion Essay

### Modern technology - A good or bad thing?

| ANSWER | COMMENTARY |
|---|---|
| A few weeks ago, I was eating lunch with my mum in a shopping centre when my mobile phone beeped. I picked it up and read a text from one of my close friends, Susanna, in which she said she was upstairs in the same shopping centre at that very minute. I called her and left a voicemail saying, 'Come down to us when you're ready.' As I hung up, Mum rolled her eyes good-naturedly. 'If you hadn't that phone with you, you'd have to make do with my company,' she said. | *Opening anecdote creates intimate, chatty style which engages reader.*<br><br>*Subject of technology indirectly introduced.* |
| My mum isn't insecure or a complainer, but she does often remark on the negatives of technology. She doesn't like that her own friends will change a meeting point at the last minute, or call into the house on five minutes' notice after ringing from up the road. Most of all, like a lot of people, she thinks that constant virtual connection has ruined my generation for real-life connection. | *Notice link from anecdote to first point.*<br><br>*The opposing viewpoint is shown in the mother's attitude to technology.* |
| I like to challenge her on this. Yes, technology has its down-sides. It can keep us glued to our computers 'chatting' when we could be meeting up in person. But much more often, it helps us connect virtually *and* in real life. To take a simple example, that day at the shops I was able to meet up with Susanna and help her choose clothes to wear to a job interview. Texting enabled us to connect and do something meaningful together in real life. If we hadn't had our phones, we would have missed out on that opportunity. | *Good linking to next point.*<br><br>*Acknowledgement of opposing view, very balanced. But stronger argument made for writer's opinion.* |
| I have heard many objections to the role technology plays in the lives of people my age, and not just from my mother. Technology makes us less social, ruins our memory, and makes us rely on calculators for even simple maths. It turns us into **atrocious** spellers and hopeless readers who can't absorb anything longer than a few sentences at a time. Not all of these complaints are far-fetched. Technology doesn't replace our social lives in the real world, but I agree that 'text language' is a serious problem and does little to help our language or writing skills. | *Paragraph flows naturally into the next.*<br><br>*Fair presentation of opposite viewpoint.*<br><br>*Balanced acceptance of some parts of opposing opinions.* |
| Allowing for that fact though, it seems that as people get older, they are more likely to exaggerate the negative side of new technology and gloss over a sea of real benefits. In fact, if technology is a sea that's bringing a tsunami, I would argue that the tsunami will change things mostly for the better. Maybe the biggest benefit is a skill called multitasking. It's true that I often text on my phone while my laptop is open in front of me and my browsers are open to three or four tabs. I can do this while carry-ing on a conversation with my mum or somebody else. True, I'm probably concentrating less on the conversation than they are, since my attention is split three-plus ways. | *Having allowed some credibility to opposing view, writer now makes strong case for own opinion.*<br><br>*Excellent image of tsunami.* |

**ANSWER**

However, brains are designed to make connections, and when we multitask, the connections are everywhere. Recently I was online sending instant messages back and forth with a friend while I read a news article about job losses for a school project. When I happened to mention what I was working on to my friend, he told me that his uncle was among those laid off in the very case I was reading about. He gave me some useful information for my project – information I was able to cross-check immediately via Google, leading me to more insights into what happened. That additional information I gathered opened up the subject for me.  All because I was doing two things at once.

This is a small, not very significant example. But it illustrates a very significant potential that technology gives us. It's as though by throwing so many things at us, technology forces us to juggle information in new ways. I expect that my generation will make many new discoveries and innovations based on this ability to mix and match information from different sources. We will find connections that haven't been understood before. We will come up with truly new ideas – like mixing separate ingredients into a cake.

What it seems to boil down to is this: technology upsets my mother's sense of order because it makes life unpredictable and much more complex. But it gives a smoother way to live to people who are able to go with the flow. Young people generally have that ability. Susanna and I are happy to find that we're out shopping by chance at the same time. We turn that into an opportunity to have a brilliant afternoon together. I can be plugged in to several devices or several websites at once, and bounce easily from one to another.

Technology, therefore, presents endless possibilities. Just as the Internet is a vast, connected network, living happily with technology means enjoying the fact that everything in our lives is connected with everything else. As Bill Gates, a leading innovator in technology, once said, 'Never before in history has innovation offered promise of so much to so many in so short a time.' I certainly agree!

**COMMENTARY**

*Notice how next idea is linked to paragraph before.*

*Anecdote clarifies and supports the point.*

*Point is well concluded.*

*Very good linking from previous paragraph.*

*Point is well developed here.*

*Good use of imagery.*

*Essay clearly moving towards a conclusion.*

*Both sides of argument presented again, but emphasis on the positives.*

*Excellent idea to return to opening anecdote in order to give unity to the essay.*

*Conclusion is logical and consistent with every-thing that has been said so far.*

*Use of apt quotation to conclude the essay.*

So how would this essay do in the Junior Cert exam according to the current marking scheme?

| | | |
|---|---|---|
| **Content** | 19 / 20 | Relevant |
| **Structure** | 15 / 15 | Excellent linking of ideas |
| **Expression** | 28 / 30 | Room for more lively expression |
| **Mechanics** | 5 / 5 | Accurate |
| Total | 67 / 70 | = 96% = Grade A |

## Sample 3: Newspaper Article

**Note:** *The text below shows how different styles can be blended in an article format.*

# Parents and Teenagers inhabit separate worlds and never the twain shall meet *by Eilis O'Hanlon*

WONDERING why that woman at the coffee shop suddenly glares daggers every time your paths cross? Maybe it's because you didn't spot the request to befriend her on Facebook which arrived a few weeks ago and now she's feeling snubbed.

As for that man who no longer returns your calls, maybe he sent you a funny message and you didn't show sufficient gratitude by adding a little cartoon thumbs up to show that you "Liked" it.

The internet makes people behave very oddly in this way – taking offence as readily as they're prepared to give it – and social networking sites are rife with the deadliest pitfalls of all. Which really ought to make it easy to answer the question: "Should you 'friend' your own children on Facebook?" Why would you willingly choose to interact with your children through this medium.

Family life is stressful enough already. Especially if your children are teenagers. How many more potential areas for conflict do you want to create anyway?

The perils don't just stop there. When my daughter joined Facebook, she persuaded her father to create a profile too so that they could 'friend' one another. Reluctantly, he agreed, then thought no more about it. Since he never logged on, or gave a second thought to what was happening on Facebook, it didn't matter. Then the emails started to arrive. Facebook had noticed that he was a friend of Miss A and wondered whether he wanted to befriend Miss B and Miss C as well. Every day, Facebook would bombard him with the names of new teenage girls that he might wish to befriend, those being the only other people on the Friends list belonging to the one user out of those hundreds of millions of accounts with whom he actually had any contact.

To say that he felt a little creeped out by the electronically-generated invitations would be an understatement – though, he suspected, nowhere near as creeped out as the teenage girls must be to receive the same random invitations from the account of some old fella who happened to be related to one of their friends. Fortysomethings and teenagers inhabit different worlds. That's the way it should be.

Sometimes, though, it seems that parents are desperate to recapture some lost youth of their own by living vicariously through their teenage children; getting their kicks secondhand by eavesdropping in on all the parties and flirtations. It's a short step from there to hitting the nightclubs together and trying to pass yourself as your daughter's elder sister. Which is demeaning for you, but, even more unforgivable, embarrassing for your children.

All that nonsense about being Best Friends Forever with your children rather than a parental figure is just misguided. Even if children think that's what they want, they don't. They want parents, whether they realise it yet or not, and you're going to have to be a parent, no matter how much easier it might be to duck the challenge.

Besides, living in one another's pockets in that way deprives them of one of the greatest pleasures any teenager can have – which is the joy of hiding things from their elders. It's not normal to share everything. Secrets make a teenager's world go round, and it's better if they can at least think Facebook is the place to stash their private thoughts and memories rather than going to greater extremes to escape prying eyes. Trespassing on that realm is only a small step up from reading their personal diaries, or putting a hidden camera in the bedroom to make sure that they're not up to mischief.

There are exceptions, naturally. If you suspected that your child was taking drugs, or suffering from serious depression – in worst-case scenarios, even making contact with unsuitable individuals online – then an argument could be made for rummaging around in their world for confirmation. It would be better to just talk to them about it, rather than snooping around like a Special Branch mole, but it may, **in extremis**, be justifiable. In those instances, after all, you're only crossing a line to save them from themselves. But it is important to recognise that there is a line, and crossing it just so that you can find out who snogged who at the last disco is probably a sign that you need to get out more.

That's why Twitter was probably right when it called it "following" rather than 'friending'. The word "follow" has the right edge of menace. Would you follow your teenage children around in real life? If not, why is doing it online any more edifying?

Having said that, there are few things more annoying than a teenager who's happy to post intimate details of their lives on Facebook and then gets indignant about alleged invasions of their online privacy by inquisitive parents.

Teenage children should be able to trust their parents to leave them alone on the internet, but good parents should also make sure their children show a matching scepticism for everyone else that they interact with out there. Which is another reason for avoiding Facebook as an adult.

If it was a neighbourhood, you wouldn't move there in a million years.

**in extremis** = in extreme circumstances

**Adapted from an article by Eilis O'Hanlon in the** *Irish Independent*

**Questions**
1. What technique has the writer used to open her article? Is it effective?
2. How would you describe the tone of the article?
3. Summarise the arguments which the writer has used.
4. What features of good persuasive argument has the writer used in developing her argument?
5. Would you describe this style as formal or informal? Give reasons for your answer.
6. Would you say that the writer is (a) serious about the subject, (b) only joking and does not really hold this opinion, (c) serious but using humour as a persuasive device?
7. How reasonable is the writer's opinion on this subject in your view? Explain.
8. Comment on the sentence structure and language used in the article.

9. How would you know that this article was written by an experienced journalist as opposed to a Junior Cert student? (Apart from the fact that it is obviously written by an adult!)
10. Did you enjoy reading this article? Why or why not?

*Having considered all your responses to the above questions, how do you think the **RAFT** system of analysis could be used to analyse this article?*

 **OVER TO YOU**

Now that you have studied and written essays in different formats, it is time for you to practise writing on the same title in different ways. This will help you to find the style that suits you best.

Take the title 'What the world needs now', which was given on a past Junior Cert exam paper.

Write the essay as:
- A persuasive speech to be delivered to a meeting of world leaders.
- An article for a magazine aimed at teenage boys or girls.
- A thoughtful, reflective piece written in a letter to a friend.

## (ii) Writing a Narrative or Short Story

When you are writing a short story or any other narrative form of writing, you are free to base it on an actual experience or to invent the characters and plot.

### Narrative essay: Key Skills

As with any form of writing, it is extremely important that you **plan** before you begin to write. When planning a short story consider each of the following:

### Plot

✴ What is going to happen in this story? Why? How? In what order? Aim for originality and try to have an unexpected ending. Avoid silly, unbelievable plots which bore the reader. For example, not very many people are going to be interested in a story where you meet and fall in love with a famous film star or where the main character emerges as a total hero or heroine, with no human weaknesses or frailties. Try to imagine events that seem possible and realistic and inject some kind of unexpected 'twist' which takes the reader by surprise. Do not create too many events. It is much better to keep the plot line simple. You can achieve this by having one major event occurring over a short period of time.

✴ Arrange the plot in a logical sequence of events. You can either tell the story chronologically (in the order in which things happen) or decide to use a 'flashback' technique. This involves beginning at a certain point in the story – usually near the end – and recounting the events which led up to that moment or point in time.

✷ In your planning make sure that you know how the story is going to end. Avoid boring, worn-out tricks like suddenly waking up and discovering that the whole thing was a dream. If the ending of your essay lacks credibility, the whole story suffers. Remember that the examiner is going to grade your essay *after* reading the final paragraph! Make the ending strong and satisfying.

## Structure

✷ Who is going to be the narrator? Do I tell the story? Will it be told by one of the characters I create?

✷ Pay particular attention to the wording of the question. Have you been told to begin or end with a specific sentence, or to include a sentence in the body of your essay? If so, make sure that you do exactly what you were told to do. Such sentences are supposed to inspire the plot of the story and cannot be ignored.

✷ Arrange paragraphs in a logical order. Do not allow the story to ramble in a haphazard way – this will not happen if you have done your planning correctly!

✷ Short stories should be structured carefully. You need a setting for the action, characters who are credible and in whom we have an interest, some suspense/dramatic action or a problem that needs to be resolved, conflict and a satisfying ending. The story will be richer and more memorable if you have a message or theme which is not stated but suggested to the reader.

## Setting

✷ Creating the setting gives you a chance to show off your powers of description. Use powerful words and phrases that appeal to the reader's senses – make them see, hear, touch, smell or taste.

✷ Well-chosen images can convey a place or an atmosphere in a very sophisticated way. Read the following description carefully. It is taken from *Lord of the Flies* by William Golding and gives an aerial view of the setting.

### Example 1

*The reef enclosed more than one side of the island, lying perhaps a mile out and parallel to what they now thought of as their beach. The coral was **scribbled in the sea as though a giant had bent down to reproduce the shape of the island in a flowing, chalk line but tired before he had finished.** Inside was peacock water, **rocks and weed showing as in an aquarium**; outside was the **dark blue** of the sea. ...*
*Beyond falls and cliffs there was **a gash** visible in the trees; there were **the splintered trunks** and then the drag, leaving only **a fringe of palm between the scar and the sea.** There, too, **jutting** into the lagoon, was the platform, with **insect like figures** moving near it.*

William Golding is a famous and experienced writer so you will not be expected to produce anything like this, but you can learn from his technique. Look carefully at the words and phrases marked in bold print. Notice the splendid image of the 'giant' scribbling in the sea. Do you see how the great vista of the island is contrasted with the 'insect like figures' of the boys? Golding does not use big or unusual words here. He uses ordinary, simple words but arranges them for maximum impact on the reader. The details build up until we get a clear impression of the setting.

The following example shows how a good student could create a vivid setting for a story about a person who cannot sleep, walking the streets of New York at night. The best word choices and images are in bold print.

### Example 2

*A day in New York begins with night, since the city's greatest fame lies in its sleeplessness. Almost all over the world, 3 a.m. is a disconcerting hour, a time when nothing stirs and those lying awake in their beds are likely to scare themselves with* **<u>black</u> thoughts of intruders, demons, bad luck**. *In New York, though, there is always comfort and company for the likes of James Harty. Instead of suffering in his room,* **taunted** *by the digital display clock, he can pull on his jeans and a warm sweater, take the keys to his apartment from the rack, and wander onto the Manhattan street, seeking the reassurance of hustle and bustle.*

*Most of the cars on the street, especially at 3 a.m., are <u>yellow</u> taxis.* **They pulse** *up the avenues* **like purposeful bees**, *carrying revellers to and from nightclubs that won't close until the sun comes up, even though it's midweek. Larger,* **<u>sleek black</u>** *cars bring* **worker bees** *from Wall Street,* **zipping** *home to catch* **a scrap of sleep** *before the work day begins again. On one block, outside a hospital's A&E entrance, an ambulance flashes* **<u>blue and red</u>** *but there is no sign of a patient, only the ambulance crew standing nearby,* **talking and laughing**.

Notice the startling opening sentence, the use of colour (underlined) to create a vivid impact, the use of strong action verbs, the use of striking imagery, the manner in which details are arranged in a sequence until we get a strong sense of New York at night.

 **You Try It**

Create a vivid setting for the following:
   **(a)** A story about a haunted house
   **(b)** A detective or mystery story
   **(c)** An exotic place you dreamt about.

### Characterisation

Try to make your characters, like your plot, credible and interesting. Even if you set your story on Mars or in an imaginary place, you still need to make the story credible as long as the reader is reading it. Think of how the *Harry Potter* novels are capable of creating a temporary 'reality' and how successful they are in making us believe in the characters and the things they say and do.

❂ Ask yourself questions about your characters. Who are they? How can I make them credible? Remember the rule about showing rather than telling the reader what to think about a character, e.g. Instead of saying *Mary Jones was a very suspicious kind of person*, you could say *Mary Jones sat glaring at me, as if I was up to something and she was the only one in the class who could see through me.*

✪ Use dialogue effectively to aid characterisation. Good writers do not tell their readers what to think of the characters, they let them come to their own conclusions based on what characters say, think and do. It is important to use good dialogue. However, too much dialogue can make the story more like a play script and hold up the plot. On the other hand, no dialogue at all is a weakness in narrative because it is impossible to imagine a world where nobody says anything. Reported speech is not as effective as direct speech and should be used sparingly. Remember **show** don't **tell**. Read the following example of a dialogue between two characters:

**Example 3**

*'Yes, that's my bike' he said irritably.*
*'It looks very like the one which was stolen from my shed,' Robert said tentatively.*
*'Are you calling me a thief?' he snapped. 'I'd watch my mouth if I was you.'*
*'No! no! Of course I'm not calling you a thief,' Robert murmured as he backed out onto the road.*

The writer uses dialogue here to give an insight into the attitude and manner of both characters. We can see for ourselves that the first speaker is an abrupt, rude character who has probably stolen the bike. Words like *'irritably'* and *'snapped'* convey his attitude and he appears to be threatening Robert if he continues the conversation. Robert, on the other hand, has sufficient courage to confront him at first, but he is intimidated. The words *'tentatively', 'murmured'* and *'backed out'* suggest fear, as does his denial that he thinks the other character is a thief.

 **You Try It**

Using the above short dialogue as an example, write a similar short dialogue for each of the following situations. Both characters must speak!
✪ One person tells another a shocking secret.
✪ An old man gives a piece of advice to a young man.
✪ A teacher questions a student about homework copied from another student.

Try to use dialogue and narration to create a strong sense of each character as in Example 3.

**Expression**

☞ **Language** You need to display a wide and varied range of language. This is a necessary skill for all aspects of short story writing. It is neither necessary nor advisable to use long, complicated words just for effect. Simple words, beautifully arranged make more impact on a reader. You could keep a special copybook for making word circles for different purposes, adding new words to them as you increase your vocabulary. After a while, you will become accustomed to varying your language and having a wide, versatile vocabulary to create vivid writing. On the next page there are examples of word circles which could be used to describe the sea in different kinds of conditions.

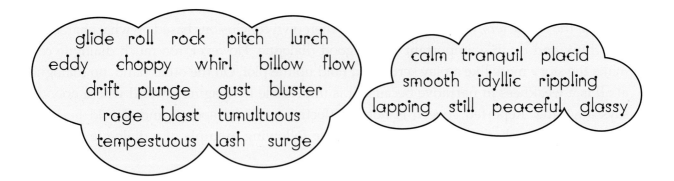

You could make similar circles with words to describe different characters, places, atmospheres, sights, smells, sounds, tastes, feelings. Use a dictionary and a thesaurus to help you gather words which you understand and can incorporate into your writing. However, do not allow your language to become forced and artificial. The reader should not get the impression that you are using words just for the sake of showing off your vocabulary. Words are for communication but they can be used stylishly and to create an impact. Here is a description based on some of the words in the circles above:

### Example 4

*In the dim light of evening, the tranquil sea seemed to beckon. Its calm, lapping waves rocked the little boats which were moored in the harbour, lifting them rhythmically in the breeze. Michael loved this hour of the evening. He plunged eagerly into the rippling surface, savouring the thrill of the cold water as it enshrouded his warm body. Further and further, the sea beckoned him onwards and outwards until the small boats became specks in the distance. As he turned to swim back, the sun disappeared behind threatening storm clouds. Waves, which had previously lapped gently over him, began to surge angrily while stinging sheets of rain blurred his vision.*

☛ Read as many descriptions as you can and underline effective words. Keep enlarging or creating new word circles. You will gain confidence from this exercise and your store of words will be of tremendous assistance in other areas of the exam, as well as in your personal writing.

### Theme

❀ Is there going to be a clear message? Am I going to use the story to make a point about some issue? If the reader is left thinking over what the story was about, the point of the story was well made.

❀ It helps greatly if you think about the title and jot down a sentence or two at the beginning of your planning, which sums up your theme or main idea. Your plot and characters can then be woven around this central idea, which will give direction and purpose to the story.

## Sample 1: Narrative Essay

# An Amazing Discovery

It was so simple, so easy to do, so instinctive, that I could not believe that I, John Mitchell, had discovered something right under our noses, that had been lying there for centuries, undisturbed in the mists of the past, covering itself with layer upon layer of earth until it was invisible – not even a tiny bump or mound in the earth!

Dad had bought me a metal detector for Christmas. He had gone to a lot of trouble to get quite a good one which wasn't going to squeak its head off at every little pin or nail on the ground.  You don't know my dad. He doesn't just grab the first thing that he sees when he is deciding to spend money. He examines each brand with the greatest of care. Dad has no interest in metal detectors himself, but he liked to encourage exploration and discovery in me. I think he might have had some idea that I was a pretty smart kid who would probably study physics or technology – something that required an inquiring mind. I had that alright! I couldn't get enough of books about discoveries and inventions and I was always messing about trying to invent or improve gadgets.

It wasn't really all that big when I took it out of its box. My hands were trembling with excitement, as I poked all the buttons to see what each one could do. There were instructions enclosed, printed on a little sheet of paper, but I couldn't be bothered with that. I like to find out how things work by messing around with them. I had expected some sort of clumsy, heavy machine. To be honest, I felt a little disappointed because it didn't look all that impressive and I had boasted so much to my friends about getting this brilliant metal detector for Christmas. They would all have a great laugh now. They were getting X-boxes and all sorts of new video games and here was I, John Mitchell, or 'Mitch' as they call me, getting all excited about something that looked more like a little kid's Star Wars' toy. All buttons and bleepers but nothing really spectacular.

As Mum prepared dinner, I rambled around the garden experimenting with the buttons. Once or twice I heard a little buzzing sound but there was nothing to discover, even when I dug down a little bit into the earth. As a matter of fact, the stupid thing stopped buzzing after I had dug up a few worms. There wasn't even a nail or a coin! It just started buzzing and stopped. I couldn't believe Dad had bought such a daft thing. It wasn't like him at all!

Dinner was the usual affair and I tried my best not to show that I was so disappointed with my present. Dad asked lots of questions and realised fairly quickly that I wasn't exactly overjoyed. 'I'd read those instructions if I were you John,' he said 'Sometimes you need a bit of help with those  things.' I shrugged. I really hate having to read instructions; they are so boring, usually complicated and anyway, I prefer to work things out for myself.

Later, I went outside to see could I make any sense out of my 'present'. When I discovered that by pressing two buttons at the same time, certain noises were emitted, I got a bit more interested. Actually, after about ten more minutes, pressing different combinations, I got excited enough to give in and speed things up by reading through the instructions. They were short and simple and I was sorry I had delayed. That day I found a few interesting bits and pieces in the fields behind our house. Nothing very exciting admittedly, but I thought I could at least have some fun with the detector. I found an old penny, buried underneath a metre of earth. It was dated 1912. Some of those old coins are worth a few bob you know, and I thought I might discover enough of them to sell on eBay.

As it was getting dark and tea was being prepared, I decided to have one quick scour around the perimeter of the field where I had found the penny. Little beeps and buzzes went off intermittently, but I ignored those. The instructions had warned me when to get really interested and when to ignore and carry on scouring. I suppose it was a good metal detector after all, not a cheap, shoddy type. I should have known to trust Dad.

Then it happened! The metal detector went crazy in my hands, almost jumping out of its metal skin. A red light flashed, faded and flashed again. The beeps got louder and the buzzing sounded like a swarm of bees had been disturbed in winter and didn't like it! I could hear Mum calling my name but I couldn't wait. I wanted to at least start my dig as it would probably take a few days. But there was something under there for sure and I was not going to risk losing the spot.

You won't believe me, but I only had to dig for about fifteen minutes and then I saw it. It was wrapped up in what looked like a few layers of old leather strips and roughly tied with what looked like leather shoe strings. I just poked it with the edge of the shovel and, yes, there was something there alright. I knew that I should not disturb it. I had read about historical artefacts. Dashing excitely into the house, I yelled for Dad. He laughed at me as I gasped, 'Come out Dad … hurry … bring your torch … I've found something.'

'Sit down and eat your tea,' Mum said. 'You're getting too old for all that silly nonsense.'

I had to sit there and eat my tea, but my heart was pounding. Dad decided to relieve me of my misery. 'We'll take a quick look,' he said 'and then you can put your mind to rest on the matter. It's probably nothing as your mother says.'

But it was! It most certainly was something. It wasn't nothing. They were wrong!

That night we uncovered a dull, mucky but wonderful ancient vessel. Not in the same league as the Ardagh Chalice or anything like that and not as old. But the people from the National Museum, whom Dad notified, said that it was of considerable historical importance. It looked like rubbish when they took it out of the hole, but I knew by the way they were quietly excited and by the way they handled it gingerly that it was no old tin can!

My find, a golden goblet, now stands proudly in a glass case, polished back to its former glory, attracting people and scholars from all over the world. I am named as the person who discovered it. Oh, and I almost forgot – we got a decent reward as it was found on our land. The newspapers carried stories about my splendid understanding and how I knew not to touch it or dig it up, but to leave it to the experts.

I'm afraid, despite my best efforts, I never discovered anything quite so exotic afterwards with my metal detector. However, I'm not giving up hope and perhaps I'll invent a superior model some day. Who knows?

**Note:** This essay is longer than what you would be required to write in the Junior Certificate exam but it illustrates some excellent narrative techniques.

● Interesting introduction which 'hooks' the reader.
● The writer has a clear plot line and has decided to write in the first person, 'I'.
● The style is chatty and gives us a sense of the character of the narrator.
● Other characters are introduced and sound credible.
● There is a varied vocabulary and varied sentence length. Very good use is made of the shorter sentences to build up suspense.
● Notice the use of simile and sensual images to create a vivid impact at the moment of the discovery.
● The writer uses dialogue effectively.
● Clear conclusion.

There are also some areas which could improve.
○ The ending is a bit predictable. Usually a short story is more interesting if something unexpected happens.
○ Tone could be livelier at times.

**So how would this essay do in the Junior Cert exam according to the current marking scheme:**

| | | |
|---|---|---|
| **Content** | 15/20 | Predictable ending |
| **Structure** | 13/15 | Excellent structure |
| **Expression** | 28/30 | Opportunity for more variety |
| **Mechanics** | 5 / 5 | Accurate |
| | | |
| **Total =** | 61 / 70 = 87 % = Grade A | |

## Writing a Narrative Essay in Diary Format

One of the titles in the list of options provided in the exam may specify that the essay must be written as a series of diary entries. Or you may simply choose to write about one of the other titles in this style.

## Diary narrative: Key Skills

✿ Brainstorm and plan as you would for any narrative. You cannot just ramble because it is a diary.

✿ The story needs the same careful structure as any short story. It cannot simply be a collection of journal entries that does not have an actual plot; there must be a definite beginning, middle and satisfying conclusion.

✿ Decide on the character who is writing the diary and try to imagine what type of person he /she is. Think about their likes and dislikes, their attitudes and emotions etc.

✿ Pay careful attention to the plot line. Focus on the major events that happen to your main character and organise them in **chronological** order. Add any notes or bits of dialogue that occur to you as you plan the outline.

✿ For a diary story, it is essential that you create a sense of an individual 'voice'. This is vital if the story is going to convince the reader.

✿ Include dialogue in your diary story. While most actual diaries do not include dialogue, a story does. Dialogue both enhances the story and makes it more entertaining and believable for the reader.

✿ The language choice should be simple and direct.

✿ The tone will be determined by what happens in the plot. For example, a sad experience will carry a sad tone, while a celebration entry may be jubilant and excited.

## Sample 2: Diary Narrative

Read the following essay and watch out for the guidelines listed on pages 50-54. The title is taken from a past Junior Cert exam paper: **You and some friends enter a major talent competition. Write a series of diary entries recording your experiences.**

**ANSWER**

**Monday, 1st December 20--**

We got through! I can't believe it. That semi-final was really nerve-wracking.

As we waited in the crowded hall, Jack, Kevin, Lisa and myself huddled together hardly daring to breathe as the judges came out to announce who was going to go forward for the final of the 'Best of Showtime' talent competition.

It's a legend that competition. Talent spotters come in droves, looking for the next big money-making hit. I could feel my heart thumping in my chest and the sticky hand of Lisa got even stickier and tighter with each passing second.

I threw a nervous glance at Jack. Trust him to be the calmest! 'Just chill out guys – it's not the end of the world one way or the other. Those other acts were pretty good too.'

I knew he didn't mean that. I could see the trickle of sweat running down the side of his face like a lost raindrop, searching for its puddle. But he insisted that there were better acts than ours.

'Rubbish! We were the best,' I hissed through clenched teeth.

Honestly. I'm not just being biased here. That awful group from St. Martin's on the Hill – they were just sickeners. Sang sentimental songs in four-part harmony with mushy lyrics. I thought they were sucking up to the judges, who were, strangely enough, middle-aged. Then those dancers from the 'Ballet and Balance' school! Ha-ha! More like 'Bimbos and Boredom'.

Okay – there were some good acts too. So I was nervous and not really expecting to be picked.

After a sickening ten hours delay – alright then, ten minutes – the main judge announced that our band,' Fresh and Frisky', had made it through to the final.

Yippee! We have to get real now about our practice sessions. I thought Lisa was slightly out of tune tonight and Jack's guitar rhythm seemed a bit 'off'. Needless to say, I was, as usual, just amazing.

**COMMENTARY**

*Date given - this is necessary for a diary entry.*

*Building of suspense good here as it engages the reader and creates mood.*

*Character introduced simply, using dialogue.*

*Use of simile effective here.*

*Well-chosen verbs.*

*Character of writer emerges in her comments.*

*Honest revelation of feelings.*

*Tendency to exaggerate clearly marked.*

*Tone of excitement and over-confidence. Adds to humour.*

| ANSWER | COMMENTARY |
|---|---|

**Tuesday, 2nd December 20--**

*Consistent dating of entry.*

Some people are such begrudgers. I expected a fanfare and whoops of congratulations from friends and foes alike. It didn't happen. Nobody seemed to grasp the stupendous achievement of last night. 'Hey, great! You must be happy' was the nearest Lisa and I got to receiving compliments. I even think there were a few sniggers when we revealed the name of our band. The cheek of them! We are 'fresh' and we are 'frisky'. So what's wrong with 'Fresh and Frisky'? Sheer begrudgery I'm telling you.

*Character of writer brought out in her writing. Clear 'voice' established.*

I'll tell you what's going on there. Jack and Kevin are… well, let's just say 'desirable'. If you prefer to exaggerate, they're 'adorable'. Lisa and I are not in love with them (they may be with us though) but there are certain people who are, and the green-eyed monster of envy is lurking in our class. That explains the dumbed-down response to our win. Lisa is convinced that they just hate me because I'm such a big-head and know-all. Wrong! I'm no such thing. I'm just confident. They're simply jealous.

*Notice variation in sentence-length and the colloquial style.*

*Effective use of image.*

Roll on Saturday. We're having a massive practice. Lisa and I have new dance moves and the lads are working out new riffs and astonishing drum effects. I can't wait.

*Tone of building excitement maintained*

**Saturday, 6th December 20--**

Don't even ask me about today's 'practice'. Jack and Kevin are jerks and Lisa is definitely singing out of tune. How dare they dismiss my brilliant suggestions in such an off-hand way!

*Effective switch of tone from excitement to disgust.*

I'm sorry I didn't enter as a solo act. I could have called myself 'The One and Only'. Forget all that 'frisky' stuff and do my own thing.

*Consistent character and voice.*

## ANSWER

**Wednesday, 10th December 20--**

Spent the whole afternoon practising for Saturday night's final.

It seems to be coming together a bit now. We've compromised. I've agreed not to do my bare-belly dance stunt (although it would have wowed the judges) and Lisa accepts that she is a bit out of tune, so I get to be lead singer and she is the backer for me. Nice one!

In order to bring out the 'Frisky' factor, we are going to do a Jedward-like bounce-about in the middle. At least Lisa and I are. The other two will emphasise our rhythm on the guitar and drums. Pity Lisa is slightly clumsy. She nearly broke her neck today. That's all we need. Lisa with her neck in one of those surgical collar things trying to outdo Jedward.

**Friday, 12th December 20--**

Don't even ask me how I'm feeling. Nerves, nerves nerves!

This time tomorrow I'll be famous. Sorry – we'll be famous. I just hope Louis Walsh has been invited – or whatshisname with the big shiny teeth. We're going to blitz that competition for sure.

**Saturday, 13th December 20--**

Where do they find those judges? Who picks them? They wouldn't know a good act if it jumped up and slapped them across the face or spat in their eye.

I'm not joking. The other acts were ... 'rubbish' is too kind; they were pathetic. Believe me about this.

Guess who won? A girls' school choir. Honestly, I joke not. They tried so hard to be cool and with-it, singing a jazzed-up version of a 1960's hit. That's why they won. The slightly hippie-looking old geezers of judges had a nostalgia trip.

You should have seen me though. I couldn't help throwing in my bare-belly number at the last minute. Unfortunately, Lisa is so clumsy she bumped into me in the middle of one of her Jedward jumps. That girl needs to go to 'Ballet and Balance' classes.

## COMMENTARY

*Humour engages reader.*

*Notice the pace of the writing, which suggests the excited confidence of the speaker and her desire to control the act.*

*Short sentences increase sense of urgency.*

*Consistent dating.*

*Effective use of repetition.*

*Tone change as date of competition approaches.*

*Notice how we are shown, not told that they did not win.*

*Comments typical of writer of diary. Very consistent.*

*Humour used here as writer mocked those classes earlier. Shows her shallowness and lack of self-awareness.*

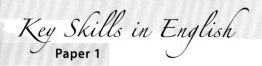
They would not speak to me after the competition. I even got a text from Kevin saying 'U suck big time'. More begrudgery. He was the one who couldn't improvise quickly enough when I started my belly dance.

I'm trying to think of a witty and clever answer. Something like, 'What a splendid head yet no brain.' Aesop said that. I think I could come up with something better. I'm just too tired tonight.

Needless to say, Jack said nothing at all. He just looked at me as if   *Effective use of image.*
I was something nasty that had crawled out from under a stone.

Tomorrow, I'm going to start working on going solo for next   *Ending is typical of the*
year's competition. I'll win. Trust me on that.   *writer's character.*

**Note:** You are not expected to write at this length in the Junior Cert exam, but this example shows the potential to write a story in diary format.

 **OVER TO YOU**

**(a)** Write a short story based on each of the following titles from past exam papers. Remember to observe the guidelines provided for narrative essays on pages 50-54.

  **1.** Write a story that features a most unlikely hero or heroine.

  **2.** Write a story beginning, 'I knew I would need a lot of courage to get through the day.'

  **3.** 'I could hardly sleep with excitement. Only three more days to go ...' Continue this composition.

**(b)** Now try writing one of the short stories listed in part (a) above in a diary format. Remember to observe the guidelines for diary entries on pages 57-58.

## (iii) Writing a Personal Essay

You will be given plenty of choice in the Personal Writing section of Paper One to write about your own experiences, attitudes or feelings. The responses to these titles are very often the best because people tend to write well about the things which they really have experienced or about which they feel deeply.

Underline all the keywords in your chosen title and organise your plan around them. Avoid turning the essay into a short story rather than a piece of writing which reveals you as a person to the reader.

**Here are some examples of titles from past papers:**

♦ *The most interesting place OR places I have ever been*

♦ *Things that make me angry*

♦ *The rudest person I have ever met*

♦ *Magical moments from my childhood*

♦ *Music in my life*

♦ *A talent I would like to have*

♦ *The best advice I was ever given*

♦ *My recipe for happiness*

**Personal Essay: Key Skills**

◎ Remember that you are not writing about events or characters as in a short story. You are **conveying** your own thoughts and feelings about a certain topic or issue. You should always try to write about something you know and are passionate about.

◎ Look carefully at the title before you write. Examine it carefully and make sure that it suits this style of writing. This kind of writing is not a short story nor an argument.

◎ A good introduction should give a little background related to the topic of the essay. It should also give the reader some clue as to why you are writing about this topic.

◎ Your conclusion should restate your main idea and give the reader something to ponder.

◎ Remember the reader. The person reading your essay will not be interested in what you did, what you saw, what you discovered etc. unless you are communicating something deeper, with which they can identify.

◎ As in short story writing: **Show, don't tell!** Create a vivid impression through description rather than simply listing things that may have happened or thoughts which you may have had.

◎ Decide on the tone or general emotion associated with the subject of your writing. Make sure that your choice of language and structure is suitable.

◎ Avoid unnecessary, boring details which reduce the impact of your writing on your reader. Only include those details which are relevant to revealing your thoughts and feelings.

◎ Take care with length of sentences and varied paragraphs.

## Sample 1: Personal Essay

We will now examine this essay using the **RAFT** technique.

### The Best Advice I Was Ever Given

**COMMENTARY**

My grandfather is the most contented person you could ever meet. He doesn't have a lot of money or own a lot of property, he's not famous for anything, and he has arthritis which seems painful enough. But he doesn't complain about any of it – on the contrary, he seems to enjoy life as though each moment were a sip of a really lovely cold drink on a hot day. And although he hasn't done anything really spectacular in his day, he does tell some terrific stories about adventures he had in his youth and during his career as he travelled around the country.  I admire my grandfather greatly and I want to be in his state of mind when I reach my golden years. So when he commented to me one day, 'If you don't expect, you won't be disappointed,' I took this seriously as some advice that I should live by. I have already found that it has helped me to be a happier person.

*Introduces in detail the person who gave the 'best advice'.*

*Excellent image*

*Notice personal tone*

I interpret my Granddad's advice like this: I think he means to say that you shouldn't live in a fantasy world. Sometimes the world will grant your dreams and things will go exactly according to plan. But most of the time, things will be at least a little bit different than you want them to be. Therefore, it's wise to take life as it comes and not expect everything to be perfect. That way, when things are perfect, you will be pleasantly surprised. When they're not, you will be ready to handle it. You will get more satisfaction out of small things, so you won't need to win the lottery to feel glad. Everything good that comes to you will be a gift. The difficult things will still be difficult, but they might not take you by surprise so much.

*Link to next paragraph.*

*Explanation of the advice and why it is so good.*

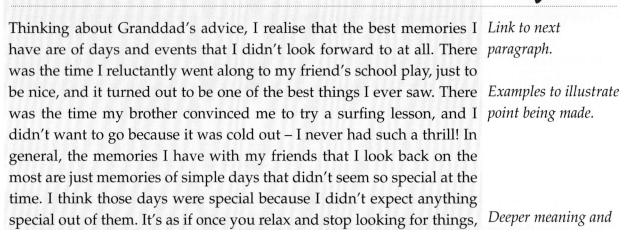

Thinking about Granddad's advice, I realise that the best memories I have are of days and events that I didn't look forward to at all. There was the time I reluctantly went along to my friend's school play, just to be nice, and it turned out to be one of the best things I ever saw. There was the time my brother convinced me to try a surfing lesson, and I didn't want to go because it was cold out – I never had such a thrill! In general, the memories I have with my friends that I look back on the most are just memories of simple days that didn't seem so special at the time. I think those days were special because I didn't expect anything special out of them. It's as if once you relax and stop looking for things, you'll find them.

*Link to next paragraph.*

*Examples to illustrate point being made.*

*Deeper meaning and reflection.*

I decided to use this wisdom to make myself happier. We were coming up to summer holidays at school and like everyone else, I begin to look forward to summer holidays in March if not earlier. My head fills with ideas about all the things I'll do for fun, like swimming, and going for cycles, and spending hours and hours with all my friends together, and seeing every movie that comes out, and maybe going somewhere interesting with my family. Every summer, I expect that each day will be bubbling over with activities and friends and fun, and every summer, I get disappointed. I don't see my friends nearly as much as I expected; I spend half the day watching telly and acting lazy; the weather isn't right for swimming or eating 99s. September arrives and I get depressed because my summer didn't live up to the brilliant expectations I built up in my head.

*Link to previous paragraph.*

*Illustration of attitude before taking the advice.*

*Outcome of previous attitude.*

I decided that this year, I would stop building up big expectations of what my summer should be. I would take it as it came, and just try to relax and enjoy whatever happened while I was out of school for three months. I told myself that my friends might not be available to spend a lot of time with me. I reminded myself that the weather could be bad and that I am always lazy. I made myself think of summer as a season of the year, just like all the others.

*Smooth linking to next paragraph.*

*Personal, reflective tone maintained throughout.*

The results were even better than I hoped. First, I enjoyed the spring much more because I stopped daydreaming about my future holidays. I knew I might not see my friends a lot during the holidays, so I appreciated seeing them at school each day before the holidays began.

*Logical linking of ideas from previous paragraph.*

Then, once the summer came, I didn't worry about how I was spending my days. I got up when I wanted, stayed indoors if I wanted, and met my friends if they were free. I wasn't trying to live up to anything, and it might be my imagination, but I think I had a more active summer than ever before. In any case, I was happier about it than ever before, and that's what counts. I made sure to visit my Granddad. I needed to thank him for letting me in on the secret to his happiness and for giving me such excellent advice.

*Conclusion prepared for.*

*Point emphasised.*

*Conclusion returns to Granddad's advice - neatly bringing the essay full circle.*

R =  **Reason** for the writing: To convey a personal response to the given title.

A =  **Audience:** Language is conversational and intimate. Addresses the reader.

F =  **Format:** The format of this writing is connected to the reason for the writing. Clear opening and conclusion. Excellent linking of paragraphs – every paragraph has one major idea and advances the essay. Varied sentence length and paragraph length.

T =  **Tone:** The tone or atmosphere created by the writer is appropriate. Tone is conveyed through the language used. The tone here is serious and reflective. Personal tone maintained throughout.

**So how would this essay do in the Junior Cert exam according to the current marking scheme?**

**Marking Scheme:**

| | |
|---|---|
| **Content** | 18 / 20 |
| **Structure** | 15 / 15 |
| **Expression** | 30 / 30 |
| **Mechanics** | 5 / 5 |
| | |
| **Total** | 68 / 70 = 98% Grade A |

## Sample 2: Personal Essay

**Here is an example of an essay on the same title but with a completely different approach:**

The Best Advice
I Was Ever Given

If there is one thing I absolutely loathe, it's people giving me advice. How dare they think that I am not able to think for myself about the issues which confront me on a daily basis! I do have a brain and I am quite good at working out how to act in practically every situation which arises in my miserable life as a secondary school student. The only person who ever gave me really good advice, the best advice I was ever given, which I didn't loathe, was Jimmy Black.

First, though, let me give you a sample of some of the advice I have been lumbered with in the past. My parents kept telling me not to get stressed. Oh yes, all very fine, but the problem was they didn't mean a word of it. They were just parrotting all the psycho-babble that goes with their job of being parents to exam students. They gave the right 'advice' but heaven help me if my grades weren't up to scratch! They were trying to swim with the current and against it at the same time. Then they wondered why I was bewildered. Believe me when I say I was very often bewildered to the point of wondering if I was sane.

So now you know why I loathe advice. It depresses me. However, back to Jimmy Black, the best friend and adviser I have ever had. He gave me gold-standard advice for getting through my Junior Cert year.

Jimmy is the kind of friend that most people would avoid like the bubonic plague. There is something contagious about his attitude to school, exams and life in general. He is every parent and teacher's worst nightmare. The reason for this is that Jimmy refuses to conform to other people's expectations of him. He has built up a natural immunity to advice from others and trusts his own instincts. He intrigues me. So, on one of my many 'down-days', I turned to Jimmy for some real advice on how to survive the plague of advice. He didn't let me down.

'Do you know what's wrong with you, Bill? You're a people pleaser!'

'Why do you say that, Jimmy?'

'Because you're always trying to meet other people's expectations of you.'

'What do you mean by that?'

'I mean that you have to fight off the advice of your parents and others and get your own life back.'

'How can I do that Jimmy?'

'Ignore them.'

Now I know what you are probably thinking by now. Jimmy Black was a bad influence and his advice wasn't exactly good advice, not to mind the 'best' advice a person could get. But you're wrong. Jimmy Black was right.

I went home that night and I thought hard about Jimmy himself. He wasn't popular and he wasn't the most scholarly of students. He avoided stress of any sort (as though it was worse than the bubonic plague). He didn't try to fit in with the crowd and he didn't try to impress the teachers or his parents. He let them think whatever they wanted to think while he managed to keep things in perspective. He never got depressed at criticism, as far as I could see, because he ignored it. In one ear and out the other was his way of dealing with criticism or advice.

To make a long story short, I took Jimmy's advice.

When my parents asked about school, I just said everything was fine. When my Christmas report came, they could see that everything was certainly not fine. The usual rant started, 'Look at all we do to give you a good education and you couldn't be bothered to work ... What's the point in talking to you ... You'll get nowhere ...' Normally, I would start arguing back and end up being upset and wishing I had said nothing. But this time I took Jimmy's advice. While they ranted I imagined Jimmy and me on a raft, sailing up the Mississippi away from slavery (yes, you guessed it, we did 'Huckleberry Finn' as our novel). I imagined all the exciting and strange places and people we would encounter together and had to try hard not to smile in the middle of the tirade. That would have started World War Three in our house.

My mock results were not much better than my Christmas tests, but there was, funnily enough, an improvement. One teacher actually wrote, 'Bill seems to be gaining in confidence'. Another strange thing is that my parents and others noticed that I wasn't getting all defensive and worked up about their advice and counter-advice, so they stopped giving it. That was just fine with me. I worked out a good revision plan for myself and decided to prove something to all of them. I wanted them to see that I could do without advice – especially conflicting, negative-sounding advice, which only made things worse anyway by destroying my self-confidence. I decided, by myself, to succeed.

Let me finish by just telling you one fact. Jimmy Black and I came out best in the Junior Cert results.

Now you decide for yourself if Jimmy's advice was the best anyone could ever get.

## 10. You Try It

Imagine that you are the examiner in the Junior Cert exam. You have been told to mark the essay on pages 66 and 67 according to the marking scheme:

| | |
|---|---|
| Content | ? /20 |
| Structure | ? /15 |
| Expression | ? /30 |
| Mechanics | ? / 5 |
| | |
| Total | / 70 |

**1.** How would you mark this essay? Give reasons for the marks you would award.

Remember that the writer decided to write a personal response type of essay to this title. That is fine, because the style of essay was not specified in the wording of the task.

Read the guidelines for writing a personal, discursive style of essay on page 63 before you begin to mark this piece of writing.

■ For **content** ask yourself if the ideas in the essay are completely relevant to the title.

■ For **structure** look carefully at the introduction and conclusion. Look at the variation in sentence length and paragraphs.

■ For **expression** ask yourself if the language is suitable for the style of essay. Are words well-chosen? Is it clear what the writer is saying? Does it sound forced or natural?

■ For **mechanics** examine the spelling, grammar and punctuation of the essay.

**2.** Now grade the essay. You might like to compare your grading with another student's grade and discuss any differences of opinion about the awarding of marks.

**3.** Finally, ask your teacher how they would award marks on this essay if they were grading it.

**4.** For another example of personal writing, read the essay which follows and pay attention to the comments in the right-hand margin.

# Sample 3: Personal Essay

## Things That Fill Me With Wonder

**ANSWER**

Wonder is an emotion that many things can prompt, as long as your mind is open to it. When I consider how many wonderful things surround me, it's overwhelming. Even in the past year alone, off the top of my head I can come up with an almost endless list of things that filled me with wonder and amazement.

The first thing, or person, that comes to mind is my little cousin, Rory. He was born a few months ago, and his tiny but perfect hands and feet amaze me every time I look at them. I'm filled with wonder when I think that just one year ago, he was not here. Now, he is here just like we are, and he is getting bigger and smarter every day. He looks at me with his bright, round eyes and I can see he is trying to figure out who I am and what everything around him is. Everything fills him with wonder, and his wonder is contagious. It is fascinating to see such a tiny person growing up before your eyes.

I also think about a trip to Italy that I took with my family last summer. In our guidebook, we read about a writer from several hundred years ago who was seized with amazement when he visited Florence and saw all the beautiful architecture. His amazement was so strong that he had heart palpitations and other symptoms of illness, which seemed to be caused by the beauty of his surroundings. I understood how he felt. I can imagine getting light-headed after looking at the cathedrals in Florence or Milan. I couldn't believe how much work must have gone into building them, and I couldn't imagine how someone could plan the construction beforehand in such detail. The fact that these buildings have remained standing for so long, without crumbling or being destroyed, is also striking. While the world is changing so fast, they stand in the same grand way they always have. This makes them a link to the past, and they make you stop and think about everything that happened since they were built, all of the many scenes they have witnessed.

**COMMENTARY**

*Opening line addresses the topic.*

*Personal tone.*

*Wording focuses on title.*

*First example introduced and developed.*

*Every sentence is built on the opening sentence of the paragraph - creates a unit.*

*Title central to main idea.*

*Smooth link to next paragraph.*

*Paragraph deals with one main idea.*

*Personal tone maintained.*

*Reflection on the experience which is linked to title.*

| ANSWER | COMMENTARY |
|---|---|
| It is especially strange to leave these historic cathedrals and step onto an airplane to fly back home. When we boarded our flight, I thought about how flabbergasted Michaelangelo would be to see a jumbo jet swooping across the sky. I've flown in airplanes quite a few times, but in spite of this I shake my head in wonder whenever I fly. In an airplane, you speed from one country to another in a matter of hours, crossing towering mountains and mighty rivers in a single bound. When I think of how many residents of Rome throughout the years would have longed for such an experience, I am full of wonder and gratitude that I am part of an amazing age. | *Link in ideas – movement from wonders of ancient world to wonders of modern world.* *Wording of title kept central.* |
| But the thankfulness I felt then was nothing compared to what I felt when I passed my Junior Cert 'mock' exams and did much better than I expected in most subjects. I had been studying quite a lot this year, but I didn't have much confidence going into the exams. A lot of important things didn't seem to be sticking in my head, but obviously I did something right! When I saw my results, I tried to imagine how I earned those grades and I couldn't quite do it. I could only wonder and be hopeful about the actual exam. | *Smooth link to next paragraph. Paragraph deals with one main idea. Personal tone maintained. Reflection on the experience which is linked to title.* |
| When I reflect on this list of things that gave me a feeling of wonder in the past, I ask myself what they all have in common. What makes something wondrous? I think wonder comes from a strong emotional reaction to something that you don't fully understand. I don't really know how my little cousin learns to smile and walk and talk, or how people managed to build huge cathedrals centuries ago, or what makes airplanes work so that humans can fly, or what enabled me to get through my mocks with flying colours. But I'm very glad all of these things happen or happened, because they make my life and the lives of many people so much richer. Some of the most important and beloved things in my life are things I can't explain. Maybe if I could explain them, I would take them for granted or consider them dull, everyday facts. But I can't explain them – which is the source of their wonder. | *Conclusion built up on the examples given in the body of the essay.* *Reflection on the meaning of the word 'wonder'.* *Ending directly linked to the concept of wonder.* |

**So how would this essay do in the Junior Cert exam according to the current marking scheme?**

**Marking Scheme:**

| | | |
|---|---|---|
| **Content** | 17 / 20 | All points relevant, but could do with more originality. |
| **Structure** | 15 / 15 | Excellent structure |
| **Expression** | 23 / 30 | There could be more variety in language use. |
| **Mechanics** | 5 / 5 | Perfect |
| | | |
| **Total** | 60 / 70 = 85% = Grade A | |

## OVER TO YOU

**Write a personal essay on at least two of the following titles taken from past exam papers:**

1. The most interesting place or places I have ever been.
2. Things that make me angry.
3. The rudest person I have ever met.
4. Magical moments from my childhood.
5. Music in my life.
6. A talent I would like to have.

## (iv) Writing a Descriptive Essay

The ability to write descriptively is essential for most genres. However, in the Junior Cert exam you are seldom required to describe anything purely for the sake of describing. Usually, you will use your descriptive skills in your narrative, personal, argumentative and opinion essays. Description, therefore, is a skill you need to master because it will improve your writing in whichever genre you choose to use.

Effective description works because it appeals to the reader's senses of sight, touch, taste, smell and hearing. By using sensory details the writer helps the reader to imagine the person, incident or scene being described as if they were there and to respond to it emotionally.

In the following brief example from a student's writing you will see how this can be achieved:

*Mrs O'Hara lived alone in a house on the corner and liked to sit out on fine days and watch all the children from the estate playing games. Usually she would bring a tin of chocolate biscuits with her and offer them to any of us who ran past her gate. If you took a biscuit, you had to listen to Mrs O'Hara talk for at least ten minutes. She liked to tell the story of how she met her husband at a dance when she was nineteen years old. She also liked to share the story of their first house, which was a small but lovely cottage. She seemed very proud of that house, because when they bought it there was grass growing out of the roof, but they turned it into the nicest house in the county.*

*Even though I heard her stories many times, I couldn't really picture Mrs O'Hara as a young woman. In fact, my brother told me once that Mrs O'Hara was the oldest old lady in the world, and for a long time I believed him. Her skin was dark and so creased that it looked scaly. Her blue eyes were cloudy, like they had got damp and musty over time. She had a hoarse voice, so that it sounded like she was straining to get the words out. But she seemed to want to talk more than anyone else I knew – she seemed to need to talk, as though talking was the thing that kept her alive.*

In this extract, the reader can imagine the old woman clearly because of the appeal to different senses. These sensory descriptions are in purple in the passage above.

You will notice that the writer does not tell us what to think about Mrs O'Hara, but allows us to picture her for ourselves and come to our own conclusions about her character from the details of the description. This is what is meant by **show, don't tell** when describing anyone or anything or any place.

**Descriptive writing: Key Skills**

◎ Use sensory images to engage the reader.

◎ Show, don't tell!

◎ Use specific details. Only emphasise the aspects that bring out the essential characteristics of whatever is being described.

◎ Take great care with word choice. Choose adjectives and adverbs carefully. Do not fall into the trap of thinking that the more adjectives you use, the better the description! This is never the case. Take for example the simple sentence, *The cat sat on the mat.* Compare this to *The fat, black cat sat on the fluffy mat.* Now compare this last sentence to *The big, fat, lazy, black and white cat sat on the large, red, circular, slightly-worn, comfy, fluffy mat.* The unnecessary adjectives make the writing sound ridiculous. Who wants to know so much about the cat or the mat? What is the importance of either? Remember – do not overdo description. Pick the details you want to zoom in on and select words carefully for exact meaning.

◎ Clever use of similes and metaphors can enrich your descriptions.

◎ Imagine that you are recording a scene with a camera: zoom in on details, pan across the scene, move from outside to inside or reverse that order. Make sure that you can see, hear, touch, taste and smell as much as possible. But do not just write a random list! Choose what is going to be the focus of your attention and decide *why* it is going to be so.

◎ A description is not a short story. Read the guidelines on pages 50-54 for writing a short story. Description can and should be an essential feature of a story, but it is not the story.

◎ When you are describing, keep in mind that you are aiming to communicate a **theme**. This is what gives depth to your writing. In the example on page 71, the writer introduces the themes of loneliness and old age. How? Through the carefully chosen descriptive details. Mrs O'Hara lives alone and watches children play; she bribes them to listen to her life story by giving them biscuits; the final sentence – *But she seemed to want to talk more than anyone else I knew – she seemed to need to talk, as though talking was the thing that kept her alive.* – is laden with suggestion concerning the themes of loneliness and old age. The writer only uses the details which will underline the theme or major idea.

◎ Create an appropriate mood for the scene you are describing. This will help to engage the reader and advance your theme or idea.

◎ Use the Rule of Three (grouping ideas in a list of three: *I came, I saw, I conquered*) to add emphasis to descriptions.

◎ Repetition can be effective. But, again, choose carefully the words you repeat in order to emphasise your main idea or theme.

You can learn a great deal about description by reading the works of great writers. Take a look at this extract from *Hard Times* by Charles Dickens. If you examine his technique, you will see why he is regarded as one of the great descriptive writers in the English language:

*'NOW, what I want is, Facts. Teach these boys and girls nothing but Facts. Facts alone are wanted in life. Plant nothing else, and root out everything else. You can only form the minds of reasoning animals upon Facts: nothing else will ever be of any service to them. This is the principle on which I bring up my own children, and this is the principle on which I bring up these children. Stick to Facts, sir!'*

*The scene was a plain, bare, monotonous vault of a schoolroom, and the speaker's square forefinger emphasised his observations by underscoring every sentence with a line on the schoolmaster's sleeve. The emphasis was helped by the speaker's square wall of a forehead, which had his eyebrows for its base, while his eyes found commodious cellarage in two dark caves, overshadowed by the wall. The emphasis was helped by the speaker's mouth, which was wide, thin, and hard set. The emphasis was helped by the speaker's voice, which was inflexible, dry, and dictatorial. The emphasis was helped by the speaker's hair, which bristled on the skirts of his bald head, a plantation of firs to keep the wind from its shining surface, all covered with knobs, like the crust of a plum pie, as if the head had scarcely warehouse-room for the hard facts stored inside. The speaker's obstinate carriage, square coat, square legs, square shoulders, — nay, his very neckcloth, trained to take him by the throat with an unaccommodating grasp, like a stubborn fact, as it was, — all helped the emphasis.*

## 11. You Try It

Find three of the features of effective descriptive writing in the above passage from *Hard Times*.

   (a) In the case of each of these three features, say how it affects the passage.
   (b) What impression of the speaker did you form from this description?
   (c) Pick three words which you found particularly effective. Explain your response.

## Sample 1: Descriptive Essay

# Sleepless In The City

*A day in New York begins with night, since the city's greatest fame lies in its sleeplessness. Almost all over the world, 3 a.m. is a disconcerting hour, a time when nothing stirs and those lying awake in their beds are likely to scare themselves with black thoughts of intruders, demons, bad luck. In New York, though, there is always comfort and company for the likes of an insomniac like James Harty. Instead of suffering in his room, taunted by the digital display clock, he can pull on his jeans and a warm sweater, take the keys to his apartment from the rack, and wander onto the Manhattan street, seeking the reassurance of hustle and bustle.*

*Most of the cars on the street, especially at 3 a.m., are yellow taxis. They pulse up the avenues like purposeful bees, carrying revellers to and from nightclubs that won't close until the sun comes up, even though it's midweek. Larger, sleek black cars bring worker bees from Wall Street, zipping home to catch a scrap of sleep before the work day begins again. On one block, outside a hospital's A&E entrance, an ambulance flashes blue and red but there is no sign of a patient, only the ambulance crew standing nearby, talking and laughing.*

*He wanders into a newsagent's just in time to see the day's papers delivered. The tabloid lettering is large and loud, something about the latest scandal involving a footballer. He has to buy something, so he chooses the least expensive thing, a packet of chewing gum. Chewing gum is always useful. It's sugar-free, and tastes of menthol, making the mouth feel like a cold wind is blowing through it.*

*Outside the shop, three young men are leaning against the wall, smoking. By keeping his eyes on the ground, James is ignored. High above the street, a light goes out in one window and turns on in the next one. It might be cleaning crews, finishing the evening's work in an office – or maybe it's an apartment building where early risers are moving from the bedroom to the kitchen, where coffee awaits. He keeps walking, south along the avenue, passing a gaggle of young people who are a little bit drunk and yelping loudly.*

*The sky begins to lighten in the east – slowly if you stop to watch it, but with shocking speed if you aren't paying attention. Streaks of ice blue slip between the buildings at each intersection. A low, revving grumble sounds as a garbage truck approaches the corner; it's followed by a high-pitched squeak of brakes, and before it comes to a complete stop, two men in dark jumpsuits spring out to collect fifteen bags of 'treasure' from the kerb.*

*Inside a park, along the road that is closed to cars, foot traffic is high. Joggers and speed walkers pass – some of them race, some of them dart, some of them plod, and some of them drag themselves with great effort. Most look quite fit and wear sleek exercise clothing that makes them look like advertisements for fitness products.*

*As noon approaches, delivery men are still busy on the side streets. They laugh and joke with each other, discussing the latest political news, as they slide large parcels from trucks to the ground along wooden runners. Outside a school, small children are lined up two by two, like colourful dominoes,*

*waiting for their tall teachers to lead them on a field trip.*

*The day has become quite warm, and in the small seating area outside a Holiday Inn, hotel guests mingle with workers eating sandwiches and holding meetings in the fresh air. The traffic is beginning to thicken. At some of the intersections, policemen make big movements with their arms, directing first this stream of vehicles, then the other, to come forward or to stop.*

*The light begins to sharpen. James is finally starting to feel like he might sleep, but dusk is his favourite time of day, so he pushes on. In the canyons formed between the skyscrapers, a pink colour shines from the west side.*

*Walking back uptown, he watches steam shoot from the manholes and sees a night work crew digging up the tarmac of the street. The bars are lively at this hour, with after-work drinkers and tourists and college students. If he walked in and tried to meet people, it probably would not be too difficult. As always in New York, he has plenty of company. But tonight, all he wants is his bed.*

## Questions

**(a)** Is the title appropriate for the essay? Explain your answer

**(b)** Which senses are appealed to in this description? Look for sights, sounds, smells, textures, tastes. What is the effect of using these sensory images?

**(c)** Do you get the impression of watching a video as you read? How is this effect created?

**(d)** Is this a story with a plot, characters, climax, dialogue, resolution etc? Should it be?

**(e)** What tense is used in this essay? Do you think it is appropriate? Explain your answer.

**(f)** Comment on the use of language and imagery in this essay.

## 12. You Try It

**(a)** Which features of descriptive writing can you identify in this extract? Check through each of the guidelines given on pages 72-73 and see which ones are being used.

**(b)** Write a description of each of the following:

- A city at night
- A troublemaker
- A storm
- A character who is old and unhappy
- A character who is mysterious
- A person who is generous and caring

- A young, frightened person
- A scene of natural beauty
- An old deserted house
- A person who is about to commit a murder
- A character who is in conflict with another character

- A cunning thief
- A scene of devastation
- A character who is old but happy

**Remember:** Do not tell a story! You are writing a description

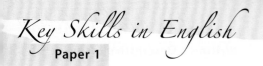
## (v) Writing an Essay Inspired by an Image

In the Personal Writing section of the Junior Cert exam paper, you can be asked to write an essay 'inspired' by an image. Unless you are specifically told to write a short story, you are free to choose the format for your essay.

### Key Skills

The guidelines for each type of essay remain the same. The only difference is that you are using a visual rather than a written prompt.

### Step One

Examine the image very carefully. Take notice of the main subject (person, animal or thing) which attracts your attention. Ask yourself questions about the subject, e.g. Who or what is this?

If it is a person or a group of people, try to imagine who they are, where they have come from, what they are doing, why they are doing it. Look at their clothes carefully and at anything they may be holding or using. What sort of facial expressions have they? Are they nice or nasty? Keep asking questions until you have given the character(s) a background and personality. Remember, you are deciding who this person is or who these people are. However, you must be 'inspired' by what you see in the image.

If it is an animal or animals, ask yourself the same questions. It may be a photo of people with animals. Invent an identity for each of them. Give them names.

If it is an object, ask yourself similar questions. Invent a history or background for this object, based on the details in the image.

Now look at the background and at any other details. What do they tell you about the setting? Where might this place be? Are there any obvious clues? If not, you decide where the setting is.

Ask yourself what type of atmosphere is in the image. What creates the mood? Is weather important? Are buildings, landscapes, seascapes, skyscapes adding to a certain mood or feeling?

Ask yourself what happened just before this image was created. Imagine something that may have taken place which has resulted in this scene.

Unless you have been told to write your essay as a story, decide whether you are going to write a debate, persuasive piece, a personal opinion piece, an article, a descriptive piece or a story based on this picture. Follow the guidelines for the type of essay you choose.

Now you are ready to plan your composition.

### Step Two

Plan the essay using one of the planning methods shown earlier in this section on pages 30-35.

Remember to base your plan closely on what you have seen in the image. Use as many of the details as you can.

## Step Three

Write your essay. If you have chosen a story, pay attention to setting, character, dialogue, conflict, climax and resolution. If you have chosen a different type of essay, use a suitable style.

**Sample Question**
Write a short story inspired by this picture.

## (c) Final Guidelines

If you practise writing in different styles or genres, you will discover which ones you are best at. You will also find that the different types of writing overlap. For example, you would need good descriptive and narrative writing skills to use an anecdote effectively in an argument.

A Chief Examiner of Junior Certificate English has noted that students who excelled in the exam indicated that they had a real grasp of style and genre coupled with much experience of writing for themselves. In many cases, however, it was noted that candidates did not vary sentence length and had a limited vocabulary.

**Take note of the following advice which has been adapted from a Chief Examiner's Report:**

■ Read, widely, enjoyably and often. Read a daily paper. You can do this for free if you call into your local library.

■ Examine the styles of different writers. Read magazines, books and instruction sheets that come with appliances and gadgets.

■ Write every day; rewrite often. Write drafts and select from them for a final version. A good style is usually the result of lots of practice in selecting one word, one phrase, or one paragraph over another. Learn to know why you make these selections; do the practice to acquire the style.

■ Take time to learn about the grammatical rules and conventions of the language. Ask your teacher to explain points of grammar which puzzle you. Experiment with tenses.

■ Take particular care with spelling and punctuation. English written in your Junior Cert exam will be more complex and varied than that used for texting on your mobile phone. Good spelling and well-used punctuation add clarity and precision to your writing.

■ Read the instructions on your exam paper closely. Answer what you are asked to answer.

■ Re-read your work, especially when writing your examination answers. Most people make mistakes when pressed for time. You want to be sure that what you have written is what you meant to write.

**Check List**

**Use the following check-list after each essay you write to ensure that you have complied with the demands of the marking scheme:**

Have I read the essay **title** correctly and underlined the key words? ❏

Have I checked to make sure of the **style** or **genre**? (If no particular style is specified, I can write in any suitable style). ❏

Have I brainstormed and **planned** my essay? ❏

Have I made sure that all my points or ideas are **relevant** to the title? ❏

Have I thought about and composed an **effective opening** to 'hook' my reader? ❏

Have I made sure to **create paragraphs** properly? One point per paragraph? ❏

Have I stated and developed **my points**? ❏

Have I **linked** my paragraphs so that the essay flows smoothly? ❏

Have I chosen **words** carefully and **varied** my expression? ❏

Have I varied my **sentence length**? ❏

Have I tried to create some **interesting, original** images in my writing for effect? ❏

Have I written a **strong conclusion**? ❏

Have I checked my **spelling, punctuation** and **grammar**? ❏

If you can tick every one of the above boxes, you will have written an effective essay which will gain excellent marks in the Junior Cert exam.

# Glossary

**allusion:** a passing reference

**anecdote:** a short story to illustrate a point

**apt:** suitable

**atrocious:** very bad, awful

**biased:** prejudiced, taking sides

**chronological:** order of events, arranged according to time

**clarity:** clearness of expression

**cliché:** worn-out, over-used phrase or saying

**coherent:** logical and consistent

**colloquial language:** casual, familiar language

**compulsion:** forced

**condescending:** acting in a way that suggests you believe you are superior to or better than others

**consistent:** unchanging, not contradictory

**convey:** made known

**counter-argument:** the opposite point of view

**credible:** believable

**genre:** type of writing

**implication:** not openly said but suggested

**rhetorical question:** a question asked for effect. No answer expected

**refutation:** to respond in a speech to an attack on a point you have made and prove the attack to be wrong

**statistics:** the study of data

# 3. Functional Writing

## Contents

## Key Exam Skills: *Functional Writing*

1 **Be aware of the content you need to include in your answer.**

Ensure that you have clearly communicated the information requested in the question.

2 **Make sure you are using the correct structure.**

For example, if your chosen question asks you to write a report, you cannot write it in the form of an email.

3 **Pitch your writing to the intended audience.**

A speech to your classmates has a different pitch to a memo to your boss at work.

# SECTION 3: FUNCTIONAL WRITING

It is recommended that you spend approximately **30 minutes** on this section in the Junior Cert exam. You will be given a choice of two or three questions. You must select and answer one of these questions. Each question is worth **30 marks**.

You must be aware of:

    **(a)** the content to be communicated

    **(b)** the correct structure

    **(c)** suitable expression and tone, depending on audience.

In the Functional Writing section you can be asked to:

- write a formal or informal letter
- write a book/film/event review
- write a speech
- write an email/fax/memo
- write a set of instructions
- use a set of pictures to inspire a specific piece of writing.
- write a report
- write the text of a brochure or flyer
- write a blurb for a book
- write a curriculum vitae (CV)
- describe a photograph or picture

**Note:** The composition types that most frequently occur in the exam are covered in this section.

You will be rewarded for:

    **1.** Well-structured answers

    **2.** Clarity of expression

    **3.** An appropriate tone

    **4.** Good grammar, spelling and punctuation.

## (a) Formal Letters

The most important element of writing a good letter is your ability to identify and write to your audience. Letters can be formal or informal.

    Formal letters are business letters. Informal letters are more chatty and are usually written to friends, relatives or people you know well.

    Always begin a new page of your answer book when writing a letter in your Junior Cert exam.

There are different kinds of formal letters. Here are some examples:

- letters of application for jobs
- letters of complaint
- letters of invitation to a formal event
- letters to the editor of a newspaper
- letters seeking information
- letters ordering or returning goods.

## Guidelines for writing a formal letter

✪ Before you begin, ask yourself the following questions: Who am I writing to? Why am I writing? What do I need to tell them? What do I want them to do?

✪ The language used should be formal and businesslike. Avoid slang or colloquial language. Do not use abbreviations or contractions. Emotional language or sarcasm should be avoided.

✪ The purpose of the letter should be absolutely clear to the **recipient**. You should state the purpose of the letter in your opening paragraph, i.e. directly after the opening salutation/ greeting.

✪ The letter should be **concise**. Do not use long, rambling sentences or lose sight of the purpose of your writing. Do not be vague about your objective. Get to the point without going into unnecessary detail.

✪ The letter should be organised in a logical manner. All letters follow a standard structure which must be observed in the exam. Examples of this structure are provided in this section.

✪ Your spelling and grammar should be free from errors. So, re-read your letter very carefully!

## Format for a formal letter:

**Read these guidelines and then check the sample letter on the next page.**

1. Your address should be displayed in the top right-hand corner.
2. The date should be displayed just below your address on the right. Skip a line between your address and the date. Give the full date, e.g. 26th March 20 – –. Avoid abbreviations.
3. The name/title and address of the person you are writing to should be displayed on the left-hand side of the letter, just below the level of your own address.
4. The formal salutation or greeting should be below the name and address of the recipient. Skip a line. When you know the name of the person you are writing to, you open by formally addressing them, e.g. **Dear Ms Collins**. If you do not know the recipient's name, address them as **Dear Sir/Madam**.
5. The opening paragraph should clearly state the purpose of the letter.
6. The following two or three paragraphs should form the body of the letter. Each paragraph should develop one major point or comment.
7. The final paragraph should conclude the letter.
8. Close formally by using the words **Yours sincerely** if you know the name of the person to whom you are writing. Use **Yours faithfully** if you do not know their name.
9. Sign your name. Write your name in block capitals underneath your signature.

## Sample Letter of Complaint

**1.** 56 Fairtree Road,
Bridgewater,
Cork

**2.** 10th March 2014

**3.** Mr John Mitchell,
52 Fairtree Road,
Bridgewater,
Cork

**4.** Dear Mr Mitchell,

**5.** I am writing to you concerning the nuisance created by your dogs barking at night.

**6.** As you are well aware, I have asked you repeatedly to bring your dogs indoors after 11.00 p.m, which I do not consider to be an unreasonable request. However, despite your assurance that you would do so, you have allowed the animals to remain outdoors, barking at passing pedestrians and road traffic.

Not only am I wakened during the night by your dogs, but so are my children, one of whom is a young baby. Several other neighbours also have young children who are being disturbed. This clearly cannot be allowed to continue.

I would very much appreciate if you would take immediate steps to **rectify** this matter. Failing any satisfactory response to this request, I will have no option but to contact the Garda Síochána and make a formal complaint.

**7.** I hope you will carefully consider and respond positively to this request as it is in everybody's interest to maintain pleasant neighbourhood relationships.

**8.** Yours sincerely,

**9.** Michael Barrett
MICHAEL BARRETT

### You Try It

You are Mr John Mitchell. Write your reply to this letter.

## Sample Letter for a Job Application

**1.** 'Laburnum Cottage',
31 Westgate Avenue,
Glendown,
Wicklow

**2.** 26th July 2014

**3.** The Manager,
Shoprite Superstore,
Park Road,
Wicklow

**4.** Dear Sir / Madam,

**5.** I wish to apply for the temporary position of shop assistant as advertised in 'The Wicklow Chronicle' on 25th July.

**6.** I have just completed my Transition Year in St. Conleth's College in Glendown and intend to continue on to Leaving Certificate with a view to studying economics at university.

During the last year I gained valuable experience working in our local supermarket at weekends. This position required me to work as a member of a team and to engage in a polite and helpful manner with customers. I am pleased to say that my employers were impressed by my work and attitude and are willing to employ me again. However, I would prefer to work full-time in a temporary position rather than part-time at weekends.

I enclose copies of references from the principal of St. Conleth's College, Mr John Hegarty, and also from the manager of my local supermarket, Ms Pauline Smith. Both of these people, who have known me for several years, consider me to be honest, hard-working and reliable.

**7.** I would be grateful if you would consider my application favourably and am available for interview at any time.

**8.** Yours faithfully,

**9.** Mark Cummins
MARK CUMMINS

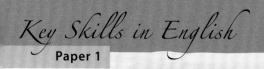

## Sample Letter Seeking Information

**1.** 21 Cherry Road,
Artane,
Dublin 5

**2.** 16th August 2014

**3.** The Manager,
Waterworld Adventure Centre,
Beach Road,
Newtown,
Galway

**4.** Dear Sir / Madam,

**5.** I am writing to you to request information on the summer courses which you organise for young people during the summer months.

**6.** I am most interested in water sports such as canoeing, kayaking, sailing and surfing. I am a good swimmer and have engaged in each of the above sports at different times in the last few years.

Could you please let me know the full costs involved regarding tuition, equipment hire and the methods of payment which you accept? I would also be interested in any special offers you may have available should I choose a combination of several activities. A brochure would be most welcome, if available.

As I do not live in Galway, I would be grateful if you could give me some information concerning accommodation within walking distance of the centre. I am aware that you do not have any accommodation at the centre itself, but perhaps there is a good hostel or reasonably-priced guesthouse nearby.

**7.** I look forward to hearing from you at your earliest convenience.

**8.** Yours faithfully,

**9.** Mary Jones.
MARY JONES

## Sample Letter of Invitation

**1.** The Young Writers' Centre,
Parnell Square,
Dublin 1

**2.** 30th April 2014

**3.** Mr John Holloway,
'The Moorings',
Dalkey,
County Dublin

**4.** Dear Mr Holloway,

**5.** I am writing on behalf of The Young Writers' Centre to formally invite you to speak at our forthcoming conference on 'Young Irish Writing Today'.

**6.** This conference will take place in The Highbury Hotel, Abbey Street, Dublin on 15th June 2014, starting at 10.00 a.m. and concluding at 5.30 p.m. If you are able to accept our invitation, we will be more than happy to offer you the speaking time of your choice. It is proposed that you would speak for approximately one hour.

The aim of the conference is to raise awareness of the diverse talents possessed by aspiring young writers, some of whom will read excerpts from their own work. We hope that there will be lively discussion and feedback from the audience. In addition, we aim to assist young writers by inviting writers of your calibre and distinction to offer advice and share insights into the art of writing effectively.

As a voluntary group, we cannot, unfortunately, pay a fee, but we would be happy to pay your travel expenses and provide a midday lunch and evening dinner.

**7.** We would be most honoured and grateful if you could attend and speak at our conference.
I can be contacted at the above address or at the telephone number or email address below.

**8.** Yours sincerely,

**9.** Michael Andrews.
Secretary: 'The Young Writers' Centre'
Telephone: 01 9487263
email: m.andrews@rmail.net

## 2. You Try It

You are Mr Holloway. Reply to this letter.

## Sample Letter to a Newspaper Editor

**Notes**

Although this type of letter is formal, it follows a different format to each of the other formal letters. In a letter to a newspaper, you:

- place the date at the top right-hand side of the page.
- open with the word **Sir** or **Madam** (omit the usual 'Dear Sir or Madam').
- close with the words **Yours, etc.** (omit 'sincerely' or 'faithfully').
- sign the letter as usual.
- write your address (which will be abbreviated by the editor) at the end, under your signature.

# LETTERS

20th July 2012

Sir - I wonder if anybody else has noticed that there are completely different coloured running torches used in the Olympic games. The Paralympic torches are silver, whilst those carried for the Olympic games are gold. Why the difference?

I can only conclude that the Paralympics are perceived by some people as being somehow less important or significant than the games for able-bodied people. We all know that silver is inferior to gold!

Personally, I find this attitude condescending as well as misguided.

While credit is due to all athletes reaching this level of competition, there is something truly inspiring and even heroic, in many cases, about the achievements of the Paralympians.

I cannot see any reason whatsoever for the difference in the colours of the running torches and would be grateful if somebody who knows the reasoning behind this distinction could enlighten me concerning this matter.

Yours etc.

Mary Kelly

Killeshandra.

Letters to an Editor can also be written in the usual formal letter format. The wording of the exam question will make it clear to you if you should write **(a)** a letter which gives a short opinion on a current issue or **(b)** a letter which invites a specific response from a reader.

**Take for example the question from the Functional Writing section of a recent exam paper.**

**Sample Question**
A national newspaper has organised a 'Person of the Year Award'. Write a letter to the editor, nominating the person you think is most deserving of this award. You should explain why you think the person deserves the award.  **JC Exam Question**

**1.** 13 The Rise,
Cornamaddy,
Athlone,
Co. Westmeath.

**2.** 28th August 2012

**3.** The Editor,
The Irish News,
Abbey Street,
Dublin 1

**4.** Dear Sir,

**5.** I am writing in response to your invitation to readers to nominate a person for the **prestigious** 'Person of the Year Award' 2012. In my opinion, nobody deserves this award more than the Irish Olympic Gold Medallist, Katie Taylor.

**6.** Katie not only bore the flag for Ireland at the London Olympics and brought home the gold medal, she also brought credit to this nation by the way she conducted herself throughout the games. She showed no arrogance in her victory and **graciously** praised the performances of her opponents, some of whom were less than gracious in defeat!

Not only is Katie a great athlete, but she is also a wonderful role model for young people, particularly young women. Boxing as a sport is not always accepted as something in which women should or could excel. Katie put an end to that particular type of stereotyping by showing that women can excel in any sport.

Another reason why I think Katie deserves the award is because she has shown that determination, hard work and the ability to overcome obstacles eventually lead to success. It is difficult to imagine that a young girl trained by her father in a small studio with only the most basic of facilities at her disposal could have the confidence and vision to take on the whole world and win.

**7.** I hope you agree with my nomination of Katie Taylor for this prestigious award. I cannot think of any other person who deserves it more. She lifted the spirit of the nation!

**8.** Yours faithfully,

**9.** Marian Duffy
MARIAN DUFFY

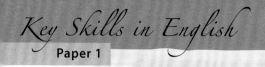

## OVER TO YOU

Practise formal letter writing by answering each one of the following questions. Make sure that you follow the guidelines for formal letters given on page 81 and check your work against each point. Strictly adhere to the format for formal letters.

1. Write a letter to the author of any text you have studied, telling him/her whether or not you enjoyed it, and explaining why. (**JC Exam Question**)

2. You need a reference letter from your principal to secure a summer job. Write the letter you would like him/her to supply you with. The address you use should not be that of your actual school, nor should you use your own name. (**JC Exam Question**)

3. A letter has appeared in a daily newspaper claiming that 'teenagers nowadays have no moral standards'. Write a letter of reply in which you respond to this charge. (**JC Exam Question**)

4. Write a letter of complaint to a shop which sold you a **defective** item. Explain exactly the nature of the problem and clarify what action you expect to be taken.

5. Write a letter to the Board of Management of your school objecting to the rules concerning having to wear your school uniform during state examinations.

**Checklist**

Use the following checklist to ensure that you have complied with the demands of the marking scheme:

Have I **read** the question very carefully and analysed **exactly** what I am being asked to do? ❑

Have I followed the **correct format** for a formal letter? (Check guidelines) ❑

Have I used **paragraphs** properly? **One idea** or comment per paragraph. ❑

Have I used formal, clear English and **avoided slang** or colloquial expressions? ❑

Have I avoided using **contractions**, e.g. 'it's' instead of 'it is' etc? ❑

Have I avoided using **abbreviations**? ❑

Have I used the **correct complimentary close**? **Yours sincerely** when I know the name of the recipient; **Yours faithfully** if I do not know their name. ❑

Have I **signed** the letter correctly? ❑

Have I checked my **spelling** and **grammar**? ❑

If you can answer 'Yes' to each of the above questions, you should do very well in formal letter writing.

Functional Writing
Informal/Personal Letters

## (b) Informal/Personal Letters

You write informal or personal letters to people whom you know or who are related to you. Some, but not all, of the rules for writing a formal letter apply. Personal letters do not commonly appear in the Functional Writing section of the Junior Cert Higher Level exam paper.

**Guidelines for writing an informal letter:**

✪ Your address should be displayed in the top right-hand corner.

✪ The date should be displayed just below your address on the right. Skip a line between your address and the date. You can write the date in full or you may use an abbreviated form, e.g. 1/3/15.

✪ There is no need to write the name and address of the recipient. This is never done in informal letters to friends and relations.

✪ The salutation or greeting should be on the left-hand side of the page, as in formal letters. You can address the person by their first name, e.g. *Dear Joe* or *Dear Granny* etc.

✪ You should use paragraphs correctly, but you are not required to state the purpose of the letter or comply with the formal letter conventions.

✪ Ensure that you are writing on the topic outlined in the question.

✪ The language register can be chatty, colloquial and intimate. However, avoid overuse of slang and **never** use obscene language.

✪ The final paragraph should conclude the letter, but it can be less formally structured.

✪ The tone can be humorous, sarcastic, mock-serious, serious or sincere.

✪ You may close informally by using such phrases as *Best wishes, Hope to see you soon, Lots of love* etc.

✪ Sign your name. Usually, your first name is all that is required, as the recipient knows you well.

In each of the sample letters on pages 90 and 91, note how each of the above points has been applied.

**Sample Question**
Write a letter to a friend inviting them to come on a holiday with you and your family.
(In a letter like this, you are free to take a light-hearted, humorous approach.)

## Sample 1: Informal Letter

23 Fairfield Road,
Newtown,
Co. Mayo.

24th April 2014

Dear Martin,

Great, great news! Mum and Dad have just told me that they are taking my sister Jill and me to Disneyland in Paris for the last two weeks in June! But that's not the best part of it, buddy – we can each bring a friend along because the deal is for a family with four kids and we have only two. You are my choice of friend, Martin, and you'd better get your parents to let you come along.

I know you're probably thinking that Disneyland is more for little kids. We've gone a bit beyond Mickey Mouse and Donald Duck at this stage of our lives. But think: PARIS! Think of all those gorgeous-looking French girls working in Disneyland for the summer holidays, with their 'ooh-la-la' – not to mention the laughs we'll have choosing between them. They might join us in the evenings for a bit of craic. Some of those thrilling roller coaster rides could be even more thrilling with a few sweet French girls screaming with excitement as we all try out the high-octane top ten! I can nearly feel the adrenaline buzz already.

I wonder will they like my freckled face and red hair. It should make a change for them anyway and as you know, I'm dangerously handsome! Pity you're so challenged in the looks department, but I'm sure we can get some poor soul to befriend you (just joking – calm down!).

Seriously though, isn't it great news? We haven't seen each other in ages since you moved to Dublin and you're not great when it comes to keeping in touch. Are your parents still banning Facebook? Tell them it's the twenty-first century we're living in, not the Middle Ages. On second thoughts, hold that until we come back from Paris. No point in getting them all sniffy and suspicious and saying 'No way' to this holiday.

Get in there right now Martin and ask them can you come. Promise them that you will swot your head off for the Junior Cert and get fabulous results. We'll be back by the time the results come out, so no worries on that score. I'm going to get an A in French, whatever about the rest of my subjects. I'm starting tonight on the vocab and phrases and I won't stop until I'm fluent. I must Google to see if there is a 'chat-up a girl' book of French phrases.

I expect to know soon as my mum is going to ring your mum this weekend. If they refuse, act like you're having a nervous breakdown, refuse to eat, don't wash, mope around and fight with your sister and that awful brother of yours. They'll crack and let you come with us – just for a few weeks of release from your rotten presence!

Au revoir, mon ami!
Jack

90

Although the student took a light-hearted approach to the subject, all the correct conventions for letter writing are present in the letter on the previous page. The tone is suitable for a personal letter and reveals the character of the writer. The letter is quite long, but could be written in 30 minutes by a student who has practised letter writing. If the student was caught for time, some paragraphs could have been shortened or omitted.

**Now look at a different approach to the same question:**

## Sample 2: Informal Letter

64 Fernview Park,
Ballybeg,
Co. Donegal

23rd May 2014

Dear Anne,

It feels so long since we last met, or even wrote to each other. How are you and all your family? We are all fine here in Donegal and send good wishes to your parents and brother.

The weather has been dreadful for the last few months. We hardly saw the face of the sun for more than a few hours this month and it's the first month of summer. However, that's all about to change I hope.

My parents are bringing us to Portugal for a family holiday in July and the best part of it is that they are allowing me to bring a friend along. Brian is outgoing and makes friends easily but I'm less confident and often end up hanging around with my parents all day. It's so boring!

I would just love it if you would come along with us on this holiday, Anne. We could do so many fun things together. There is a fabulous beach near our apartment and we also have our own swimming pool. It's not very big, but it is wonderful to cool down in when the sun is scorching. We are quite near to an old village complete with cobble stones which has some lovely little shops and boutiques and the clothes are quite cheap. I know you love clothes!
In addition, we can go for long walks, chat, listen to music and catch up on the gossip. There are a few activities for teenagers in the next resort, but I know you're a bit like me when it comes to deafening disco music and non-stop guzzling of junk food. It's just awful. Most of those teenagers are just acting a part and following the crowd I think.

Please ask your parents if they will allow you to join us. We're going from the 10th to the 24th July. My parents will pay for the tickets etc. All you need to do is pack and make sure you bring enough money to shop in the boutiques.

I am looking forward to hearing from you soon. Please come.
Love,
Jennifer

## 3 You Try It
You are Anne. Write your reply to Jennifer.

This letter is approximately the correct length. The tone is quite different from the previous sample but it addresses the task set in the question. The language here is more restrained and is effective in conveying the quiet, refined but slightly judgemental writer. One gets the sense that she is pleading for company and is a lonely kind of person. All standard letter writing rules are observed.

A good personal letter will always reveal something of the character or personality of the writer and their relationship with the recipient, unlike a formal letter which is more businesslike and detached in approach.

## (c) Reports

**Reports are written for several reasons:**
• To present ideas, information, facts and findings in a logical way.
• To research some issue or problem and come to conclusions based on this research.
• To make recommendations for improvements.
• To record information for various purposes.

### Format for reports

The format for any report is related to the type of report that is being written. A police report following a violent assault would be quite different from a report researching an accident in a factory in order to make recommendations for safety improvements. Similarly, a newspaper report on some matter of public interest has its own structure which differs from other types of report writing.

   In other words, there is no 'One size fits all' formula for writing reports.

### Guidelines for writing a report:
✪ You must be conscious of the reader and write in a formal, clear and simple style.

✪ Unless your readers are experts on the subject of the report, avoid all use of jargon or technical terms which could confuse them.

✪ Write in a structured format that allows you to communicate the information clearly and efficiently.

✪ Reports should not be written in the first person (i.e. **I**). Using '**I**' can make the content sound less objective.

✪ Good spelling, punctuation and grammar are essential in report writing.

In this section, guidelines for four report styles are provided. These styles are:
**(i)** Report based on research or a survey
**(ii)** Report based on an eyewitness account
**(iii)** Report to be published in a school magazine
**(iv)** Report to be published in a newspaper

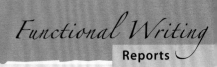

## (i) Format for reports based on research or a survey

**This type of report requires:**
- A clear layout
- A title which indicates the issue being researched and reported
- A date
- The name of the author or authors
- The name(s) of the person, people or group who commissioned the report.

## Guidelines for writing a report based on research or a survey

### STEP 1

Before you begin writing, ask yourself the following questions:
- Who requested the report and why did they request it?
- What is the purpose of this report?
- Who engaged in the research and what methods were used?

The answers to these questions are called the **Terms of Reference** and they will help you to decide how you should gather information for your report.

### STEP 2

The next step is to plan the report.
- Begin by deciding on an appropriate title as this ensures a sharp focus.
- Decide on what information, facts, evidence etc. are relevant and essential. Be **selective** as the report must be concise and clear.
- Organise your material into a logical sequence.
- Before you begin writing:
    - decide what you learnt from your research (e.g. in relation to the sample question given below: the majority of students surveyed avoided using the school canteen).
    - draw logical conclusions from this (e.g. students do not like the food or decor of the school canteen)
    - decide which recommendations to make (e.g. a new caterer should be hired and the canteen should be redecorated).

### STEP 3

The next step is to write the report
- Maintain an objective approach.
- Present the report in a visually pleasing way. Use headings and sub-headings if necessary as well as bullet-pointed lists; allow plenty of 'white space'. It can be very off-putting to see large chunks of printed text.
- Check grammar, punctuation and spelling.
- Sign the report.

**Sample Question**
You have been asked by the Board of Management of your school to investigate the canteen facilities for students in the school and to make recommendations for improvements based on your findings.
Write the report which you would submit.

## Sample Report I

### Report on Canteen Facilities at St. Brigid's College, Wexford

#### Terms of Reference
This report was commissioned by the Board of Management, St. Brigid's College, Wexford in order to evaluate the canteen facilities in the school and to make recommendations for improvements based on the findings.

#### Procedure
The researchers interviewed a cross-section of 20 students from each of the 6 year groups in the school, making a total of 120 students. Researchers asked students the following questions:

**Food:**
1. How would you describe the quality and choice of food offered in the canteen?
2. Do you consider that the food is good value for money?

**Environment:**
3. What aspect of the canteen environment most needs improvement?

(**Note:** Students were asked to respond using the words Poor, Good or Excellent.)

#### Findings:
1. In answer to the question of quality and choice of food:
   - 91 described it as Poor
   - 25 described it as Good
   - 4 described it as Excellent

2. In answer to the question of value for money:
   - 93 considered it Poor
   - 23 considered it Good
   - 4 considered it Excellent

3. As regards the aspect of the environment which most needs improvement:
   - 75 referred to the lack of adequate space in the canteen.
   - 25 referred to the dark decor and peeling paintwork.
   - 20 referred to the inadequate maintenance of proper order when queuing.

#### Conclusions:
1. The quality and choice of food on offer in the canteen is generally unsatisfactory and needs to be reviewed.
2. The price of the food on offer needs to be revised as it exceeds the value to be had elsewhere.
3. The lack of sufficient space in the canteen needs to be addressed and the decor needs upgrading.

#### Recommendations:
1. Students should be offered a wider variety of nutritious options. While some students enjoy fried foods such as burgers and chips, others would prefer grilled or baked hot dishes and some vegetarian choices. Salads would be a welcome addition.

2. The company which runs the canteen should lower prices in keeping with the value offered in the local garage shops and supermarkets.

3. As the canteen becomes over-crowded, consideration should be given to the possibility of staggering lunch times for seniors and juniors. As school numbers are growing, a new, larger canteen will need to be built eventually.

4. The canteen urgently requires to be painted. We suggest that this is a project which Transition Year students could undertake with appropriate supervision.

5. More adult supervision is needed to ensure orderly queuing.

**Report compiled and signed by;**

Gillian Adams          Anthony Burke

Michael King          Rosemary Murphy

*All of the above students are members of the School Student Committee.*

*Date: 18th September 2014.*

## 4. You Try It

Review the guidelines on page 93 for writing this type of report. Do you consider the sample report above to be effective?

### (ii) Format for reports based on an eyewitness account

An eyewitness report is a first-person account of an event you personally witnessed. The aim is to provide accurate details about the event in a clear, concise manner.

- Eyewitness reports are often used by police and are crucial to solving crimes or clarifying the facts surrounding road accidents etc.
- They can offer important information for newsworthy stories.
- Eyewitness reports are also used as part of incident reports, e.g. bullying at school or details explaining how a fight started etc.

### Guidelines for writing an eyewitness report

◎ Before writing the report, ask yourself exactly what you saw and the order of the events. Jot down as many details as you can before you begin writing. Remember, you must not base your report on anything that has actually happened or name any real person in your report. This is a functional writing exercise. Use your imagination, but aim for realism.

◎ Unlike a report based on research or a survey, you must write your eyewitness report in the first person. Confine your description to what you actually witnessed. Avoid **dramatising** or **sensationalising** and **never** give your personal opinion.

◎ Give specific time and date information when writing about the incident, your full name and contact information.

◎ Use precise language. If you're describing clothes, don't just say someone was wearing an old jacket. Give the colour and type, e.g. He was wearing an old, black jacket which came to his hips.

◎ You may name others who were present and who can back up your account. You may not repeat or include anything they said.

**Sample Question**

You have witnessed a serious fight which took place on the school premises. The principal of your school is compiling a report for the Board of Management, which will also be given to the parents of the students involved. You have been asked by the principal to write an eyewitness report of what you saw and heard. Write the text of your report.

## Sample Report 2

CONFIDENTIAL

### Fight in Students' Locker Room

On Wednesday, the 24th March at approximately 2.00.p.m., I was in the Junior Students' locker room collecting my books for the afternoon classes.

As I was closing my locker door, I heard somebody shouting outside the door of the room and another person shouting back at them.

A group of students suddenly entered the room and I noticed that one of the boys, Michael Aherne, was holding an open pen-knife in his hand and pointing it at John Roche, who was holding a hurley. Other students who were present included Alan Casey, Niall Corbett and Peter Lynch.

Niall Corbett tried to intervene but was threatened with a blow from the hurley held by John Roche.

I tried to exit the room but could not do so because the door was being blocked by Michael Aherne. Both boys were shouting loudly and threatening to kill each other.

John Roche knocked the pen-knife out of Michael Aherne's hand with the hurley, but Michael Aherne managed to retrieve it and they both began to physically attack each other. I saw blood pouring from the side of John Roche's face and observed him swinging the hurley, which hit Michael Aherne's head. Alan and Niall tried to break the fight up, while Peter managed to exit the room.

Within minutes, two teachers, Mr O'Connor and Mr Murphy, arrived. They attempted to break up the fight but both boys continued until Mr Murphy grabbed the hurley from John Roche's hand. John Roche was bleeding badly at this stage. Michael Aherne then threw the pen-knife to the ground and sat on one of the benches with his head leaning against the wall.

Mr O'Connor noticed me and asked me if I had witnessed the entire fight. I told him that I had only witnessed what had taken place in the locker room. He asked me to accompany him to the principal's office. As I left the locker room, Mr Murphy was phoning for an ambulance, while Alan Casey and Peter Lynch were talking quietly to Michael Aherne. Two other teachers, Ms O'Brien and Mr Burke, arrived in the locker room just as I was leaving with Mr. O'Connor.

Signed: *Patrick Foley*

You will notice that the writer of the report on page 96 has:
- given a logical account of the fight which he witnessed.
- not used any exaggeration or dramatic expressions.
- not offered any opinion on who was to blame for the fight.
- named other witnesses to the fight.
- only referred to his own situation in order to explain why he did not leave the room.
- written in clear, simple language.

## 5. You Try It
Write a police report on an accident you witnessed.

### (iii) Format for reports to be published in a school magazine
You may be asked to write a report for a school magazine in which you comment on a school tour, a sports event, a fashion show or musical etc.

This type of report has more in common with writing an article, such as we have seen in the Personal Writing section on pages 48-49.

### Guidelines for writing a report to be published in a school magazine
- Give your report a title.
- Clearly identify the focus of the report, e.g. Annual Ski-Trip to Austria, Transition Year Fashion Show etc.
- Begin with an overview which sets the tone and acts as a 'hook' to grab the readers' attention and makes them want to read on.
- Include essential information such as the dates on which the event took place, who organised the event, who took part in the event, how successful the event was etc.
- You should add some anecdotes which will be interesting to your readers.
- Give your personal experiences and reaction to the event and those of your friends or parents.
- Language should be clear and conversational in style and will not require the conciseness or formality of the other style of reports.
- Layout: This report is quite different to a research/survey type of report or an eyewitness report. It allows you to report on an event or situation in an informal manner and express personal opinions. The layout is really that of an article.

### Sample Question
Write a report on a recent school trip for your school magazine.

**Sample Report 3**

School Mag

# Ski Trip to Austria 20--

## Every year, students eagerly anticipate the school ski trip to Austria, and this year did not disappoint our high expectations.

On 27th March, we travelled by air and coach until we reached the beautiful little village of Itter, set in the Austrian Tyrol. Some sunny weather had melted the snow on the lower slopes. However, most of us had some previous experience of skiing, so we were able to go further up the mountain where the snow was deep and thick.

Our instructors were really fantastic. The fact that our only injuries were a few bumps and bruises speaks volumes for the expert tuition we received. Ms Cotter, armed with her first-aid kit, was able to deal with every situation that arose and, thankfully, we did not need to visit the local hospital.

Evening activities were varied and extremely enjoyable. We had lots of fun playing competitive games against the teachers- especially when we beat them more often than not!

Our reluctance to leave Itter and journey home was only relieved by the day we spent shopping in Munich, which is a truly beautiful city.

We are all grateful to the teachers who organised and accompanied us on the trip. They do this every year in order to allow us to have such a wonderful and educational experience.

Thanks are also due to our drivers, Bill and Tom, who tolerated our raucous singing and managed to get the broken DVD player replaced. Their good humour and patience added to the success of the whole trip.

We all have happy memories from our week in Austria and hope next year's group have as good a time as we did.

## (iv) Format for reports to be published in a newspaper

News reports usually employ the classic inverted pyramid where all of the 5 'W' questions are answered first. This is followed by further important details and concludes with background information or other material which could be omitted without affecting the facts on which the report is based. Editors can print the entire story or easily cut from the bottom section.

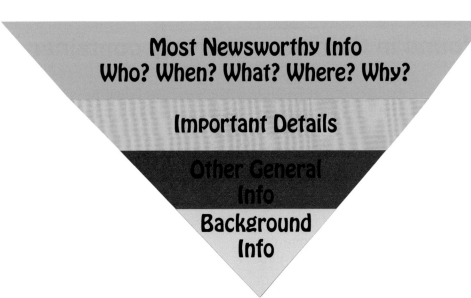

## Guidelines for writing a report to be published in a newspaper

A news report informs readers of the facts surrounding various events and who or what may be affected by these events. The two most important elements of a news report are facts and style.

**Facts:**
◎ The facts of any given news event can be gained quickly by asking the 5 'W' questions 'who, what, when, where, why.'
◎ Writers must ensure that the facts they report on are accurate (or, for exam purposes, believable).
◎ Avoid sensationalism.
◎ News reports deal with the truth and should not contain any **bias** or personal opinion.

**Style:**
◎ The style of a report should be direct and concise.
◎ Avoid using unnecessary words or engaging in lengthy description.
◎ Use clear expression.
◎ Paragraphs should be kept short and contain one main point.

**Note:** The news report on page 100 is quite brief, but it demonstrates all of the guidelines for writing a news report.

**Sample Report 4**

# NEWS

## Snake found in Guinness delivery container

Workers at the Guinness brewery in Dublin were a little shocked to discover a snake at St. James' Gate.

The reptile was found yesterday while staff at the Diageo logistics centre were unpacking a delivery container which had arrived from Texas.

The DSPCA was called out to remove the reptile, which has now been christened JR because of his place of origin.

He was then taken to vet Bairbre O'Malle, one of Ireland's leading authorities on exotic pets.

She has identified him as a non-poisonous corn snake, who was a little underweight and somewhat dehydrated.

JR is now being nursed back to health.

Source: BreakingNews.ie

**Note:** A good news report will have a strong 'lead' or opening sentence in order to grab the attention of the reader. In the above sample, the first sentence encourages the reader to read on.

 **OVER TO YOU**

1. Imagine you are a journalist with your school magazine. Write a report of a recent sports event involving your school team. Try to capture the atmosphere of the event for your readers. (**JC Exam Question**)

2. You are a member of your school's Student Council. As there are now students from a range of different nationalities attending the school, your principal has asked you to come up with some suggestions to help your school to develop as an intercultural community. Write a report to be submitted by the Student Council to the principal outlining your ideas. (**JC Exam Question**)

3. Imagine you are a journalist with a local newspaper. Write a short report on a criminal offence which was committed in your neighbourhood.

**4.** The Transition Year class in your school carried out a survey of how the students in third year spent an average of €10 pocket money per week. Based on the figures supplied below write a report on this survey for your school magazine. **(JC Exam Question)***)*

| Pocket Money Survey | Males (€) | Females (€) |
|---|---|---|
| Food/Soft drinks | 3.90 | 2.40 |
| Leisure goods and services | 2.70 | 1.90 |
| Clothing | 1.00 | 2.40 |
| Personal goods | 1.40 | 2.30 |
| Transport | 1.00 | 1.00 |

## Checklist

Use the following checklist to ensure that you have complied with the demands of the marking scheme:

Have I **read** the question very carefully and **analysed** exactly what I am being asked to do? ☐

Have I followed the **correct format** for the report? (Check guidelines) ☐

Have I used **paragraphs** properly? (**One idea** or comment per paragraph.) ☐

Have I maintained **objectivity** and avoided bias? ☐

Have I used **formal, clear English** and avoided slang or colloquial expressions? ☐

Have I avoided using **contractions**, e.g. 'it's' instead of 'it is' etc? ☐

Have I avoided using **abbreviations**? ☐

Have I **signed** the report correctly? ☐

Have I checked my **spelling** and **grammar**? ☐

If you can answer 'Yes' to each of the above questions, you should do very well in report writing.

## (d) Reviews

A review is an individual response to a book, film, occasion etc. The reviewer expresses his/her judgement on the work presented. A review is, therefore, **subjective**.

Different reviewers may respond differently to the same book/film/occasion.

In this section guidelines for three review styles are provided

These styles are:

(i)   Book reviews

(ii)  Film reviews

(iii) Event reviews.

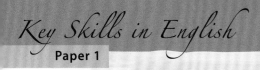

### (i) Book reviews

**Guidelines for writing a book review**

◎ Brainstorm and plan your ideas before you begin writing.

◎ State the title of the book and the name of the author in the first paragraph.

◎ What is the genre of the book: science fiction, thriller, mystery, adventure?

◎ Give a brief outline of the setting and plot but do not write a summary and **never** tell how it ends.

◎ Describe the main characters. Are they realistic or stereotypes? What is their importance to the story?

◎ Comment on the major themes. What sort of ideas and issues does the story deal with? What does the book make you think about?

◎ Comment on style. Is the story written in the first or third person (**I** or **he/she**)? How did this affect the story? Is the setting described in detail? Are emotions and attitudes described in depth?

◎ Personal response: Think about why you enjoyed or did not enjoy the book. Did it affect you in any way? Could you identify with any of the characters and the situations in which they found themselves? Have you learned anything from the book (e.g. about yourself, other people, life in general)?

◎ Give the book a rating, e.g. 4/5, three stars etc.

## Sample Review 1

The book which I am reviewing is 'The Boy in the Striped Pyjamas' by John Boyne, a fictional story set during the time of the Holocaust.

When Bruno, the main character, is forced to move away from his Berlin home with his family, his life changes forever. His beautiful home in Germany is replaced by a much smaller, duller house, which is also the location of his father's downstairs office. His father does not explain or discuss his occupation with his children. However the reader soon realises that Bruno's father is a Nazi Commandant in Auschwitz.

Despite the setting, the reader is spared many of the horrific details of what actually took place in the concentration camp itself. This, I believe, increases the shock when we discover exactly what is going on there.

I found the book intriguing and a real page-turner. However, it was difficult to fully believe that a nine-year-old, intelligent boy like Bruno could really be so naive as to think that all the people were wearing pyjamas instead of prison uniforms. It was also very difficult to believe that Bruno and Schmuel, a young prisoner whom he befriends, could meet, have conversations and play games without being noticed by anybody. The adult characters were, however, far more **credible** and created a major contrast to the two boys.

The style of the writing is clear and straightforward because it explores and captures the mind of a child. The deliberate mistakes of 'Fury' for Fuhrer, and 'Out-With' for Auschwitz are funny in a dark sort of way and made me feel a strong sense of foreboding right from the start.

Although the book is easy to read, it deals with some very serious themes and issues which I found disturbing.

I would consider this book unsuitable for any reader under the age of eleven or twelve. It is, however, a very good, thought-provoking read for teenagers.

I would recommend it and would give it a rating of 9 /10.

## ✎ You Try It

Using the guidelines on page 102, write a review of a book you read and enjoyed recently.

### (ii) Film Reviews

### Guidelines for writing a film review

The guidelines for writing a film review are similar to those for writing a book review. The major differences are:
- ◎ Instead of referring to the author, you refer to the director of the film.
- ◎ You name the lead actors who play the different characters in the film.
- ◎ You could refer to costumes, make-up, set design, music, special effects etc.

## Sample Review 2

'The Boy in the Striped Pyjamas', directed by Mark Herman, offers us a fresh look at the <u>horrific atrocities</u> of the Holocaust. In just 90 minutes, it manages to create <u>heart-breaking poignancy</u> similar to that of 'Schindler's List' or 'The Diary of Anne Frank'.

Bruno, played by Asa Butterfield, is a German nine-year-old. His father (David Thewlis) is an SS officer who runs a concentration camp. The drama unfolds through the boy's innocent, confused eyes. Part of the power of the film is due to the fact that we, the audience, know what is going on whereas Bruno does not. We understand the significance of the death's head on the collar tab of the uniform which his father wears.

The city setting in Berlin, where Bruno plays happily with his friends, is captured well in the opening sequences but the location changes dramatically when the family move to the countryside near Auschwitz. Bruno, who thinks the place is called 'Out-With', can see what he thinks is a farm from a window that his mother (Vera Farmiga) has sealed. He can see what he believes are 'striped pyjamas' of the inmates, pyjamas similar to those worn by Pavel (David Hayman), the frail old man who works in their garden.

Loneliness and curiosity drive Bruno to explore beyond the bounds of his garden fence. He discovers a quiet, unguarded area of the fence where he meets Shmuel (Jack Scanlon), a boy his own age, who is equally confused by the events taking place around him.

Mark Herman directs the film using a simple, uncluttered style which <u>heightens the profound impact on</u> the viewer. He allows us to see the horror of the Holocaust through the unknowing eyes of a child. We see Bruno peeping in the door as his father and other soldiers watch a Nazi propaganda film about the camp. We sense his fear of the brutal staff officer (Rupert Friend) who describes Jews as being 'evil' and we can almost smell the smoke which he sees curling from the chimneys in the death camp.

The film focuses on complex emotional issues of evil and the Holocaust and raises questions about the nature of man. I found it disturbing but deeply thought-provoking.

I would highly recommend 'The Boy in the Striped Pyjamas' to anybody over the age of 13.

My rating is 5 out of 5 stars.

Glossary
**horrific atrocities:** horrible events **heart-breaking poignancy:** tragic effect
**heightens the profound impact:** emphasises it even more

### ✍ You Try It

The review above is based on the film of the novel which was reviewed on pages 102-103. Compare and contrast both reviews.

### (iii) Event Reviews

#### Guidelines for writing an event review

Magazines, newspapers and other media publish reviews of events in order to give readers information on what is available for entertainment in their area. Writing a vivid review allows readers to imagine they were at the event themselves and may encourage them to avail of future opportunities which come their way. Of course, the reverse is also possible and may have the effect of discouraging the readers from attending a particular event!

◎ Give essential information at the beginning of the review. You could use the 5 'W's' system used by journalists: **W**hat was name of the event? **W**here was it held? **W**hen did it take place? **W**hy? (perhaps to raise funds for a charity etc.) **W**ho was involved?

◎ Give the review a title.

◎ Next, write about the event and say whether it was a success or a failure. Give reasons for coming to your conclusion. Be as specific as possible and include details to fill out the review. Make a special effort to catch the atmosphere of the event.

◎ Use the past tense as the event has already happened.

◎ Maintain some objectivity. Although a review is a statement of opinion, you cannot appear to be biased. The reader needs to feel that they can trust your judgement. You can create trust by backing up your opinion with facts. Don't just say the event was 'badly organised' – give specific examples of the lack of organisation.

◎ Remember that a review must be structured appropriately. You need an introduction, body paragraphs and a clear conclusion.

## Sample Review 3

**Note:** The following review is an edited version of a longer review which first appeared on a website, npr.org.

# A Raucous, Riotous and Audacious Opening Ceremony

Here's what Danny Boyle got right in his raucous and riotous opening ceremony extravaganza for the London Olympics. Boyle brought wonder and whimsy and wit to the proceedings, without skimping on any of the patriotic touch points that are a must at any Olympic opening ceremony.

If I gave you a list of the ingredients that were part of this rich menu, you would be hard pressed to imagine how they could all come together. The much-mentioned sheep, cows, maypoles and pastoral idyll formed the early part of the show, and it was hard to imagine how this scene of a Britain of times gone by could possibly be transformed into anything resembling the last two centuries of British history.

In an astonishing display of audacity and bravado, we were soon entering the upheaval of the Industrial Revolution, with the green pastures of the shire replaced by the ferocity of industrial destruction and creation.

Top-hatted **plutocrats** sashayed across the stadium, as the workers of Britain's industrial heights forged iron that transformed into a ring that formed the fifth Olympic ring, rising majestically above the stadium to join the other four rings, with fireworks exploding as they were suspended high in the air.

Throw in some Mr. Bean, Mike Oldfied's tubular bells, a medley of the last 50 years of British music – rock, pop, ska, and grime – and there was something for everyone.

What was amazing about the whole thing was that it worked.

It was dazzling and grand and heartwarming and emotional and fun, all at the same time. And it was the fun that came through the most. People seemed to be having fun. Danny Boyle gave us the Britain we have all heard about, but he wrapped it up in his unique creative style. I wasn't sure what to expect from him, but the fact that he got James Bond to escort the Queen to the Olympics is enough to earn my respect and my gratitude. It was an entertainment worthy of the spectacle.

**plutocrats** = powerful, wealthy people

**Source** = **www.npr.org.**
Review by Madhulika Sikka
(Adapted)

**105**

## 8 You Try It

Did the review on page 105 succeed in creating the atmosphere of the event? You must give reasons for your answer and refer closely to the review.

## (e) Blurbs

A blurb is a short description of a book, written on the back cover of the book. It is intended to encourage a person to read the book.

Blurbs do not have to follow any particular formats, as in letters or reports, but you should be aware of basic guidelines.

### Guidelines for writing a blurb

- ◎ Blurbs should be very concise and simply written. Keep sentences very short.
- ◎ You should use some persuasive techniques to encourage the reader to read the book.
- ◎ What is left unsaid can be just as important as what is said and can create a sense of mystery to 'hook' the reader.
- ◎ Never give any clues in a blurb as to how the book will end.

**Note:** The following blurb is taken from goodreads.com, an Internet website. You can find plenty of such examples on the Internet, or just look at the blurbs on the books in your school library or at home.

### Sample Blurb 1

## Personal Effects
by E.M. Kokie

After his older brother dies in Iraq, Matt makes a discovery that rocks his beliefs about strength, bravery, and honour in this page-turning debut.

Ever since his brother, T.J., was killed in Iraq, Matt feels like he's been sleepwalking through life — failing classes, getting into fights, and avoiding his dad's lectures about following in his brother's footsteps. T.J.'s gone, but Matt can't shake the feeling that if only he could get his hands on his brother's stuff from Iraq, he'd be able to make sense of his death. But as Matt searches for answers about T.J.'s death, he faces a shocking revelation about T.J.'s life that suggests he may not have known T.J. as well as he thought. What he learns challenges him to stand up to his father, honour his brother's memory, and take charge of his own life. With compassion, humour, and a compelling narrative voice, E. M. Kokie explores grief, social mores, and self-discovery in a provocative first novel.

**Note:** This next blurb is the text from the back of the book *The Boy in the Striped Pyjamas*:

**Sample Blurb 2**

## The Boy in the Striped Pyjamas

The story of 'The Boy in the Striped Pyjamas' is very difficult to describe. Usually we give some clues about the book on the cover, but in this case we think that would spoil the reading of the book. We think it is important that you start to read without knowing what it is about. If you do start to read this book, you will go on a journey with a nine-year-old boy called Bruno. (Though this isn't a book for nine-year-olds.) And sooner or later you will arrive with Bruno at a fence. We hope you never have to cross such a fence.

## You Try It

1. Compare the two sample blurbs. Which is the most effective in your opinion? Give reasons for your answer.
2. How does each blurb correspond to the guidelines given on page 106?
3. Write a blurb for a book you have read.

## (f) Brochures and Flyers

In the Functional Writing section of the Junior Cert exam, you could be asked to write a text suitable for a brochure or a flyer.

A **brochure** is a document containing pictures and information about a product or service, e.g. a holiday brochure. It is usually folded so it looks like a small booklet.

A **flyer** is a single sheet advertising an event or a product.

Brochures and flyers are used to inform, educate or persuade the reader. They attract attention through eye-catching design and must contain clear, focused writing because they are so short.

### Guidelines for writing the text of a brochure or flyer

◎ Keep your focus on the type of brochure and examine the exact wording of the exam question.
◎ Write a headline for the cover of your brochure which is short, snappy and 'hooks' the reader. Use large writing for the headline.
◎ As people only skim brochures, it is important that you communicate the facts very quickly. Keep text brief and to the point. A little text goes a long way. Use short sentences of 20 words or less per sentence. Use short paragraphs of no more than three sentences.
◎ Build up details as you go along. But do not give too many details. Brochures have limited space and most of the space is taken up with photographs or graphics.
◎ Use sub-headings that grab the interest of the reader. Make sure they are clear and short.
◎ Tell the reader everything that he/she needs to know about the subject. Apply the 'who, what, where, why and when' formula.
◎ Speak directly to the reader. 'You' is the most important word in persuasion. Focus on the benefits. Emphasise what the reader will gain.
◎ Use bulleted lists. These are commonly used to highlight important information.
◎ Write in a conversational style.

## (1) Sample brochure

**Front cover/ Page 1**

# Welcome to Kruger National Park!

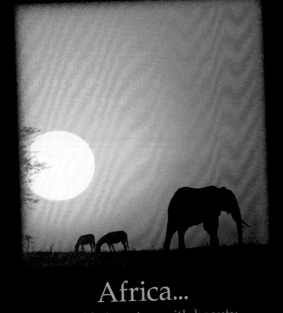

## Africa...
a land brimming with beauty, hospitality and adventure.

**Page 2**

Journey to a place where wildlife is preserved and cherished.

Experience for yourself how ancient tradition Is very much a part of today.

## Welcome to Africa! Welcome to Kruger Park!

**Page 3**

# Kruger National Park

South Africa's Kruger National Park offers one of the best wildlife experiences on the continent.

Pack up and leave behind the hustle and bustle of modern city life and head to one of the world's most exciting safari destinations.

See if you spot the 'Big Five' - lions, leopards, rhinos, elephants and buffaloes.

After dark, enjoy a delicious meal before sleeping soundly in a comfortable lodge.

**Back cover. Page**

- Go in search of Africa's Big Five
- Take an exciting and memorable safari
- Enjoy traditional South African food and hospitality.
- Experience the park after dark - if you dare!

## Don't delay!
Avail of huge discounts on trips tailored especially for YOU!

Contact: Global Travel Agency
Tel: 012-345-678
email: info@global.com
Website: www.global.com
Address: 40 Dublin Road, Newtown, Co. Cavan.

## (2) Sample flyer

# Last of the Summer Wine!

## DONEGAL SINGS AND DANCES

### Darren O'Donnell! Mary Shine! The Blackthorn Ceili band!

You, your family and friends are invited to a wonderful night of

## *traditional music* **& *dance***

Venue: The Park Hotel, Main Street, Donegal.
Date: 28th August 2013
Time: 6.30 p.m -11.30 p.m.
Admission: €10

Other artists include:
**The Dunraven Singers, Buncrana Folk Group and
The Mary Dillon Dancers.**

## *Come and enjoy the last of the summer wine!*

For bookings and more details, contact John Roche at The Park Hotel, Main Street,
Donegal: Tel: 2345678.  email: jroche@memail.com

# (g) Speeches

In the Junior Cert exam, speeches written in the Functional Writing section should be shorter than those written in the Personal Writing section. Remember: Do not get carried away and exceed the time limit of 30 minutes.

## Guidelines for writing a speech

◎ Read the question very carefully, underlining key words.
◎ Decide on a title for your speech.
◎ Do not make too many points during your speech. This could result in the audience becoming bored. Remember that a speech is meant to be heard.
◎ Keep your audience in mind.
◎ Address the audience frequently in the course of the speech.
◎ Use a conversational tone. This engages the listener more.
◎ Use short, simple **anecdotes** to illustrate your points. This creates more interest, as most people enjoy stories.
◎ If you are trying to argue or persuade in your speech, you could use some of the persuasive techniques outlined in the Personal Writing section on pages 40-41.
◎ Use humour if appropriate but do not force it!
◎ Aim for a strong conclusion that reinforces your message. The conclusion should emphasise your central message.

**Sample Question**

The principal of your school is leaving. You have been nominated by the Junior Certificate students in your school to prepare a speech for the occasion. Write out the speech you would make to a gathering of staff and pupils on the principal's final day in the school.
**(JC Exam Question)**

FAREWELL TO MR CLANCY
Teachers and fellow students, we are assembled here today to mark the retirement of our esteemed principal, Mr George Clancy.

Albert Schweitzer once said that, 'Example is leadership'.
When I was asked to speak to you all today, I looked up a few quotations about leadership, many of which were long and boring, but the words of Albert Schweitzer just about summed up what Mr Clancy has been for the last 20 years as principal of St John's College. He has led, not by giving orders, not by issuing threats, not by going on power trips, but by example.

One of my first memories of starting secondary school is of being gathered in the hall, just like we are today, and hearing Mr Clancy's words of welcome. I had expected a slightly intimidating lecture about behaviour and dire consequences if rules were broken. But I was so wrong! Mr Clancy spoke to us, not down to us.

He was warm and welcoming and I wondered if a man who seemed so gentle and relaxed could possibly manage to control 400 pupils, not to mind the teachers!

I found out very early on that Mr Clancy was not a man you'd want to meet if you tried to get away with skipping a class or taking an unauthorised day off! It wasn't his anger that made me respect him when I was caught in the locker room dodging my first French test. It was his calm, rational approach as he explained the importance of facing up to things that we find hard. I wasn't frightened of him; I was frightened of letting him down. I never skipped a class or a test again.

Mr Clancy, teachers and fellow students, is a gentleman of integrity and honour. He is also great fun, as we discovered on the school tour to France. Do you remember his reaction when we thought it would be smart to lock ourselves into the small hostel and lock the teachers out? We all waited for the thunderbolts which never came, much to our disappointment. He just left us there while he enjoyed coffee and croissants on the outdoor veranda with the other staff members, laughing and chatting, while we looked at each other feeling very silly and bored!

We are all feeling sad today because we know that we are losing not only a great principal who did great things for this school, but a friend who cared about every one of us. He taught us all how to take responsibility, as he did for the running of the school, to admit mistakes and to keep trying harder.

Example is leadership, as Schweitzer said. Mr Clancy was a leader. We wish him health and happiness in his retirement. He will be missed by us all.

## OVER TO YOU

Read the guidelines for writing speeches on page 110 and answer the following questions:

1. You are the captain of a team playing in the final of a major competition. Your team is losing at half-time. Write the pep talk you would give to the team. **(JC Exam Question)**

2. You have been asked to nominate a pupil in your class for the 'Student of the Year Award'. Write in a persuasive style the nomination speech you would make in favour of this individual. **(JC Exam Question)**

3. You have been asked to give a five minute talk on why we should do Media Studies in school. Write out the talk you would give. **(JC Exam Question)**

4. You have been asked to address the Board of Management on the subject of banning school uniforms in your school. Write the text of the talk you would give.

5. Write the text of a speech you would make to incoming first-year students. You should give them advice and tips on how to cope with their first year in the school.

## (h) Short Articles

An example of an article can be found on pages 48-49 of the Personal Writing Section. Just remember that you only have **30 minutes** to complete a Functional Writing task, so it's important to keep an article very short.

### (1) Writing a short magazine article

**Sample Question:** You have been asked to contribute a short article to your school magazine giving advice to students who suffer from low self-esteem. Write the text of the article you would write.

### Sample Article 1

## • Building your Self-Esteem •

Do you find yourself taking things very personally and seeing yourself as a victim? Are you constantly looking for approval? If you find yourself answering 'Yes' to these questions, you may be suffering from poor self-esteem.

So what can you do to change how you view yourself? Start by writing down three things about yourself that make you happy. Do this once a day and you will begin to focus on what is positive in your life.

It is always a good idea to get involved in a variety of activities. Many teens have fought over the years to avoid activities, but later in life are thankful that they did do them. Just give yourself a chance. You might be surprised to discover that you really like some sport or group activity and you are sure to make some friends. Even if you don't play a team sport, physical activity is a must. Not only does it improve your physical health, but also your mental health.

In addition to engaging in activities, you might like to do some voluntary work during holiday periods. Try working with groups that help the homeless or with disadvantaged children. Not only will this help you to think beyond yourself, it will also help you to appreciate the good things in your own life.

Our happiness in life is never guaranteed because we cannot control everything that happens to us. But we can and should develop ways of viewing ourselves positively and believing that we can not only cope with life but enjoy it to the full.

*So, get out there, get busy and build up your self-esteem.*

## (1) Writing a short newspaper article

## Sample Article 2

# NEWS

### Broadband Key to Building our Future

The Government's plans to roll out high-speed broadband, with every citizen in the country having access to broadband speeds of at least 30 megabits by 2015, will ensure that future economic growth will not be hampered by lack of access to this crucial piece of infrastructure.

Under the plans announced yesterday by Communications Minister Pat Rabbitte, half of the population will have access to 100Mbps broadband by 2015.

However, while the private sector will provide high-speed broadband in built-up areas, state support will be required to provide high-speed broadband in rural areas.

The total investment required will be approximately €350m, split equally between the State and the private sector.

Even in the hard times we are currently enduring, this will be money well spent.

In the new knowledge-based economy high-speed broadband is a necessity rather than a luxury.

If we are to compete in the markets of tomorrow then it is vital that all companies and individuals have access to high-speed broadband.

Now that he has announced his ambitious broadband targets, Mr Rabbitte must ensure that they are achieved.

It is only by doing so that Ireland will be in a position to benefit when the global economy begins to recover.

[Source: *Irish Independent*]

## ⏰ You Try It

(a) Write a short magazine article entitled, 'Technology – we can't get enough of it!'

(b) Write a short newspaper article using the headline, 'Beating Bullying in Schools'.

## (i) Memos and Emails

Memos and emails are short pieces of writing commonly used in functional writing.

## (1) Writing a Memo

A memorandum, usually called a memo, is a short piece of writing which is rather like a note. It is used in business as a means of communication. A memo can be used to convey requests, arrangements, complaints, notice of meeting, suggestions etc.

### Guidelines for writing a memo

◎ The content must always be clear, concise and written in simple English.

◎ No formal opening is required but do end your memo in a pleasant way, e.g. *Many thanks*.

# Move! Dance Company

To:     Members of cast of *The Wizard of Oz*
From:   The Director
Date:   03/03/2014
Re:     Postponement of rehearsal session

Please note that next Friday's rehearsal will not take place as scheduled.
This is due to the fact that the hall will not be available because of essential renovation work.

The rehearsal has been re-scheduled for 22nd March from 6.30-9.00 p.m.

Please make every effort to attend as time is slipping away and we are behind schedule already.

Thanks to all
Mary Madden

## (2) Writing a Business Email

### Guidelines for writing a business email

◎ Give the message a subject/title. E-mail messages without a subject may not be opened because of a fear of viruses.

◎ Keep the subject short and clear.

◎ Opening/Greeting: Begin the message with a greeting which creates a friendly but business-like tone. If you know the person well, you may use their first name, e.g. Dear Thomas or Hello Thomas. If the person receiving the email is unknown to you or more senior, it would be more appropriate to use the surname together with a title, e.g. Dear Mr Smith, Dear Ms O'Connor.

◎ Use concise, clear expression. Nobody wants to wade through a long, rambling email.

◎ Purpose: Clearly indicate what the message is about in the first paragraph. Give full details in the following paragraph(s).

◎ Action: Any action that you want the reader to take should be clearly described, using polite phrases such as Could you... **or** I would be grateful if....

◎ Attachments: Make sure you refer in the main message to any attachments you are adding.

◎ Pay attention to correct spelling and grammar.

◎ Conclusions: Conclude the message politely. Common endings are Yours sincerely, Best regards, Best wishes, Regards.

◎ Sign the message: Include your name at the end of the message. It is very annoying to receive an email which does not include the name of the sender.

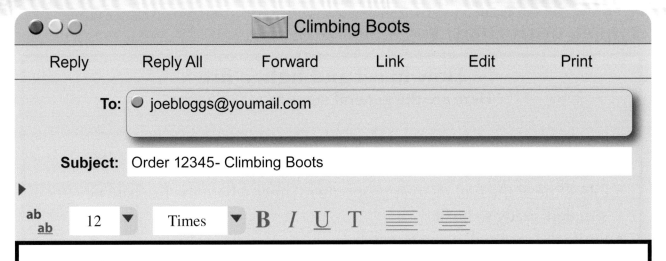

Dear Mr Bloggs,

I refer to my recent order, Ref. 12345, for a pair of climbing boots manufactured by your company.

I received an acknowledgement but, unfortunately, the description of the boots did not represent those which I ordered.

It is possible that the catalogue numbers did not correspond accurately. For clarity, the boots I require are Catalogue No. 9876 in Size 12.

I would be grateful for confirmation that this order is now amended. Can you also provide a date on which I could expect to receive them.

Yours sincerely,
John Hennessy

## 11. You Try It

Write an email OR a memo to a colleague enquiring about the progress of a business deal. Remind him/her of an upcoming meeting and mention some points which you think could be raised at this meeting. Revise guidelines for memos and emails on pages 113-114 before you write.

## (j) Instructions

Instructions help people to perform an action that accomplishes a specific result, e.g. maintain safety in a laboratory or kitchen, make a cup of tea, set up a computer, bake a cake, assemble a toy or a piece of furniture etc.

**Guidelines for writing a set of instructions**

◎ Break instructions into short, simple steps.
◎ Start all sentences with a verb, e.g. **Put** water into a kettle **or Check** that you have received all the necessary parts etc.
◎ Make sure sentences are concise and clear.
◎ Use *If* to indicate something that may or may not occur. Use *When* to indicate something that should occur. For example: **If** the pieces do not slot together easily, do not force them; **When** you have slotted the sections together securely, proceed to the next step.
◎ Check spelling and grammar.

## Sample Instructions 1

# How to set and light a fire
### Here are the general steps to make a fire:

- Choose and prepare a location for the fire.
- Gather fuel.
- Pile some of the fuel in an appropriate manner where the fire is to be situated, ready to be lit.
- Ignite the material, using a match.
- If necessary, blow on the material to create a small flame.
- Build up the fire by adding extra fuel.
- Maintain the fire as needed.
- Put out the fire or allow it to burn out when no longer needed.

## Sample Instructions 2

# Safety Guidelines in Science Laboratory

**Follow all instructions carefully. If you don't understand what you are expected to do, ask your teacher before proceeding.**

- Conduct yourself in a responsible manner whenever you are in the science laboratory.
- Do not touch any equipment or chemicals until you are told to do so by a teacher.
- Keep your hands away from your eyes, mouth and face when using chemicals or handling specimens.
- Keep hair tied up and away from your face.
- Keep your work area neat and clean.
- Know where the safety equipment including the eyewash station, safety shower, fire extinguisher and fire blanket is located.
- If a fire drill occurs during a laboratory period, be sure to close all chemical containers, gas and electricity.
- Wash your hands with soap and water before leaving the laboratory.
- Wear goggles when instructed by your teacher. There are no exceptions to this rule.
- Make sure your hands are dry before removing an electric plug from a socket.
- Report any damaged electrical equipment, including frayed wires and loose connections.
- Be very careful when using a gas burner. Keep hair, clothing and your hands safely away from an open flame.
- Never point the open end of a test tube that is being heated at yourself or anyone else.
- Leave your work area clean and tidy at the end of class.

**Note:** You can find many samples of instructions in user manuals, recipe books and school textbooks – including this one! Read a wide variety of instructions paying close attention to the language and format.

## (k) Images

### (1) Writing a photo/image description

A photo/image description is an ideal way of practising your English skills and vocabulary. Remember you are writing a factual description, so do not engage in interpretation.

### Guidelines for describing an image

◎ Have a close look at the image provided and decide on how to structure your description. What is the focus of the image? What is important or special? What should the viewer pay attention to?

◎ Give a general introduction, e.g. This image shows that ...,  In this image I can see ...

◎ Describe the place or setting of the image, e.g. I can see a rough path with a wooded area in the distance etc.

◎ Use adjectives and comment on colour, light and shade and the atmosphere created.

◎ Mention the angle from which an image is captured, e.g. an aerial shot, a close-up etc.

◎ When describing people, mention their approximate age, clothing, gender, posture, actions etc.

◎ If people have clearly defined roles in the image, state what these are, e.g. a teacher with a class of children, a doctor examining young, malnourished children etc.

◎ Make sure that your image description is logically structured, e.g. from left to right from the background to the foreground and from the middle to the sides. Which structure you finally choose depends on the image you are describing.

**Sample Question**
Write an accurate description of the following image:

**Sample answer:**

*The picture depicts a small church, surrounded by trees and shrubbery. In the foreground of the picture, there is a still lake, which reflects the image of the small church. Fine ripples can be observed on the surface of the lake. The water is lighter to the right of the picture, where we see the reflection and darker to the left. Small shrubs grow along the perimeter of the lake and the land.*

*The church can be seen in the middle ground, right of the picture. We see it from a side angle. It has a high-pitched roof, which appears to be made out of slate. The brick-work is grey and we can see a lighter brick, where the angles of the walls meet. One entry, facing slightly towards the left front, has been blocked up. The curved arc above this previous doorway and the sides can be clearly seen. The rest of this wall is covered in shrubbery. The church has double wooden doors, with a rounded arch entrance. Large bolted hinges can be seen, holding the doors in place.*

*There is a neat, well-kept lawn in front of the church. Small trees stand on the lawn and there is a small bench, supported by three legs or blocks. The background shows a low mountain, with channels created by little rivulets. The terrain is rough and wild and shown with a soft focus, which makes it appeared blurred. No people are present in this picture. The atmosphere is one of serenity, beauty and calm.*

## 12. You Try It

Write accurate descriptions of the following two pictures:

## (2) Writing a short dialogue based on an image

In the exam, you may be required to write a short dialogue based on an image. This should be written as a script.

### Guidelines for writing a script based on an image

◎ Give names or some form of identity to the people, animals or objects which are supposedly having the dialogue.

◎ Arrange the script by putting the name of each speaker in the left-hand margin and inserting a colon (:) after each speaker's name.

◎ Keep what each character is saying short. Do not write large chunks of dialogue.

◎ Conversational tone is appropriate. You may use contractions, e.g. **I'm** instead of **I am**.

◎ Create as much interest as you can in the conversation, making each comment meaningful and moving the dialogue forward.

◎ Do not insert unnecessary comments, e.g. 'Good Morning. How are you?', 'I'm fine. How are you?' etc. This makes for a very boring script. Be creative and original.

## Sample dialogue based on a picture:

[Characters are Jenny and Catherine. They are both young businesswomen working for a large corporation based in London.]

**Jenny:** It really isn't my imagination Catherine, they are excluding me and I don't know why.

**Catherine:** Listen, Jen, when I came here last year, I was convinced of the same thing. They aren't deliberately brushing you off. They have been here a few years now and have formed a close business relationship. They often discuss things together like that.

**Jenny:** Well I don't think it's very good manners to sit in a group, having conversations about things which I haven't the foggiest notion about. So much for team work! I feel like a spare part around here. How did you deal with it? You seem fine with them now.

**Catherine:** I felt a bit like you but I decided to pretend I didn't notice that they were ... well, sort of ignoring me. I inserted myself into their conversations, asked questions, made them tell me what was happening. I even offered opinions! Can you just imagine what they must have thought about me – butting in like that! To be fair though, they eased up a bit and they include me in the decision-making now.

**Jenny:** I wish I had your confidence to make them take notice of my presence. I just find that Nora is very cold. I know she's older and more experienced. I don't expect her to befriend me or anything, but it wouldn't hurt her to smile back at me and give me some encouragement at times. She's so intense. She scares me sometimes.

**Catherine:** You need to develop a thicker skin around here. I'll tell you what I'll do. When we are having a coffee break later, I'll ask them straight out if we could have a few more opportunities to share ideas and discuss projects. I could say that you and I were chatting about the big order from John Thomas Ltd. and you came up with a brilliant idea how to get the contract.

Jenny:    What brilliant idea? What do you mean?

Catherine:    Just leave it all to me. I have a great idea, which is going to be yours. They'll be impressed. Just you wait and see.

Jenny:    Gosh Catherine! That's very decent of you, but I wouldn't be comfortable with that. I think I'll just have to assert myself a bit more. Make them notice me.

Catherine:    Well, if that's how you want it, but don't miss coffee break with us anyway. You're a bit shy you know. I'll make those guys come down from their high perches!

Jenny:    Thanks for the moral support Cath. I'm glad you're around here or I think I'd go crazy.

## 13. You Try It

Write an imagined dialogue based on the following picture:

# Glossary

**anecdotes:** short stories to illustrate a point
**bias:** taking sides, prejudiced
**concise:** to the point
**credible:** convincing, believable
**defective:** faulty
**dramatising:** making something dramatic (overreacting)
**graciously:** with charm and politeness
**prestigious:** inspiring respect and admiration
**raucous:** harsh and loud noise
**recipient:** person receiving a letter
**rectify:** to make right, correct
**retrieve:** get something back, regain possession
**selective:** choosing the most suitable or best
**sensationalising:** making something more exciting and dramatic than it is
**subjective:** from a personal point of view

# 4. Media

## Contents

## Key Exam Skills: Media

1 **Analysing and responding to print media**
Newspapers and magazines

2 **Analysing and responding to broadcast media**
Radio and television

3 **Analysing and responding to digital media**
Online content

4 **Analysing and responding to advertising in media**

5 **Analysing and responding to cartoons and comic strips**

# SECTION 4: MEDIA

This section of the paper is worth **40 marks**. You have **30 minutes** to complete this section. You usually get a choice of **two** questions from which you choose **one**.

Each question is divided into two parts, usually with the marks being divided evenly: 20 for part (a) and 20 for part (b). However, this may vary so look carefully at the marks provided in brackets after each question.

Read each question very carefully before you choose which one to do. Underline the task and key words in each part of the question and make sure that you understand what is being asked of you.

This section of the paper is very broad and questions do not always follow predictable formats. The best way to prepare for it is to familiarise yourself with various forms of media. Most of the questions require you to use your own common sense.

Media analysis is relevant to many aspects of daily life. Learning how to analyse allows you to see the many ways in which the media influences opinions and decisions in modern life.

The guidelines in this section will give you the essential information you need to provide a good answer for this section in your Junior Cert exam.

### Background
The word **media** refers to mass communication. It can be divided into three different sections:
  (a) **Print media:** newspapers, magazines, brochures, newsletters, comics, print advertising (e.g. posters, billboards etc).
  (b) **Broadcast media:** television, radio, film or any other form of electronic broadcast.
  (c) **Digital media:** this combines aspects of print and broadcast media (e.g. reading newspapers online, watching films on a laptop) and also includes such services as email, blogging, websites, social networking sites etc. This form of media can often be accessed through a smartphone.

In the Junior Cert exam, you can be asked questions which involve a thorough understanding of these three sections of the media.

## (a) Print Media
### Newspapers
Newspapers are national and local printed texts that contain news, articles, information, advertisements, entertainment, sport columns and opinion sections (i.e. editorials and letters).

Newspapers can be owned by individuals or by large commercial organisations/corporations. As they are free to report news and to express opinions, this gives them a powerful influence over the way the general public interprets events.

In general, newspapers can be divided into two major groups: tabloids and broadsheets. However, some newspapers do not fit neatly into either of these categories as they combine elements of both groups, e.g. *The Sunday Times*

The major differences between tabloids and broadsheets can be seen in the following table:

| TABLOIDS | BROADSHEETS |
|---|---|
| Small, magazine-size format. | Size is double that of a tabloid. |
| Front page is generally eye-catching. Use of colour, white print on black background. Red banners. Focus on one main story. | Front page is usually filled with dense text. More print is used than in tabloids and more stories are presented. |
| Headlines use different **font** sizes and can dominate the page. They often contain only one or two words, e.g. *Smash n'Grab! Lying Lennie!* | Headlines are not as large in size as in tabloids and are usually longer, e.g. *Minister of Health calls urgent meeting of HSE.* |
| Photographs and other types of visuals are given more space than printed text. | Text usually takes up more space than photographs. |
| Stories tend to be dramatic and deal with human interest or celebrity issues. | Stories tend to deal with national and international news as well as political and business issues. |
| Feelings and opinions are more dominant than factual information. | Factual statements are more dominant than feelings or opinions. |
| Language tends to be emotive, dramatic, informal, sometimes **biased** and often witty. | Language is formal and balanced in tone. It is more varied. |
| **Puns** on words, **alliterations**, over-use of personal pronouns, questions and exclamation marks are used throughout. | Puns, alliteration, exclamations etc. are rarely used. |
| Verbs can be omitted from sentences, e.g. *Secrets and Lies! Angry with Angie!* | Verbs are included in sentences, e.g. *Ireland's borrowing costs rise sharply, Man and woman arrested on suspicion of criminal damage.* |
| Stories and articles tend to be short and sub-divided, using sub-titles. | Stories and articles are developed in more detail and depth. They tend to be much longer and are not sub-divided. |
| Sentences and paragraphs are short. | Sentences are more complex and varied. Paragraphs are longer. |
| Tabloids can engage in obvious bias and often take strong positions on a variety of issues. | Bias is less obvious and, where it does occur, is not revealed in emotive language. |
| Tabloids are generally aimed at a readership who seek to be entertained. | Broadsheets are generally aimed at a readership who seek to be informed. |

When you are reading a news report from either a broadsheet or a tabloid newspaper, it is very important that you ask yourself the **5 Ws and How?** questions.

✳ **W**ho is this story about?
✳ **W**hat happened?
✳ **W**hen did it happen?
✳ **W**here did it happen?
✳ **W**hy did it happen?
✳ **H**ow did it happen?

## 1. You Try It

Read this news article and answer the questions which follow:

# Armed Robbery in Meath Bank

An armed gang made away with €20,000 following a bank raid at approximately 11 a.m. on Wednesday morning.

The robbers entered the National Bank in Barretstown, County Meath, and shouted at staff and customers to lie on the ground while one of the gang forced a cashier to put the cash into a large bag. They later fled the scene in a black Renault Scenic car which had been stolen in Dublin the previous day.

Garda Inspector Mark Glavin said the thieves had warned the bank staff not to raise the alarm, threatening that they would not hesitate to shoot if their orders were disobeyed. He described the robbery as a serious incident, which thankfully had not resulted in any injury, but had left people shocked and distressed. He praised the reaction of the bank staff and the customers who were in the bank at the time of the robbery. 'People did not panic but obeyed the orders of the thieves,' he said. 'Bank staff followed all procedures correctly and this helped avoid violence.'

Garda sources have linked this robbery to a series of similar bank raids which have taken place in recent months. They are following several lines of inquiry to investigate if it is the work of the same gang.

Members of the public who may have noticed unusual or suspicious activity in or around Barretstown on Wednesday 20th November, between 9 a.m. and 11 a.m. are asked to contact the Gardaí at Barretstown Garda station.

**Questions:**

**(a)** What is this story about? Summarise it in three or four sentences.

**(b)** When and where did the event take place? Give full details.

**(c)** Who were the main people involved in this event?

**(d)** Is this report written in a tabloid or in a broadsheet style? Give reasons for your response.

**(e)** You are the reporter. Write a fuller version of this story. You could give more details of the actual robbery, describe the scene shortly after the robbery took place, relate witness accounts etc.

## News sources

1. Local or national reporters, who research events and matters of public interest.
2. Press conferences held to inform journalists about any matter of public importance.
3. International news agencies such as the Associated Press or Reuters, who charge fees for providing international stories to newspapers.
4. Freelance reporters in different parts of the world or individuals who wish to publicise or highlight an event or issue.
5. Sometimes, a news story can break as a result of a 'leak' (something secretly disclosed to a journalist to create a sensation or to cause discomfort or embarrassment).

## Which stories make the news?

Editors and journalists are very aware of what their particular readership expects and what is considered newsworthy. Media researchers have identified certain types of stories which generate the most interest and which usually make the front pages of a newspaper. Some newsworthy stories relate to:

(a) **Negative or bad news:** catastrophes, tragedies, deaths, political or social uprising, natural disasters such as earthquakes, floods etc.

(b) **Breaking news:** Recent events are reported on more frequently than past events.

(c) **Continuity:** This refers to stories that are likely to be ongoing and which will provide major public interest, e.g. the destruction of the World Trade Centre in 2001.

(d) **Simplicity:** Stories that are simple are preferred to those which have a more complex background. More complex stories can be analysed in supplements, features or articles.

(e) **Celebrity appeal:** Stories that concern well-known people, e.g. politicians, film-stars, royalty etc., have news appeal – particularly for tabloids.

(f) **International importance:** Stories of international importance are often newsworthy. The more powerful the nation involved, the more interest will be generated by the story.

## Front Page Layout

1. **Masthead:** The masthead is usually printed at the top of the newspaper and refers to the name of the newspaper.
2. **Date** and **edition numbers** are always printed close to the masthead.
3. **The blurb:** This is the term used to describe the pictures and text directly under or close to the masthead.

1. ⟶

4. **Banner headline:** This refers to the main story headline. Other headlines can be used for stories of lesser importance. Banner headlines can sometimes be followed by a sub-headline, which gives more detail on the story to follow.

5. **A sub-headline** is printed directly below and gives further essential information.

6. **Photographs** can be connected to one of the front page stories, but can also be linked to an inside story or be totally independent. They usually have a short title or description written above them with a longer explanation appearing underneath them.

7. **Captions** are sentences which describe a photograph or other illustration. Captions are placed below the photograph. The name of the photographer or the source of the image is acknowledged.

**Caption:** *Kilkenny captain Eoin Larkin holds up the Liam McCarthy cup as the team parade through the city on an open top bus to celebrate their All-Ireland senior hurling championship win.*

**Photograph:** INPHO/ Cathal Noonan

8. **Advertisements** often take up a considerable portion of the front page of a newspaper. The bottom right-hand corner of the front page on page 127 contains a large advertisement.

9. **A by-line** indicates the name of a reporter. It is placed directly underneath the title of the story.

10. A newspaper story is often presented in **columns**. The space given to the text is known as 'column inches'.

11. The bottom of the page contains short information about some of the inside stories. This acts as a type of **'teaser'** to encourage readers to buy the paper. In the example on page 127 it is divided into the main sections of Home, World, Business and Sports news.

**Example of a broadsheet newspaper:**

Notice the following features:

♦ Plain masthead at top of page.

♦ Use of colour photographs, but densely packed text.

♦ No dramatic language. Headlines are factually stated.

♦ No use of abbreviation in headlines.

♦ No capitalisation in headlines; normal punctuation used.

♦ Dealing with serious news of political and social importance.

♦ Font size of headlines varied depending on importance of story.

♦ Section at bottom of page indicates the main content of the paper.

**Example of a tabloid newspaper:**

Notice the following features:

♦ Colourful, eye-catching presentation.

♦ Dramatic language of headline, e.g. 'grim sickness', 'secret' etc.

♦ Use of capitalisation in headline.

♦ Dealing mainly with celebrity issues rather than serious news.

♦ Large font of headline.

♦ Use of reverse print, i.e white text on black or strong coloured background.

♦ Very little text.

## 2. You Try It

Examine the front page of a tabloid newspaper and the front page of a broadsheet newspaper – both published on the same day. Compare the layout features of the two front pages. (You can use online versions of these newspapers if more convenient.)

## Other Essential Newspaper Terms

It is useful to know the following terms:

→ **Editorial team:** This refers to those people who are closely involved in preparing material for publication which contains news, information or comment as opposed to advertising. It includes the editor (who has overall responsibility), sub-editors for sections such as sports, news, business, features, pictures etc. and members of the graphics department.

→ **Editorial:** The editorial is a newspaper article which expresses the editor's opinion on a **topical** issue. The following is an example of an editorial:

# Taxi monopoly has to be broken

The behaviour of the taxi drivers at Dublin Airport, who have been refusing to pick up incoming passengers since Wednesday, is utterly **reprehensible**.

It was said of the old French royal family the Bourbons that they had learnt nothing and forgotten nothing. The same seems to apply to the taxi drivers. A dozen years after they tried and failed to block **deregulation** it seems as if a hard core are still wedded to their bad old habits.

For most of the Bourbons the price of their refusal to move with the times was to end up a head shorter. While we are not recommending anything so drastic for the taxi drivers, it is clear that the **monopoly** which they enjoy on public transport links to and from Dublin Airport must be decisively broken once and for all.

That can only happen when Dublin follows the example of virtually every other European capital and constructs a fixed-line link to the airport.

Now that Metro North has been finally abandoned, the path is clear to do what should have been done decades ago, run a spur from the DART at Baldoyle to Dublin city centre. This would allow passengers to travel by rail between the airport and the city centre in less than half-an-hour.

Irish Rail submitted a proposal to do just that almost a year ago. It costed the new line at just 200m.

Whatever doubts existed about the merits of this scheme have been banished by the events of the past few days. The sooner construction begins and the taxi drivers' monopoly broken, the better. *[Irish Independent]*

Glossary
**reprehensible:** deserving punishment, blameworthy
**deregulation:** removing from state regulations  **monopoly:** a group that has control over a service

→ **Fillers:** Short pieces of information used to fill small spaces.

→ **Supplements:** Any additional newspaper inserts which are enclosed but separate from the main body of the newspaper are known as supplements. Different supplements are offered at different times during the week and deal with subjects such as sport, business, property, fashion, farming etc.

→ **Taglines:** A slogan or catchphrase, often used in tabloids and placed under or near to the masthead.

→ **Typography:** This refers to the style and appearance of the printed text. It is particularly important regarding the lettering used for headlines and captions. Big, bold letters are used for headlines to make them stand out, whereas smaller bold lettering can be used for subheadings. Introductory lines are often printed in a different font style to the style used in the remainder of the news story or article.

*Key Skills in English*

Paper 1

### Functions of a newspaper

✿ To inform the public by circulating information about local, national and international events.

✿ To explain or comment on the significance of certain events – particularly through opinion pieces.

✿ To act as 'watchdogs' for the public by highlighting and exposing matters of public interest.

✿ To provide entertainment through the use of humorous articles and reports, crosswords, games, puzzles, horoscopes etc.

✿ To provide a platform where members of the public can express personal views on matters of interest, e.g. the letters page.

✿ To provide a vehicle for advertising. The main income of newspapers is from advertising.

 **OVER TO YOU**

**Question 1.** Read these two **news reports** and answer the questions which follow:

**Report A**

# Beaked Putin to fly with cranes

Russian President Vladimir Putin is reportedly planning to put on a fake beak and fly a motorized hang-glider to lead a flock of endangered Siberian white cranes on part of their migration to Asia.

The cranes, raised in captivity, do not know how to fly south, and environmentalists have to devise an imitation lead crane to show them the way.

Mr Putin's spokesman Dmitry Peskov told the Interfax news agency on Wednesday that the flight is to take place "one of these days".

The newspaper *Vedomosti* said it is expected before Mr Putin chairs the Asia-Pacific Economic Cooperation summit in Vladivostok beginning on Friday.

Mr Putin has become alternately notorious and beloved for an array of macho stunts, including posing with a tiger cub and riding a horse bare-chested.

Some of the stunts, such as petting a polar bear tranquillised in the wild, have purported scientific connections. But Mr Putin last year was caught out when one of the events was revealed to be a setup.

In that case, he was shown scuba diving and bringing up fragments of ancient Greek amphorae. But Mr Peskov later admitted the artefacts had been planted on the sea floor for him to grab.

The stunts irritate Mr Putin's opponents, who regard them not as benign political entertainment but as part of an establishment of a cult of personality **lionising** an authoritarian leader.

Masha Gessen, author of a book critical of Putin, left her post as editor of the travel and science magazine *Vokrug Sveta* (Around the World) this week, claiming she was fired for refusing to send a reporter 2,200 miles (3,500 kilometres) north-west of Moscow to Yamal Peninsula to cover Mr Putin's flight with the cranes.

The magazine said she left by agreement with management because of "differences" on the separation of editorial and publishing powers.

[**Source**: Associated Press]

Glossary
**lionising:** to treat somebody as a celebrity

130

**Questions on Report A:**

1. Would you consider the style of this report to be typical of tabloid or broadsheet reporting? Give reasons for your answer.
2. How many of the '5 Ws' are addressed in this report. Be specific.
3. How would you describe the tone of this article?
4. Do you consider this report to be newsworthy? Why? / Why not?

**Report B**

# Cops nab banana throwing race thug

GARDAI have snared the racist thug who threw a banana at a black Manchester City player in Thomond Park, it emerged last night.

Sources say the suspect, a **habitual criminal**, has admitted chucking the banana at Gael Clichy when the Premier League champions played Limerick FC in a pre-season friendly on August 5.

It's understood the 20-year-old, from the Moyross area of the city, is known to cops.

"He has a record as long as your arm — but all for petty stuff," a source told *The Star* last night.

Officers are now preparing a file for the DPP and expect charges to follow.

However sources revealed last night the rap is most likely to be a public-order one, which often gets a fine of as little as €100.

Gardai based at Roxboro Road have been scouring CCTV footage of the match at Thomond Park looking for the culprit — and it has emerged that the suspect's name was also given to them.

But they had no power to arrest him as there is no specific race-hate legislation here. Instead they interviewed him under caution this week in Limerick — and the suspect admitted throwing the banana.

There was uproar after it was thrown at Clichy 30 minutes into the friendly, which Manchester City won 4-0.

Such racists taunts have mostly been stamped out in British and Irish football, but often occur in Eastern Europe.

Last month's incident in Ireland made global headlines and Limerick FC and Thomond Park management slated it.

The joint statement said: "An incident of this nature is completely unacceptable. It is deeply upsetting that the actions of one individual have soured the experience for all those in attendance."

A witness who saw the thug throw the banana said he was one of a gang hurling racist abuse at black players.

The eyewitness also revealed the thugs didn't know the names of a single player in the Limerick FC team.

[Caitriona Giblin, *Irish Daily Star*]

Glossary
**habitual criminal:** someone who has repeatedly committed crimes

**Questions on Report B:**

1. How would you describe the use of language in this report? Give specific examples and explain your response.
2. How many of the '5 Ws' are addressed in this report? Be specific.
3. Do you consider this report to be newsworthy? Why? / Why not?

**Question 2.** Read this **newspaper article** and answer the questions which follow:

# . . . on having enough

**A FEW WEEKS AGO,** my boyfriend started baking bread every day. He makes two kinds, a soda bread he learned how to do on a cookery course and a friend's failsafe seeded bread. Neither are breads that require proving or, for that matter, kneading. It's just simple bread for a life we are trying to live as simply as we can.

Things are different now: he bakes his bread. I make our lunches from dinner leftovers to bring into work. We bring coffee in a flask when we go to the park. Instead of wandering into shops and making impulse purchases, I wander into shops and look at all the things I used to think I needed.

Sometimes I even stroke them. I pick up neon nail varnishes and carry them about in the shop as though I were headed to the tills. I feel the perceived loss of things less when I do this. It feels like a choice. I could have you, I say to the fake fur **gilet** that would never have suited me anyway, but instead I choose to put you back. Bye now.

The taxi drivers of Dublin are in mourning, having lost one of their best customers. My friend doesn't know what to make of it. "Are you in a taxi?" he used to say when he called. "You are always in a taxi." Now, I am on the bike or on the bus and the bus drivers of Dublin are sick of this woman asking questions about where the bus goes to and how long it takes to get where I'm going. I didn't come to this point gracefully. I was pushed, I didn't jump. But here I am. Feeling oddly giddy at a fourth day in a row spending exactly no money. Here I am, appreciating everything much more, from the €2 coin found down the back of the sofa to the bag of ingredients for tumeric tea with the recipe written on the side given by a friend to cure a raging sore throat.

It's not all Enid Blyton, home-baked produce and lashings of ginger beer around here. It's not all *Little House On The Prairie*, although with a name similar to the Ingalls you'd be amazed how often in my life myself and little freckly-faced Laura have been compared. There are challenging days when the smell of fresh bread does nothing to relieve the stress of an unexpected but necessary expense, but so far – mostly – this new approach has given us far more than has been taken away.

It's shown me the unexpected beauty in how the kind-of-sort-of running programme I've been doing costs nothing except commitment. I put on my runners and go out into the night and I kind-of-sort-of run. Simple.

Exactly one year ago today I wrote an article for the features section of this newspaper about the philosophy of "enough" or what's known in the trade as "enoughonomics".

Anne B Ryan of the National University of Ireland, Maynooth, who has been researching this notion for more than a decade, gave me tasks so that I could try living for five days with enough. I did, but I was a five-day wonder and I only started

**Glossary**
**gilet:** sleeveless jacket

thinking about it again yesterday. The bread was enough, and the not spending was enough, and enough was also the night spent recently with a friend sipping tap water – "tap water?" asked the unsmiling bar person – during which I laughed so much I thought my head was going to explode.

"We tend to be overloaded with expectations, information, people, decisions, choices and time demands," Ryan told me at the time. "The overall effect is to make us feel emotionally overloaded, because we end up feeling that we are not good enough or not coping well with all the demands. Exploring the concept of enough is about asking questions of ourselves, what do we really need, what can we do without? What in every area of our lives is really enough?"

She told me something else. That the phrase in Irish for enough, go leor, is the same word used for "plenty". Enough is plenty. And I forgot all about it until the smell of bread freshly baked every morning emerged as a symbol of the enoughness I've finally learned not just to embrace but to appreciate.

There are positive **repercussions**. Because he makes the bread, I eat less bread than I used to. You don't tend to plough as greedily through the stuff when you know and love the person who made it. Also, the children now think this is where bread comes from. From his hands. From our oven.

"Daddy's Bread" they cheer when it's placed on the wire rack as though he were Johnston, Mooney and O'Brien all rolled into one.

The bread rises and I ask myself questions. What do I really need? What can I do without? I don't need any more nail varnishes. I don't even like gilets. There's bread in the oven. It's go leor. It's plenty. It's enough.

{Róisín Ingle,

*The Irish Times*]

Glossary

**repercussions:** unintended consequences

**Questions**

1. In what way is a newspaper article different to a news story or report? Explain your response.
2. How would you describe the style and tone of this article?
3. In what sort of newspaper would you expect to find this article? Give reasons for your answer.
4. Would you expect to find this article on the front page of a newspaper? Why? / Why not?
5. Could this article be published online as well as in a printed newspaper? Why? / Why not?
6. Could this article be printed in a magazine? Why? / Why not?

## 3. You Try It

 **A.** You have been asked to write a news report based on the following details:

1. Train crashes into car at level-crossing
2. Driver of car survives but is seriously injured
3. Two witnesses to accident make statements
4. Driver of train interviewed.
5. Police make comment.

Using the inverted pyramid format,
write your news report:
   **(a)** in tabloid style
   **(b)** in broadsheet style.
   Give each report a headline.

**B.** Write a newspaper article which offers advice to parents on how teenagers can be encouraged to eat healthily.

## Magazines

A magazine is another form of print media. Unlike newspapers, which are published daily, magazines are a periodical publication, i.e. they appear weekly or monthly. They contain articles, illustrations and advertisements, often on a particular subject and aimed at a target audience: a women's magazine, teen magazine, computer or technology magazine etc.

### The major differences between magazines and newspapers

| Feature | Magazines | Newspapers |
|---|---|---|
| Publication | Monthly or bi-monthly, weekly | Daily |
| Format | Smaller than newspapers<br>More visually attractive<br>Better bound<br>Good quality paper | Larger<br>Less visually attractive<br>Not bound<br>Poorer quality paper |
| Price | Variety of prices, ranging from €1 up to €10 | Cheaper than magazines<br>Prices ranges from €1 to €2. |
| Content | Focus on features and articles relating to the interests of their particular readership, e.g. sports, weddings, cars, films etc. Content is thus less varied throughout magazine. | Deal mainly with breaking national and international news stories |
| Entertainment | Magazines are concerned with entertaining the reader, with some limited information pieces. | Newspapers are concerned with informing the reader, with some entertainment pieces. |
| Target audience | Magazines target specific age groups, genders and interest groups. | Newspapers appeal to a wide variety of age groups and interests. |

## Front Page Layout

**Masthead:** This is the name of the magazine displayed in a special font. It has a style unique to the magazine.

**Left third:** The left third of the magazine cover has a particular function. Because the entire cover is not always shown in full when displayed in shops, the left third must give some indication of the title and the contents.

**Main image:** This is a large, dominating image to attract the audience. It usually promotes the content or theme of the magazine. Notice its size and its position. What does this tell the reader?

**Anchorage text:** A text line used to give an image meaning so it cannot be interpreted in any other way.

**Colour scheme:** What moods do the colours used create?

**Cover lines:** These are lines which let the reader know about the features inside. Language is often exaggerated.

**Hyperbole:** Examples of this include 'Ultimate', 'Best', 'Shocking', 'New', 'Exclusive' etc. These words are used to 'hook' or grab the reader's attention.

**Slogan:** Slogans usually take the form of a boast or a claim that the magazine is special or unique in some way.

**Price:** This is displayed prominently when magazines are cheap. However, expensive magazines show their price in small print.

**Layout:** Covers can be formal or informal in the way they are organised. Some covers are aimed at older or more serious readers (e.g. *TIME* magazine or *National Geographic*). Other types of magazines tend to maximise impact or 'shout' at their readers. Always analyse the layout to get a sense of who the target audience is, and look for some of the following features: font size, font style (e.g. italic script, large block capitals, small print), colour, boxes at different angles.

**Direct address:** Some magazines directly address the reader by using personal pronouns such as 'you' or 'your'. On many magazine covers, the cover image person makes direct eye contact with the reader or a main product is presented dramatically to entice the reader.

**Barcode:** This is a machine-readable code located upon the front cover.

**Look at this analysis of the magazine cover on page 136 and notice the annotated features:**

1. **Masthead:** The masthead has a unique style for this film magazine. Large block capitals in red are used to attract attention.
2. **Main image:** The picture of Batman promotes the content of the magazine. It draws the reader's attention to the theme.
3. **Anchorage text:** This line gives the image meaning and context.
4. **Colour scheme:** Black conveys a sense of something sinister or hidden.
   Red implies danger or violence.
   The use of blue and yellow fonts creates contrast and makes those cover lines stand out.
5. **Slogan:** The Ultimate Exclusive

6. **Price:** This appears in small print because the publisher may not want to draw attention to the price.
7. **Cover lines:** These give the reader a brief impression of the articles inside the magazine.
8. **Use of exaggeration:** Ultimate, exclusive, special, best
9. **Creative layout** using a different graphic image of a bat, a photo in which the movie star makes eye contact with the reader, different size and colour of fonts, text boxes set at varying angles, use of columns.
10. **Bar code:** Magazine publishers are legally required to show a barcode and it cannot be covered by text.

## Magazine Articles

◎ The article has a title or headline. This grabs the reader's attention and persuades them to read on. It also highlights the main idea or theme.

◎ Opening paragraphs often provide background information.

◎ Style is usually simple and conversational in tone and often uses descriptive techniques.

◎ Text is illustrated by photographs, diagrams, graphs etc. which relate to the content.

◎ Light-hearted, humorous articles use exaggeration for comic effect.

◎ Sub-headings are commonly used for longer articles.

◎ Quotations and interviews, **anecdotes** and personal experiences are used to develop the theme.

◎ Memorable conclusions leave a lasting impression on the reader.

◎ There is very little difference between article/feature writing in newspapers and magazines.

# A Bullying Victim Faces the Crowd

## Robert Ferris, a teen from Dublin, tackles bullying head on.

Life gave few breaks to Robert Ferris. Born with cerebral palsy, he was given up by his biological mother and spent three years in foster care before being adopted by Margaret and Jack Ferris. At school, he was teased for his small size and pronounced limp.

By the time he was a teenager, he had grown painfully shy and withdrawn. 'The feeling that there are people who will love you and care for you no matter what – I never had that,' said Robert. 'I was convinced that everyone either hated me already, or would hate me in a matter of time. "Insecure" doesn't begin to describe it.'

### LOST SELF-ESTEEM

When he started secondary school, things got worse instead of better. Robert's timidity drew the bullies' scorn, and his self-esteem plunged further. He was called 'cripple,' 'ugly dog' and worse. Those who didn't mock him ignored him. 'I couldn't reach out; I didn't have the confidence. So I had no friends,' he said. Soon, he was missing one to three days of school a week. Margaret couldn't bear to force him to attend. 'Often, the stress literally made him physically sick. Other times he just couldn't face it,' she said. 'I should have gone in to the principal and told him how upset Robert was, but I suppose I assumed they could do nothing.'

In newspapers and online, Robert read about other bullied teens and the damaged lives they led. At first, he thought some of their methods of coping, self-harming or even contemplating suicide, were extreme and shortsighted. But as feelings of hopelessness set in, he got more distressed himself.

137

## SHARING THE PAIN

Then, one winter night, a Google search on depression led him to an essay by a woman whose son's life had been made a misery by bullying. The woman described her anguish that her son had never come to her to confide his feelings. 'The last thing I wanted to do was to talk about how I felt, but I knew I owed it to my mum,' Robert said.

Soon after, he sat down with Margaret and told her how desperate he was. Though alarmed, she reacted calmly and told him she would be taking him to a counsellor immediately. Over the next few months, Robert worked with the counsellor to change his outlook. The sessions helped dispel his darkest thoughts, but he told his counsellor he still felt helpless.

## AN ACTION PLAN

'My counsellor said, "Why don't you come up with an action plan?" ' Robert recalled.
So he did. The 'action plan' involved speaking out at school about how the bullying affected him and trying to make a better environment for all students. The young man who lacked the self assurance to socialise found it in himself to approach the principal of his school and request the chance to address his fellow pupils. To his amazement, Robert managed to stand in front of all of them and tell his life story.

'What made it extraordinary was his manner,' said Elaine Dwyer, Robert's English teacher. 'He wasn't making accusations. He was very dignified. He just explained things from his perspective, why he had been feeling so alone. He was matter-of-fact, and the students responded to that in a big way, because he clearly wasn't feeling sorry for himself or angry at them.'

Robert believes giving the speech was the hardest thing he'll ever do. But he's glad he went through with it, and says the best thing that other teens in his position can do is to face their fears head-on and refuse to be intimidated. 'I've never been more nervous, but when I was up there speaking, funny enough I felt quite normal,' he said. 'I think everyone saw that, too, because they treated me differently afterwards. They started speaking to me and I made friends at last. It's like they realised that I am, in fact, normal. Or at least as much so as anyone else.'

'I couldn't reach out; I didn't have the confidence. So I had no friends.'

**Worth noting:**
- ✿ Dramatic title
- ✿ Different fonts to arouse interest and highlight sections.
- ✿ Use of illustration to create human interest and prompt an emotion.
- ✿ Sub-titles used to break up text. This encourages the reader to continue reading by giving a hint of what is coming next.
- ✿ Notice use of colour to highlight sub-titles.
- ✿ Use of dialogue.
- ✿ Simple conversational style creates a sense of intimacy between the writer and reader.

# A Fast Escape from Fast Food

Marie Glancy makes a quick escape from the junk food scene - before it's too late!

I suddenly imagined that I could glimpse all the grease, chemicals, preservatives, and other damaging ingredients I was putting into my system. I started to change my ways.

It was difficult at first, because I craved the salty, greasy meals I'd grown so used to.

Glossary
**indispensable:**
necessary

Not long ago, I could have been the spokeswoman and poster girl for my local chip shop!

I made a faithful pilgrimage there after school every day. My usual order was a large bag of chips with garlic mayonnaise. I loved their piping hot temperature and the perfect crispness of each chip- I even loved the grease that soaked the bag they came in.

But my love affair with fast food didn't stop there. Any time I was in the city centre, a stop at McDonald's was **indispensable**.

I'd go for a Big Mac and a shake and wait for the flavours to work their magic. Here came that tangy special sauce and that sweet, frothy shake: Voila!

All my problems dissolved in deliciousness.

Just the thought of fast food lifted my mood. I certainly didn't feel the same way about food I got at home. Dinner was mostly pasta with canned sauce, tasteless boiled veg, and dodgy meat. Who could blame me for seeking adventure somewhere else? I knew that fast food could make me unhealthy – in theory. Truthfully, since I only weighed about seven stone and wasn't especially worried about getting fat, the other health concerns didn't seem real.

Then, I watched **Super Size Me**, a documentary film by Morgan Spurlock. Spurlock decides to eat only McDonald's food for every meal, every day for one month. At the beginning of the month, he has a doctor check his health and it all looks fine, as you would expect for a fairly young man who eats mostly healthy food.

During the course of the month and at the end, Spurlock has his health checked repeatedly.

The doctor is able to measure Spurlock's health deteriorating as the weeks go on. By the end of the month, he has gained nearly two stone and suffers from high cholesterol and other problems that he didn't have before his experiment.

Watching **Super Size Me**, I was shocked. Thirty days is a very short span of time in which to see your health and figure ruined entirely. Spurlock shows us how violently his body reacted to the extreme diet.

Watching that, I felt disgusted with myself and my way of eating.

OK, I was young and slim – for now. For now, you couldn't see the terrible effects of my dietary choices. But I suddenly imagined that I could glimpse all the grease, chemicals, preservatives, and other damaging ingredients I was putting into my system. I saw a mess where my healthy body should be. I knew that if I didn't change my ways, eventually the inside would be reflected on the outside and I would not only be, but also look, an absolute sight.

I started to change my ways. It was difficult at first, because I craved the salty, greasy meals I'd grown so used to. It was also tough because many of my friends enjoy eating fast food. A couple of them had watched the film with me, but it was just entertainment to them. Their eyes weren't opened to the horrors of bad food the way mine were.

But because I really did have a revelation, I'd look at the same foods that used to make my mouth water and feel my stomach sink. I'd think about the fats building up in my blood vessels and feel ill instead of excited.

I needed something else to raise my mood now, so I took up football. At first I was so out of shape that I could barely trot the length of the pitch. That's when I knew I'd been right to worry about my health. I can tell you I was proud when, after just a month, I was as fit as some of the best players on the team.

I still go to McDonald's or Burger King occasionally with friends. I even buy my old treat sometimes, but it doesn't hit the spot like it once did. My body seems to object, like it has woken up and knows what its rights are. If I could just move the social scene somewhere else – like to the football pitch – this story of transformation would be complete, and not just mine alone.

## Questions

1. How would you describe the style of the above article? Explain with reference to the article.
2. What techniques are being used by Marie Glancy to grab the reader's attention at the beginning of the article?
3. What target audience is intended for this article? Give reasons.
4. What differences do you notice in this article and the one before it on pages 137-138? Consider language, use of dialogue, theme, tone etc.
5. In what ways are these articles similar?
6. Write an article for a teen magazine which you think would appeal to your readership.

## ADVANTAGES OF PRINT MEDIA

Newspapers and magazines are traditional forms of media which are usually well-researched, reliable sources of information.

Newspapers can report on local news and advertise local services. Family notices, such as births, deaths and anniversaries, and small classified advertisements are easily accessed.

Newspaper supplements provide more in-depth reporting and analysis in various areas of interest, e.g. sport, business, farming, property etc.

Print media can cater to the needs and interests of different groups of people and create loyal readerships.

Print media is easy to carry around, handle, read and re-read. Magazines and newspapers can be left in waiting rooms which increases exposure.

Print media is not very expensive and is widely available in newsagents, supermarkets, airport shops and other outlets.

## DISADVANTAGES OF PRINT MEDIA

Because large corporations fund and own newspapers and many magazines, a certain bias can operate in the way news is reported.

Because newspapers have to be designed and printed, news can be outdated before it even reaches the public. Lack of space can result in stories being left out.

Print media can rely too heavily on advertising to cover costs and advertisement 'clutter' can result. Big advertising agencies can also influence content.

Tabloids and broadsheets target different groups, and so do magazines. This can reduce their general appeal to different age groups and readerships.

Waste paper can build up and create a nuisance for households and businesses. There is also the negative environmental impact as paper is made from trees.

Print media costs can add up when buying daily newspapers or monthly magazines. Delivery to outlets is an added cost.

## (b) Broadcast Media

Broadcast media refers to forms of electronic media such as radio and television. Each form has its own advantages and disadvantages.

## ADVANTAGES OF RADIO

Most people listen to radio broadcasts at work, at home and while driving.

Programmes can have a local interest and appeal and cater to the needs of specific communities.

It is a relatively cheap form of broadcast media.

## DISADVANTAGES OF RADIO

People may listen to the radio while driving or doing other activities and this may affect concentration and create hazards.

Radio depends heavily on quality of signal reception. This is not always reliable and can be frustrating. Even household appliances can interfere with radio signals.

## ADVANTAGES OF RADIO

People can call in and engage in discussions. Programmes like *Liveline* on RTÉ Radio One attract listeners and encourage interaction.

Radio is not as addictive as television. People can listen to radio and work at the same time. News can be quickly updated.

Specially targeted programmes can cater to different interest groups, e.g. gardening, classical or popular music, political discussions etc.

Children are not as negatively influenced by radio as they are by television because of the lack of visuals.

Radio can stimulate the imagination. Readers listening to drama or book readings have to use their imaginations more (a bit like reading in print).

## DISADVANTAGES OF RADIO

Although it is cheaper to buy and operate a radio than to buy and operate a television, the lack of visuals can lessen impact and appeal.

Radio is often not listened to with full concentration which reduces its impact on the listener.

People with hearing disabilities cannot engage with radio as easily as they can engage with television (which offers sub-titles) or with print media.

News reports are not as wide-ranging in appeal and impact, as the visual aspect is removed.

Some programmes can be influenced by bias and **prejudice**. This is not always as obvious as in other media where body language, facial expression etc. are seen and can be interpreted.

Children engage better with television. Visuals, graphics and special effects can be used for educational purposes.

## ADVANTAGES OF TELEVISION

Television is an extremely popular form of media with universal appeal. It can offer a variety of programmes that appeal to different ages and interest groups.

Television combines visual and audio input. News can be quickly updated and covered **extensively**. Newsreaders' scripts are usually carefully written and edited to present facts as objectively as possible.

## DISADVANTAGES OF TELEVISION

Bcause of its wide availability and popularity, television can become addictive. People can become 'couch potatoes' and live unhealthy lifestyles.

Live news is not as carefully edited as print news. Situations can be seen from certain camera angles which could create bias. Large corporations own television networks and can sometimes influence the way stories are reported.

| ADVANTAGES OF TELEVISION | DISADVANTAGES OF TELEVISION |
| --- | --- |
| Social issues can be explored in discussion programmes and documentaries which raise social awareness. Current affairs and history programmes can educate the public. | Violence and other social problems can be seen as 'unreal' because people can view them from the comfort of their own homes. Children's attitudes can be influenced by over-exposure to violence etc. |
| Television appeals to multiple senses through the combination of text, images, sound and motion. People who have problems reading print media can easily understand news and other programmes. | Television can damage the quality of family life. Time spent in discussion and sharing family meals can be interrupted by television viewing. |
| Sporting activities can be enjoyed by larger audiences without having to travel to venues or purchase tickets. | Television can bring sport into the home but it does not always result in encouraging people to engage in sporting activities themselves. Because watching television requires so little input from the viewer, laziness and inactivity can develop. |
| Television is an excellent medium for entertaining and educating young children. Special programmes are also made to fit in with the school curriculum, e.g. history and geography programmes, plays, films, documentaries etc. | Young children cannot distinguish between what is real and what is unreal. This can lead to fears, insecurity and even danger, as children try to imitate what they observe onscreen. Stereotyping can also have a negative effect on children. |
| People who live alone or in remote areas often feel less isolated by watching television. They can also be made aware of services and products which could improve their quality of life. | Television can sometimes become a substitute for socialising with others. Visitors may not feel as welcome to call on friends or neighbours in case they interrupt their favourite programmes. |

## (c) Digital Media: the Internet

Digital media refers to text, graphics, audio and video transmitted over the internet or computer networks. This form of media began in the US after the Second World War as a government project. The intense development of the World Wide Web during the last decade of the twentieth century has made the internet accessible to all. It is a rapidly developing form of media.

You need to be informed concerning the role of the internet in media studies as it is such a strong influence in people's lives. The worlds of business, politics, education, entertainment and social networking are changing very quickly as more and more people use this form of communication.

## Words you need to know

**Network:** A network refers to a group of computers connected to each other by telephone lines or cables.

**Server:** A server is a powerful computer which runs one or more networks. It acts as a 'host', meeting the needs of other computers on a network. Servers provide essential services to organisations or to private individuals through the internet.

**Email:** Email is a very popular form of communication. Individuals can send messages to each other from their computers by using email addresses. An email address is composed of two parts: a user name and a computer name. These names are separated by the sign @, e.g. joebloggs@eircom.net

**Chatrooms:** Chatrooms are live discussion areas or meetings which allow you to type messages or comments on your computer which are seen immediately by other internet users. People can engage in discussion with others who are interested in the same subjects.

**Newsgroups:** A newsgroup is another form of discussion board (group) but these messages are saved and can be read repeatedly by other visitors to the site.

**Data:** Data refers to the information stored on a computer.

**WWW** (World Wide Web): The World Wide Web gives people access to information on the internet.

**Website:** A website refers to a specific address containing a page or pages on the internet where an individual or company has posted information.

**Web browser:** A browser is a programme that allows you to read web documents, e.g. Internet Explorer, Firefox, Safari.

**Search engines:** A search engine helps you to locate information quickly. These engines visit many websites and organise them into catalogues which you can examine to find the information you are seeking. Google and Yahoo are well-known search engines.

**Social networking:** Social networks are places where people can communicate online, e.g. Twitter, Facebook. Social network sites are a popular means of communication, providing people with ways to use instant messaging, make friends and share thoughts and comments. People can sign up, create a profile (identity), post pictures, draw images, share links and write about whatever they enjoy.

**Blogs:** A blog refers to a web log or web diary. One person writes a blog on a topic that interests them and people can read it and respond to it. Other bloggers can respond to posts and opinions can be exchanged and debated. Some people have private blogs – a type of internet diary – which they share with family and friends. Other blogs are run by large companies and organisations. Newspapers, universities, media outlets, interest groups and many other institutions use blogs to share information and circulate ideas. Twitter is a type of newsblog which can be quickly updated.

**Virus:** A virus is a small computer programme which is deliberately developed to damage other computers. Anti-virus programmes help to protect computers from viruses.

**Hackers:** Hackers are people who can access the contents of other people's computer from their own computers without permission. They can then read, copy or alter these contents. A special firewall programme can be used to protect computers from hackers.

## Why is digital media important in media studies?

Digital media plays an extremely important role in mass communication. Online content can reach a worldwide audience in seconds and can be a powerful influence in many areas of modern life. Like all forms of media, digital media has advantages and disadvantages.

### ADVANTAGES OF DIGITAL MEDIA

The internet is a major source of information on just about every subject. Research is easy and quick.

News agencies, television networks and newspapers can instantly bring breaking news stories to an international audience. Live video can be streamed (sent), interviews conducted and photographs shown to millions of people at the same time.

Advertisers can advertise and sell their products on websites. People can make purchases without having to leave their homes.

Entertainment is accessible online. Music, films and games can be purchased and downloaded. Many are available free of charge.

Researchers, doctors, scientists and other experts can share information on different projects and connect with each other without having to travel abroad.

Business meetings can be held online. Members of a business team can speak to each other, see each other and make decisions on business deals or matters without the need to travel. Some businesses can even operate from home.

People can 'socialise' online and keep in touch with family and friends. They can also have 'virtual friends' with whom they can chat and share ideas. Sometimes people get to know each other well and form online relationships, some of which end up in marriage.

### DISADVANTAGES OF DIGITAL MEDIA

Not all of the information available on the internet is completely reliable. On many websites, anybody can upload information which means content can sometimes be inaccurate or even completely wrong. Users can be misinformed and need to be aware of such misinformation.

While news can be easily accessed, it is not always reliable or properly edited. People can affect the quality of news reporting by using such sites as Twitter. Stories based on nothing but rumour can go viral and spread lies. Trustworthy news outlets have to compete with the speed of less reliable sources.

Shopping online can become addictive with people buying goods they do not need. Advertising can be very aggressive online and scams are commonplace.

It is possible for users to download copyrighted films, music and video. This is a type of theft of other people's creative work. Games and other entertainment can become addictive and waste vast amounts of time.

Viruses and spamming can completely wipe out valuable research documents and can cause computers to crash.

The internet can be used for criminal activities, organising riots and other social nuisances.

Some people can become addicted to social networking and 'virtual' worlds. They may become detached from the real world. People may spend an excessive amount of time playing games alone or chatting to virtual friends and neglect their 'real world' friends.

**145**

| ADVANTAGES OF DIGITAL MEDIA | DISADVANTAGES OF DIGITAL MEDIA |
|---|---|
| The internet provides a platform for people to express their views on many different subjects and to learn about the views of others. | The internet can be abused as a platform for personal expression. Prejudice and stereotyping can be spread. Cyber-bullying is also becoming a serious threat, especially for young or vulnerable people. |
| Specialist interests can be followed without the need to buy expensive books or magazines. | Often, one has to scroll through hundreds of poor quality pages before finding reliable, quality material. |
| Banking services can be availed of online and save time. Users can access their money 24 hours a day and pay bills, make transfers etc. from home. Tax returns can also be made online. | Internet thieves roam the World Wide Web. Credit card information can be robbed and used illegally to defraud people. Financial scams are commonplace. |
| Emails and messaging are **instantaneous** and have none of the disadvantages of post or 'snail mail'.  | Email messages can be forwarded in error to the wrong people. Because of speed and convenience, proper expression and grammar is sometimes neglected causing the reader to be confused or misinterpret the contents of the message. |

**Note:** As digital media is a rapidly growing form of media, new advantages and disadvantages can constantly be added to the above list.

## (d) Advertising

Advertising is an important area of print, broadcast and digital media. **Persuasive** techniques are fundamental to advertising as their purpose is to sell a product or service.

**AIDA** is an acronym. It a useful way to think of how to create a good advertisement.

A  **Attention:** Grab the attention of the customer.

I  **Interest:** Provoke customer interest by focusing on and demonstrating advantages and benefits of the product or service for sale.

D  **Desire:** Persuade customers that they need and desire the product or service.

A  **Action:** Encourage customers to take action and/or purchase the product or service.

### (i) Print Advertising

Advertisers create an advertisement (ad) by:

1. Identifying the target market.
2. Selecting a benefit with some type of emotional appeal.
3. Writing persuasive copy (text) accompanied by startling or appealing illustrations (pictures).

The end result is to ensure the ad has a memorable impact on people, encouraging them to buy the product/service.

## Advertising Terms/Lingo

- **Target audience:** The potential buyers of the product or service being advertised.
- **Copy:** The text or writing in an ad.
- **Denotation:** What you see or read on the page.
- **Connotation:** What the advert makes you think of (associations).
- **Facts:** Things that can be proven to be true.
- **Opinions:** Things that are not necessarily true.
- **Slogan:** A short, catchy, memorable phrase, e.g. Beanz Meanz Heinz, Under the tree at Spar, Because I'm worth it etc. Slogans often use rhyme, puns, repetition of words, alliteration, **assonance** etc. to make them memorable.
- **Buzz words:** Words which are repeated for emphasis, e.g. New, Latest, Ultimate, Best, Supreme etc.
- **Caption:** A short line or two of text describing a photo or illustration.
- **Illustration/Image:** Photographs or any type of image used in the ad.
- **Graphics:** The designs used in the ad, e.g. shape of boxes, type of font style etc.
- **Logo:** A graphical design associated with a specific company, product or service.
- **Bleed:** An illustration or design that goes to the very edge of the page without any borders or margins.
- **Brand:** A product manufactured by a specific company, e.g. Coca Cola, Benetton, Ford, Renault.
- **Characters:** People or animals used in the ad.
- **Jargon:** Specific words or expressions associated with a product. Gives the impression of expertise, e.g. use of mechanical terms when selling cars.
- **Persuasive techniques:** Any technique that encourages a person to buy the product or service.
- **Stereotyping:** An often completely false image or idea of a person or thing, e.g. a kind, old granny; a tough young man; a dumb blonde etc.
- **Typography:** The style and appearance of the words on the ad. Look at the size and colour of the fonts; use of capital letters, bold, italics, underlined words.
- **Rhetorical questions, alliteration, rule of three:** All used to create a particular effect.

## Guidelines for analysing an advertisement

**First, ask yourself:**

- ♦ What is being advertised? A product or service?
- ♦ Who is it aimed at (the target audience)? Who is likely to buy the product?
- ♦ What are the benefits for the buyer according to the ad?
- ♦ Where might this ad appear?
- ◆ Look at the language used in the text. What is the headline or main statement? Is there an effort to appeal to a person's self-image or emotions?
- ◆ Can you identify any use of flattery? exaggeration? rhetorical questions? sensual appeal?
- ◆ Underline any repetition, key or 'buzz' words, e.g. new, best, special, exclusive, bargain etc.
- ◆ How often are these words repeated?

- Is there any use of figurative language, e.g. **similes**, **metaphors**, symbols?
- Examine the different types of print or fonts. Are letters presented in bold, italics or underlined? What size are the letters? Where is the text placed? Why is it placed there?
- Is there a slogan? Where is it placed and why?
- Is there any use of humour evident in the text? How does this create an impact?
- Ask yourself if there is any stereotyping in either the language or the illustration. Identify it.
- Carefully examine the main illustration and any other pictures. How are they connected to the text?
- Look at the colours used in the illustration or picture. Do these colours have special connotations (associations) or effects on the reader? (Look at the list of colour associations below.)
- Look at any people pictured in the ad. Are they happy, sad, lively, healthy, excited, young, old, children etc?
- Have any celebrities or 'experts' been quoted or are they shown in the illustration? Have beautiful or attractive people been used to sell the product?
- How are people positioned in the ad? Why are they positioned in this way? Also examine how any animals are positioned. Ask yourself why.
- Examine body language, facial expression, clothing, etc. Does the clothing suggest a particular image, e.g. a sharp suit = a business person; stylish clothes = a person interested in appearance and image.
- Is there a logo? Where is that placed and why?
- Is this a visual ad? Advertisements do not always use words to sell their products. Sometimes the illustration cleverly contains the appeal, creates the need and sells the product or service.

## Colour associations

| | |
|---|---|
| **Red** | The colour of fire and blood; associated with energy, war, danger, strength, power, determination, passion and love. |
| **Yellow** | The colour of sunshine; associated with joy, happiness, intellect and energy. |
| **Orange** | Blends the energy of red and the happiness of yellow; associated with joy, sunshine, enthusiasm, happiness, creativity, determination, success and stimulation. |
| **Green** | The colour of nature; associated with growth, harmony, freshness, fertility and safety. |
| **Blue** | The colour of the sky and sea; associated with depth, trust, intelligence, faith, truth, and heaven. |
| **Purple** | Combines the calm of blue and the energy of red. Purple is associated with royalty. It symbolises power, nobility, luxury, and ambition. It conveys wealth and extravagance. Purple is also associated with wisdom, dignity, mystery and magic. |
| **White** | Considered to be the colour of perfection; associated with light, goodness, innocence, purity and virginity. |
| **Black** | Associated with death, evil, mystery, power, elegance and formality. |

**Sample Question:** Examine this advertisement carefully. Do you find it effective? Explain why/why not.

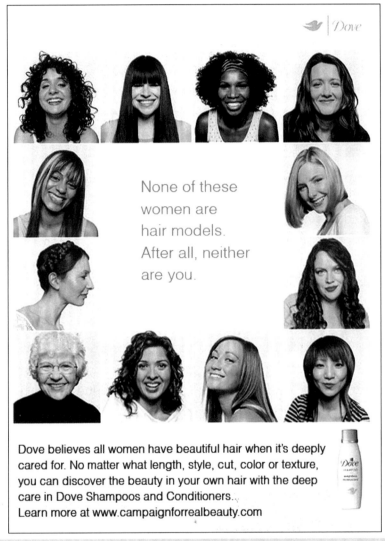

## Analysis of a Dove advertisement:

**A** **Attention:** Grab the attention of the customer.

**I** **Interest:** Provoke customer interest by focusing on and demonstrating advantages and benefits of the product or service for sale.

**D** **Desire:** Persuade customers that they need and desire the product or service.

**A** **Action:** Encourage customers to take action and/or purchase the product or service.

**Target Audience:** Women of any age with any type of hair.

**A** The attention of the target audience is captured by the use of 12 colour photographs of the heads of women forming a box around the headline. The fact that the women are from different cultural groups, have different hairstyles and textures, have different coloured hair, wear their hair at different lengths and are different ages widens the appeal of the advertisement and creates variety. It is interesting to notice that only one woman could really be described as elderly, which suggests that the advertiser is placing more emphasis on youth and beauty in order to sell the product. Attention is also stimulated by the text placed within the photographic arrangement. The reader is directly addressed as 'You' which personalises the message and creates a friendly atmosphere.

I    The interest of the customer is provoked by the use of words and phrases which have positive connotations – *beautiful hair, deeply cared for, beauty in your own hair, deep care.* There is no doubt that the advertisement is suggesting that the product will provide exceptional care  resulting in beautiful hair.

D    The desire to use the product is created by the persuasive tone of the language and also by the fact that all the women in the pictures are smiling happily, which suggests that happiness is linked to having beautiful hair. The statement that women 'can discover' the beauty in their hair by using the shampoo suggests that they have not yet discovered that beauty and need to buy the product in order to do so. The emphasis on 'deep care' also suggests that the care provided by other products is not as good.

A    Action is stimulated by encouraging the customers to 'Learn more' by visiting the website. The image of the product is carefully positioned in the bottom right-hand corner, (which is where the eye naturally rests when reading from left to right). One can clearly see what the container looks like, so it can be easily spotted on shelves in pharmacies or supermarkets.

## Points of particular interest

◎ Different sized fonts are used for the headline in the centre and the wording in the rest of the text. This creates a visual variety and contrast.

◎ The headline is written in a shade associated with gentleness and naturalness – a pale blue, dove-like colour, which is also the colour of the logo and the top of the bottle. All of the women pictured look gentle and polite in keeping with the atmosphere created by the use of  this colour.

◎ The logo of a dove and the specific script for writing the word *Dove* are seen twice on the advertisement. They are positioned above the square of photographs at the top right-hand side of the illustration and can also be seen on the front of the bottle on the bottom right-hand side.

◎ With the exception of one woman, who has a side profile, all the women are looking at the camera, which suggests an open, friendly, confident manner. The suggestion is that women will grow in confidence by having the beautiful hair which the product claims to create. The woman who is photographed from the side has a gentle, old-world look that suggests refinement. Her hair is carefully groomed and formally arranged in an 'up-style' in contrast to the more casual look of the hairstyles of the other women. This broadens the appeal of the product by attracting all types of women to buy the product.

◎ The claim that 'all women have beautiful hair' is a statement of opinion, not fact. This is acknowledged in the phrase 'Dove believes ...'. However, it is a matter of fact that not all women have beautiful hair, regardless of what products they may use on it. Some women suffer from alopecia (hair loss) or have other illnesses which may affect the quality of their hair. The advertisement is ignoring this fact and using a generalisation ('all') to sell the product. This is misleading, but is not actually a lie (because of the use of the word 'believes').

This advertisement is effective in its impact on the target audience as it taps into some
women's desire to look their best, regardless of age, and to be open, friendly and confident.

## Minimalist ads

Some ads use very little text and depend totally on the illustration to convey their message. These ads are known as minimalist and are becoming increasingly popular.

**4. You Try It**

Canal+ is a French premium pay television channel. It offers subscribers the opportunity to watch their favourite sports on their smartphone.

**A.**

1. How effective do you think this ad is in encouraging customers to buy the product offered?
2. What aspects of the ad are particularly effective in your opinion? Give reasons for your answer.
3. Would this ad benefit from having more text added? Why?/Why not?
4. Who is the target audience for this advertisement?

**B.**

1. How effective is this ad in your opinion?
2. How closely does it reflect the advertising approach in AIDA? Consider how the attention of the customer is grabbed, how interest is achieved, how desire is created and how action is suggested.
3. Comment on the positioning of the product and the logo in this advertisement.
4. If you were asked to write a short text to accompany this ad, what would you write? Keep in mind the features of ads listed earlier in this section.

**C.**

1. How is the text in this ad linked to the illustration?
2. Comment on the use of setting, colour and camera focus in the illustration.
3. Who is the target audience for this ad?
4. Where would you expect to find this ad? Give a reason for your answer.

## Posters

A poster is any piece of printed paper, bill or placard usually displayed in a public place. The most important difference between the poster and other print advertisements is that the poster is aimed at the audience 'on the move.' A passerby will not stand to read a poster very carefully. The poster, therefore, must capture the attention and get the message across instantly. Keep in mind all the skills which apply to effective ads.

Posters can be used for purposes other than simply advertising. They can be used to raise awareness of important health or social issues, e.g, anti-smoking or anti-bullying campaigns, road-safety reminders, election campaigns etc. The **AIDA** technique also applies to posters.

### Features of a good poster

- It grabs attention immediately.
- The message is communicated quickly and is not complicated.
- It convinces the reader of the benefits of the product/service.
- Colour is used effectively to hold the reader's attention.
- The KISS technique is used: **Keep It Short and Simple.**

### Consider the general impact of a poster.

◎ Who would you say is the target audience for the poster?
◎ What does the poster want to achieve?
◎ Is the intention clearly communicated by the poster?
◎ Is the message of the poster communicated primarily by images or words?
◎ Is a political or social purpose served by the poster?
◎ What is your general opinion of the effectiveness of the poster?

## OVER TO YOU

Look at the following posters and answer the questions:

**A.**

1. How does this poster grab the viewer's attention? Explain your response.
2. What is the message of this poster? Is it clearly presented?
3. Is this an effective poster? Explain your answer.

Cigarette butts make up almost half of Dublin's litter

**Source:** Dublin City Council

**Source:** Simon Community

**B.**

1. Do you find this poster effective? Explain your response.
2. How is this poster different from a print advertisement?
3. Comment on the type of lettering and the text used in this poster.
4. What main message is this poster trying to communicate?
5. Would this poster encourage you to take any action? Explain.

## (ii) Broadcast Advertising

Broadcast advertising uses a form of mass communication which is electronically transmitted, i.e. it uses an electrical current to work. The most common places to use broadcast advertising are on the radio and television.

The tables on pages 158-161 sum up the major advantages and disadvantages of each of these forms of media.

### Guidelines for writing good advertising copy for broadcast media

Plan carefully before you begin to write.

* Identify the key points about the product or service which you are selling.
* Observe the KISS rule: **Keep It Short and Simple.**
* Keep in mind the format you are using, e.g. if it is a radio advertisement you cannot use any visual aids.
* Do not try to include too many details or use too many words. People will not take time to read or listen to too much text.
* Grab consumers' attention immediately. You could use a rhetorical question, e.g. **Are you spending too much on health insurance?** or **Would you like to be the envy of your friends and neighbours?** or you could quote a startling statistic or fact or make a shocking statement etc.
* Try to create interest and curiosity so that the consumer will be motivated to take some action. You don't need to try to sell the product immediately, just encourage the reader or listener to take some form of action. (See ad for Dove Shampoo on page 149.)

 ❋ Repeat the name of the product, service or company at least three times in the ad.
 ❋ Give contact details as briefly as possible – a memorable telephone number or a web address.

When studying and revising advertising for your Junior Cert exam, it is important that you read and examine as many forms of advertising as you can. Compare and contrast each form and be clear as to the advantages and disadvantages of each type. Practise writing copy or text for all types of ads. Review the lists provided on pages 158-161 on the advantages and disadvantages of each type of media form.

**Sample Question**
Write the text for a radio advertisement which aims to sell holidays abroad.

### Sample: Radio advertisement script

*(Sound effects: heavy rain in background)*

**Announcer:** Are you sick and tired of the sound of summer rain?

Want to escape grey skies and depressing weather forecasts?

*(Sound effects: change to bright, cheery music)*

**Announcer:** Well call 'Sun Travel Holidays' now!

This year we have incredible offers for holidays in the sun.

Whether you want to explore exotic, far-flung destinations like Africa or Australia, or you just want a family holiday to the sun, NOW *(emphasised)* is the time to get a fabulous deal.

You cannot beat Sun Travel Holidays for good value and superb service.

Both our tailor-made offers or our package deals ensure total satisfaction.

*(Sound effects: thunder and heavy rain)*

**Announcer:** What are you waiting for? Call us on 1800 12345 or visit our website at Suntravel.ie

*(Next line is sung to happy, memorable tune which drowns out the sound of the rain)*

Sun Travel: Don't delay! Get away!

## OVER TO YOU

1. Write the copy (text) for a radio ad which aims to sell clothing to teenagers.
2. Write the copy for a print ad which aims to sell a new type of mobile phone. Indicate the type of illustration that would be included and the colours that would dominate the illustration. Explain how the illustration and copy are connected to each other.
3. Describe the different types of advertisements which are commonly found on websites. Explain how these are different from other forms of ads found in print media. Discuss the advantages and disadvantages of digital advertising. (You may wish to review the lists on pages 158-161 before beginning this question.)

4. Write the text of an article for a teenage magazine entitled 'Manipulation by Media - Don't buy it!'

5. Select an ad from any newspaper or magazine and annotate it carefully. Point out the key features of the ad and the impact they make on the reader.

### Product Placement

Product placement refers to the insertion of a product into films, television programmes, video games, social media, internet, books etc. It is a special, subtle type of advertising technique which does not make direct reference to the product, as in other types of advertising.

A good example of product placement is the use of a specific type or make of car, driven by a major actor or important character in a film. The car's logo will be seen repeatedly throughout the film.

Another example is the use of certain products in a kitchen scene, e.g. certain brands of kitchen equipment, foods etc. Soap operas on television are ideal places for such product placement as scenes can be set in one location for a few minutes or longer. The scene can also be re-visited in the programme. Reality shows are also useful locations for product placements. To spot product placement watch out for the logo or name of the product being repeated in the programme as well as being always clearly visible to the audience.

Video games can also be used for product placement. For example, certain car companies work with gaming programmers to incorporate their make of car into the games.

Product placement can use books as an indirect means of advertising. Take for example a book called *The Oreo Cookie Counting Book* by Sarah Albee. The blurb tells parents that, 'Children will love to count down as ten little OREOs are dunked, nibbled, and stacked one by one ... until there are none!'

### Methods of Product Placement

(a) The product can be placed in the programme so that it is clearly seen by the audience.

(b) The product can be shown in use by one of the actors.

(c) The product can be mentioned by name in the dialogue.

(d) The product could be subtly or openly placed in a book illustration, e.g. children playing with a certain toy or eating certain brands of sweets or foods.

(e) The product could be described or mentioned in the course of a narrative such as a short story or novel.

## Advantages of Product Placement

(a) Because the product is part of a film, programme or game, the impression is subtly given that it was chosen for its own worth and that it is not a marketing trick. This could influence the target audience into buying the product as they would assume that there is no bias operating.

(b) The product can be advertised without interrupting the programme or game and this means that viewers are unlikely to switch channel or mute the sound, as they can do during ordinary commercial breaks.

(c) Many people feel overwhelmed by advertising and try to ignore it. Product placement is less invasive and irritating so it can make an almost silent impact on the target audience.

(d) The use of a product can give a sense of realism to the film or programme, e.g. a bottle of Pepsi is more realistic than something that has no name at all on it. You might notice though that the can or bottle is held in such a way that you can clearly read the name of it.

(e) Integrated product placement is less expensive than traditional commercials.

## Disadvantages of Product Placement

(a) Items such as guns, alcohol or cigarettes, even if not specifically brand-named, can influence social acceptance of such products.

(b) It is possible that people could form negative associations with the product if it is shown in a certain social context or being used by an unlikeable character.

(c) Too many brands competing for space in popular films, shows etc. might create a type of visual 'clutter' which dilutes the effect of the product's impact on the viewer. Take for example the children's film *ET*. In this film, the main character, the alien called ET, ate a certain type of sweet called Reese's Pieces, which had the effect of driving up the sales of that brand of sweets. If he had eaten a variety of different sweets, the impact would have been lost.

(d) Product placement can work strongly on children who see other children visiting fast-food chains, theme parks like Disneyworld or playing with certain types or brands of toys. This can create the same 'pester power' as generated by more traditional advertisements.

## Control of Product Placement

Because of its potential to reach millions of people through cinema, television, internet, gaming and books, product placement needs to be controlled.

Recent EU regulations require that product placement is properly flagged to audiences.

**Under recent broadcasting rules**

(a) Programmes must notify the audience at the start that such product placement will occur.

(b) A 'PP' logo must flash on the screen after commercial breaks.

(c) The product placement deal must be acknowledged in the film or programme credits at the end.

## Advantages of all advertising

❀ **Creates employment:** Jobs are provided in all forms of advertising media.

❀ **Creates competition which can benefit consumers:** More variety of products and services and lower costs are better for consumers.

❀ **Finances most forms of mass media:** Most forms of media (e.g. newspapers, magazines, websites, TV programmes) could not survive without the revenue they receive from advertisements.

❀ **Must meet legal standards and cannot lie:** However, they may use persuasive techniques to encourage the consumer to buy their product/service.

❀ **Can be a creative area of the media:** Many ads are clever, colourful and can be dramatic/funny.

❀ **Can encourage healthy habits,** e.g. fresh organic food products etc.

❀ **Can help with sponsorship** for sporting and charitable causes.

## Disadvantages of all advertising

❀ **Can take advantage of gullible people:** It aims to manipulate the consumer, often in devious ways. It can make people long for unnecessary products.

❀ **Can make people feel inadequate:** Many ads play on people's insecurities and encourage them to live beyond their means.

❀ **Can encourage a materialistic attitude to life:** It can suggest that people do not belong, lack adequate cleanliness or beauty, are unfashionable etc. unless they buy the product being sold.

❀ **Can cater to a desire to indulge oneself:** 'You know you're worth it!'

❀ **Advertisements aimed at children can create 'pester power':** This is particularly evident at Christmas when advertisers invest enormous amounts of money to attract children to their products. Parents may feel pressured into giving their children toys which 'everyone else is getting'.

❀ **Advertisements often try to sell lifestyles:** They can suggest that if you buy a certain product or service, your life will be happier, healthier or the envy of others.

❀ **Advertising can create waste:** Ads often suggest that the newest, most convenient or most popular version of something is far better than the original, e.g. the constant release of new types of smart phones, computers, software etc.

❀ **Advertisements are often for alcohol and junk food:** These can have negative effects on the health of consumers.

❀ **Although they cannot openly lie**, ads can mislead by suggestion and persuasion.

# Advertising: Advantages

| Print | Radio | Television | Internet |
|---|---|---|---|
|  |  |  |  |

## Print

1. Advertising generates essential **income** for newspapers and magazines.

2. Ads are often very **creative** and amusing as they need to make a strong visual impact on the reader.

3. As they are printed, ads are capable of being **reproduced** many times and can be distributed as leaflets, brochures, flyers etc.
Ads which appeal to particular interest groups can be inserted in supplements and hobby magazines.

4. As print media can be placed on coffee tables in waiting rooms or in other places where people gather, ads can be given **extra exposure**.

## Radio

1. Advertising generates essential **income** for radio stations.

2. Radio advertising has the advantage of being very **mobile**. People listen to radio ads on their way to work or school, in waiting rooms, in shopping centres, while gardening or doing housework.

3. Radio ads can be **repeated** and organised to appeal to **different target audiences** at different times of the day and night.

4. Advertising on radio requires **creativity** in the use of **sound** effects and tones of voices, volume, pitch etc. as the ads depend totally on what the listener hears.

## Television

1. Advertising generates essential **income** for television stations.

2. TV advertising can be **extremely creative**. Advertisers can create stories to sell their products, incorporate characters and exploit the capacity for dynamic movement.

3. TV ads can be repeated and organised to appeal to **different target audiences** at different times of the day and night. Ads can be carefully scheduled to fit in with certain types of programmes, e.g. ads aimed at children can be shown during commercial breaks in cartoons.

4. TV advertising appeals to **sight** and **sound**, which creates a powerful impact on the viewer. Advertisers can use text, images, sound and motion.

## Internet

1. Advertising generates **income** for websites.

2. Ads can be **sent directly** to consumers through emails. Additional products can be offered based on people's buying history, e.g. phrases like 'People who bought X also bought Y' or 'You may like…' encourage buyers to purchase more than originally intended.

3. Different types of websites can attract **specific** types of advertising, e.g. a website devoted to history can advertise books, films, tours, posters, maps, replicas and other products associated with history. Other special interest sites can also be specifically targeted, especially social networking sites.

| Print | Radio | Television | Internet |
|---|---|---|---|
|  |  |  | 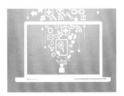 |

| Print | Radio | Television | Internet |
|---|---|---|---|
| 5. People can browse printed ads at their **leisure** which increases the likelihood that they will concentrate more on details. | 5. Listeners are **less likely to switch** channels during radio ads, as they are usually very short. | 5. **Most households** have a television which ensures an audience for ads. | 4. A major advantage of internet advertising is that it can reach a **global audience**. Online retailers like Amazon and eBay can ship products all over the world. |
| 6. Posters can catch the eye of people passing by them and can make an **immediate impact**. | 6. Slogans and jingles which are sung and repeated can **stick in the memory**. | 6. Television can combine the immediate impact of posters with the memorable use of slogans and jingles, thus **combining** the advantages of print and radio ads. | 5. Due to the rapid expansion of computer use and its value as a teaching and research tool, many universities, schools and libraries have made computers available. Target **audiences** are thus **increased**. |
| 7. Posters can be a **cheap** way to advertise sporting events, charity fund-raisers, music festivals etc. | 7. Radio advertising can **target a market** relatively cheaply and can promote national and local charities. | 7. Although more expensive to produce, TV ads reach **huge audiences** and have been proven to boost sales. | 6. Advertising on the internet allows for all the advantages of **print** and **broadcast** media, along with the added advantage of **interactive features**, pop-ups, banners etc. |
| | | | 7. Internet ads can be quickly and cheaply **updated**, which gives an advantage over other forms of media. |

# Advertising: Disadvantages

|  |  |  |  |
|:---:|:---:|:---:|:---:|
| **Print** | **Radio** | **Television** | **Internet** |

## Print

1. The shelf **life** of printed media is very **limited**. Newspapers, for example, arc usually thrown out after one day.

2. Print media does **not** always provide **a wide reach**. Not everybody reads a newspaper and many readers just skim over ads or completely ignore them as they are more interested in the other features of the paper.

3. Planning of ads can take many weeks or **months**. Tight printing deadlines do not offer a lot of flexibility.

4. Ads can get **lost** in the rest of the written texts and have to compete with other ads on the same page.

## Radio

1. Radio ads, although they can be repeated many times, are a **fleeting form** of media. They can be missed completely by listeners who are interrupted during driving, doing chores etc. Details have to be remembered as there is no pause or rewind facility and people seldom listen to podcasts just to hear ads.

2. Radio advertising has a **limited reach**. People change channels regularly while listening to radio and can mute the ads or pay little attention to them.

3. Planning of ads can **take time** and are not easily updated.

4. Some people find radio ads very **irritating** as sound effects, voice tones, pitches and accents can be over-done.

## Television

1. Like radio, TV ads are **fleeting** in nature and have to be repeated many times to ensure maximum impact.

2. Although TV ads have a wider reach than print or radio ads, there are many channels for consumers to choose to watch, especially on cable channel networks, so exposure can be **diluted** somewhat.

3. TV ads are very **expensive** to produce and cannot be updated or changed without incurring substantial expense.

4. TV ads can cause **annoyance** for viewers as they interrupt programmes. Muting of sound or channel-hopping helps avoid them. Recorded and saved programmes help consumers to avoid ads completely as they can fast forward through the commercial breaks.

## Internet

1. Internet ads can be viewed multiple times and are not as fleeting in nature as radio or television ads. However, **quality** can be poor and not the work of professional advertisers in some cases. Advertisement **clutter** is common, with many sites being crowded with ads, reducing effect.

2. **Not everybody** browsing the web for serious research or information purposes is going to take notice of ads, no matter how prominently they are displayed.

3. Internet ads can show special offers for very limited periods and **pressurise consumers** to make an impulse purchase.

**Print**

**Radio**

**Television**

**Internet**

### Print

5. Print media advertising is completely dependent on text and illustration. It **cannot capture** the imagination through use of sound, audio and motion.

6. Print ads use paper which is made from trees, so it is **not** very **environmentally** friendly.

7. A lot of **waste clutter** can arise from print media. This can be recycled, but has to be collected and sorted.

8. Magazines and books can take up a lot of **space** for storage.

### Radio

5. Slogans and jingles can sometimes contribute to **irritation** through over-use.

6. Radio advertising depends totally on **audio**. Scripts have to be very well written and delivered in order to capture the attention of listeners without the use of visuals.

7. As radio ads have to be **repeated** in order to have maximum impact, this increases **costs**. Often they need to be aired on different channels, which is another cost factor.

8. **Interruption** of radio signals can interfere with the quality and effectiveness of an ad. Some ads could be missed entirely at times.

9. For maximum effect, ads need to be aired at **costly time slots**, e.g. rush hour traffic in the morning and evening; spots just before news.

### Television

5. TV ads have many advantages over print and radio advertising as they have visuals and motion. However, this **increases the cost** of making ads for TV.

6. TV ads are **not as permanent** as printed ads and, like radio, are fleeting in nature. This requires **constant repetition** which is costly.

7. Children can be more easily manipulated by television advertising. 'Pester power' arises as children see toys in use or watch families having meals in fast food chains etc.

8. As with radio, there is fierce competition for the prime advertising spots. This drives up the **cost** of already expensive ads.

### Internet

4. Internet ads may repeatedly pop up along with banners flashing on the screens. Animated characters can interfere with browsing. Many users simply **click off** ads without even bothering to read them.

5. Advertisers can gain access to users' email addresses if they have previously made purchases on the web. Users may then receive **unwanted junk mail**.

6. As **children** become more skilled at using computers, they can become exposed to very **aggressive advertising** for toys, clothes, computing games, apps and music etc.

7. Competing websites can push up the **costs** of placing ads online. For example, it is now quite expensive to buy space for an ad on a social networking site.

## (e) Cartoons and Comic Strips

A **cartoon** is a drawing which is intended to create humour by simplifying or exaggerating. A cartoonist is an artist who creates or draws cartoons.

A **comic strip** is a narrative sequence of funny drawings in a comic, newspaper or magazine, usually with captions, speech or thought bubbles.

The study of cartoons is an important area of media studies because cartoons make their point very quickly and are viewed by millions of people all over the world. This gives them powerful influence when dealing with political or social matters. Cartoons or comics which are created simply to amuse or entertain the reader can also have powerful effects, especially on children.

### Types of cartoons

**1. Humorous:** These cartoons are meant to simply entertain the reader by making a joke.

This cartoon pokes fun at the way the Olympic Games coverage can control domestic life. While it highlights the obsession with the games, the aim is to amuse and entertain the reader.

**2. Satirical:** These cartoons deal with social and political issues and are capable of making a personal comment on them. They are often critical and sarcastic or cynical in style. Exaggeration is a key element of such cartoons.

Here, the International Monetary Fund, which is based in Washington, is shown in a cynical way. Instead of supposedly offering help and assistance to a country in financial difficulty, it is portrayed as a terrifying creature which aims to inflict austerity by insisting on increased taxes, cuts in spending and the surrender of savings.

The humour is created by the **parody** of the stereotypical Easter bunny who traditionally brings chocolate and treats. The pun on 'Easter' which is changed to 'Austere' adds to the humour, as does the reference to 'eggs'.

The exaggerated expressions on the faces of the vulnerable, frightened family, trying to conceal their savings is contrasted with the grim, threatening expression of the 'Austere Bunny' who is bounding along, wielding a knife.

The clothing of the 'bunny' represents the stars and stripes of the US (where the IMF is based), while the patch on the trousers of the man depicts his national identity.

The speech bubble with the words 'Happy Austere' emphasises the satire. Although the cartoon is funny and clever, it makes a serious point and expresses a point of view about austerity measures.

**3. Caricatures:** Some cartoons show caricatures of a well-known person or a political figure. A caricature means that some feature or quality of a person which identifies them or reveals their character or personality has been exaggerated. Often, caricature is used for satirical purposes.

In this cartoon, we see how the cartoonist has exaggerated the physical features of Barack Obama and Mitt Romney, so that they are both instantly recognisable. The long face and big

ears of Obama are pronounced, as are the jutting chin and thick eye-brows of Romney. Obama looks as though he is under pressure due to his closed eyes and furrowed brow, while Romney has a broad, confident but artificial smile.

Both are dressed in almost identical suits and stand at identical podiums. The background is deliberately plain. All these similarities serve to emphasise the canister of oxygen beside Obama.

The cartoon clearly caricatures both politicians, but places the emphasis on Obama's apparently poor, lifeless performance in a past presidential debate. It suggests that he needs some assistance if he is to remain alert and capable of thinking clearly. The important effects of physical features, clothing and accessories are evident in this cartoon.

### Comic Strips

Comic strips usually tell their stories in three or four panels.

**Opening panel:** Sets the scene

**Centre panel/s:** Develops the plot

**Final panel:** Creates a response or punchline.

### Comic Strip (a)

## Comic Strip (b)

## Cartoon Lingo

- ◘ **Frame/Panel:** Both of these words refer to the box that contains the illustration. Each of the frames or panels advances the storyline and builds up to the punchline. In comic strips (a), and (b), the frames are rectangular or square and drawn with straight lines. However, the cartoonist often uses wavy, jagged or blurry lines to suggest time changes or changes in the development of the action. At times, these varied lines are only used to create visual variety, but always examine them to see if there might be a good reason for their changed appearance.

- ◘ **Action marks:** Movement or action in cartoons is created by the use of simple marks. Different cartoonists use different marks, but they are always fairly obvious as regards meaning. For example, in comic strip (a), the cartoonist has used a creative technique to show how the rabbit is shadow-boxing and turning from side to side. An arrow indicates this movement and so does the changed position of the gloves. Little notes indicate that he is singing a tune as he boxes. Also notice the rays of light spreading out from behind the bear to show that he believes he has received some special insight.

- ◘ **Characters:** All cartoons use characterisation. Characters can be suggested through the use of facial expressions, physical features, posture, gestures, clothing, actions and the reactions of other characters. Emotions are always depicted in an exaggerated fashion. In comic strip (a) the aggression of the rabbit is shown in his facial features in Frame 1. The change to a surprised expression is caught in the second frame, where he seems amazed that a war could be won without fighting at all. Frame 3 changes the expression to one of confusion, as he wonders what one can do without aggression. The last frame shows his disbelief that watching jokes on a phone could be seen as a substitute for self-defence. The bear, on the other hand, seems more placid and content. His attitude is one of laziness, as he finds a good excuse not to have to exert himself. He uses the words of an ancient Chinese philosopher, Sun Tzu, who taught that fighting is unnecessary but really he is simply dodging having to fight with the rabbit. He prefers to google LOL Cats, as it suits his lazy attitude to exercise. The zagged speech bubble 'Me can has cheezburger?' is associated with the silly content he is watching, even though he is spouting grand philosophical statements. His last comment contains the punchline. He now considers himself superior to the aggressive, energetic rabbit. In an amusing, subtle way, the cartoonist is showing how people can twist anything to suit their own agenda. None of these characters is complex and only essential details are drawn by the cartoonist.

In comic strip (b) the man is the stereotype of a frustrated father forced to read the same bedtime story every night to his son. Notice how his attempt to convince his son to read a different book is shown in Frame 2. He has his arm extended in a gesture of appeal to Calvin. His dress, body language and speech reveal his character in a simple way. The child is also the stereotype of a stubborn kid who screams and yells to get his own way; this is seen by his wide open mouth as he yells. The expressions of confusion and perplexity on both Calvin and Hobbes's faces in Frame 4 suggest that Calvin somehow failed to get his own way but has not yet figured this out. None of these characters is complex and only essential details are drawn by the cartoonist.

◻ **Background:** Cartoons and comics tend to use plain backgrounds, only sketching essential details in order to create a clear setting. The cartoons and comic strips on pages 164 and 165 show this clearly. Too much background detail causes confusion and takes the focus off the main subject. Light or dark backgrounds can help with setting the time or mood. Notice how in the Calvin and Hobbes cartoon the dark background in Frame 4 suggests night. Sometimes, no background at all is necessary.

◻ **Speech and thought bubbles:** Not all cartoons need speech to make their points, but when speech or thought is required certain techniques are used. Text in speech and thought bubbles is always kept to a minimum to avoid boredom and save space. Speech bubbles have a pointed tail, which indicates the speaker, whereas thought bubbles have a wavy outline and a trail of bubbles leading to the person having the thought.

Speech Bubbles

Thought Bubble

The bubbles are the means by which a character can become real and reveal their personality or inner selves. The bubbles should be placed in such a way that nothing is obscured, the speakers are clearly indicated and characters are revealed.

## Positive aspects of cartoons and comic strips

✳ Cartoons can be used for educational purposes. Children often understand and grasp concepts better if a familiar cartoon character is explaining something. Watching television cartoons can help children to absorb information quickly. Many entertaining and educational programmes for children use cartoon and comic techniques.

✳ Cartoons and comic strips are entertaining and can lighten the depressing effect of some social and political issues for adults by injecting them with humour.

✳ Because of their witty and instant quality, cartoons are memorable and can, therefore, **exert** an influence on public opinion. Political and social issues can be highlighted in cartoons in a simple, accessible way.

✳ Cartoons and comic strips can contribute to the sale of newspapers. This generates employment for cartoonists.

**Negative aspects of cartoons**

✪ While cartoons can amuse and entertain, they can also be unfair and hurtful in the way they distort or exaggerate personalities or issues.

✪ Caricatures can be insulting and personally humiliating as they ridicule individuals and can often present a biased attitude to the public.

✪ Children can be negatively affected by cartoons and comic strips which confuse reality for fantasy. In many cartoons, characters fall over, get knocked down etc but these accidents rarely hurt them – unlike in real life.

✪ Cartoons and comic strips can present violence as being acceptable and funny.

✪ Satirical cartoons tend to over-simplify social or political issues which can then influence a reader's perception of those issues.

✪ Stereotypes can be reinforced in cartoons. Stereotyping refers to forming a quick, superficial image of a group of people which is usually based on false or incomplete information. Different races, religions, genders etc. can be stereotyped. Stereotyping implies a value judgement about a person or group. Because it can give a limited or over-simplistic view of people, it is usually not a good way to describe someone.

## OVER TO YOU

### Questions

**1.** Explain the joke which is made in the cartoon.

**2.** Find three ways in which this cartoon is different from the others already discussed in this section.

**3.** You have been asked to create thought or speech bubbles for the man, the monster fish and the worm (bait). Write the text of your speech/thought bubble. Show clearly which bubble belongs to each character.

# Glossary

**alliteration:** repeating the same sound in a series of words, e.g. sneaky snakes.

**anecdotes:** short stories used to illustrate a point

**annotated:** to have made notes while reading a text, e.g. writing notes in the margin of a book, underlining key words

**assonance:** repeating the same vowel sound in a series of words e.g. the long, broad tunnel

**biased:** took sides, prejudiced

**connotations:** the implication of a word other than its main meaning

**conveys:** makes known

**exert:** make an effort; to force

**extensively:** covering or taking over a large area/amount; widely

**font:** typeface; a set of letters in a particular size and style

**gullible:** naive; easily convinced to believe something

**instantaneous:** immediate

**metaphors:** images which compare two things without using 'like' or 'as'

**parody:** a humorous imitation of a person, event, piece of writing etc.

**persuasive:** convincing, forceful

**prejudice:** bias, taking sides

**puns:** word play, when a word or phrase could have more than one meaning

**rhetorical questions:** asking questions simply for effect, no answer expected

**similes:** images which compare two things using 'like' or 'as'

**topical:** a current subject of interest

# Paper Two

This paper is worth **180 marks**.
There are **three sections** in Paper Two:

**Section One:** **Drama (60 marks)**

**Section Two:** **Poetry (60 marks)**

**Section Three:** **Fiction (60 marks)**

Paper Two is worth **180 marks**. Each section is worth 60 marks.
You will have 2 hours and 30 minutes to complete Paper Two.
You should spend approximately 45 minutes on each section.
This allows you some time to check your work at the end.

**Section One: Drama**
**In the exam:**
Question One: Unseen Drama (30 marks)
Choice of 2 unseen extracts: Shakespeare OR Other

Question Two: Studied Drama (30 marks)
Choice of 2 questions

**Section Two: Poetry**
**In the exam:** Question One: Unseen Poem (30 marks)
Question Two: Studied Poem (30 marks)

**Section Three: Fiction**
**In the exam:** Question One: Unseen Extract (30 marks)
Question Two: Studied Novel/Short
Story (30 marks)

# 5. Drama

## Contents

## Exam Key Skills: *Drama*

### Understanding and responding to:

1. Setting
2. Characterisation
3. Plot
4. Mood/Atmosphere
5. Stage directions
6. Stagecraft

# SECTION 1: DRAMA

It is recommended that you spend approximately **45** minutes on this section. It is worth **60 marks**: 30 for Question One (Unseen Drama) and 30 for Question Two (Studied Drama). You must answer a question on Unseen Drama **and** a question on Studied Drama.

In Question One, you will choose between (a) a question on an extract from a play by Shakespeare OR (b) an extract from a play by someone else. It is likely that you will never have seen either of these extracts before. Each question is usually divided into three parts. This is the Unseen Drama Question.

In Question Two, you will choose between two questions on a play which you have studied. Each question is usually divided into two parts. This is the Studied Drama question.

## (a) Unseen Drama: Question One

Always remember that plays are written to be performed on stage. When you are responding to questions on drama, imagine that you are a member of the audience. Do not write about a scene from a play in the same way that you would write about an extract from fiction. Show awareness of the fact that it is written to be performed on stage before an audience.

### KEY SKILLS

#### 1. Setting

Ask yourself if the setting (i.e. the time and location) of the play is important and be able to comment on its importance.

The setting of a scene is not always of great importance. However, if the introduction provides details about the setting, you must look for a reason for this. The setting can create a certain atmosphere or give an indication of the time, place, period in history or any other information that may influence how you interpret events and characters. For example, a daughter arguing with her father in a modern setting creates a very different situation to a daughter arguing with her father during earlier centuries, when daughters obeyed their fathers without question. Likewise, the theft of a small item that takes place against a background of wealth and luxury may be interpreted differently from a similar theft in a setting which depicts poverty.

If the setting influences the plot, the characters, the atmosphere or any other aspect of the play or extract, you must be able to discuss it and demonstrate its importance.

#### 2. Characterisation

If you are asked to discuss characters in a scene you should ask yourself:

(a) What are they doing?

(b) What are they saying?

(c) How are they speaking? (language used and tone of voice)

(d) How do they relate to other characters?

(e) How do they change or develop in the extract?

(f) What motivates their actions and words?

**171**

(g) Do you like or dislike a character? Why/Why not?

(h) What impression do you form of a character and why?

When you are writing about characters, do not tell the story of the extract or summarise what a character says or does. You must try to answer each of the questions listed in (a) to (h) above and make points which you can support from the text. Your task is to show that you can interpret and form opinions about the characters, their motives and their relationships.

### 3. Plot

Many students fall into the trap each year of providing a summary of the extract. It is extremely unlikely to be required in your answer. If you find yourself writing a summary, stop and carefully read the question again. Are you really being asked to summarise? You should pay careful attention to each of the following questions:

(a) Is there any conflict, suspense or tension in this scene? Where? Why?

(b) Is the conflict meant to be serious or comic in its effect on the audience?

(c) Does tension build up? How does it build up?

(d) Does tension reach a climax? Where?

(e) Does the tension relax in the scene? Where and how does it relax?

(f) Does anything happen which has an impact on the plot?

(g) What might happen next?

(h) Is there any underlying message or theme in the extract?

### 4. Mood or Atmosphere

The mood or atmosphere in a scene creates a big impact on the audience. Ask yourself questions about the mood.

(a) What is the mood at the beginning of the extract?

(b) How is this mood created?

(c) Does the mood change in the course of the extract?

(d) How does it change?

(e) Why does it change?

(f) Is the audience aware of something that the characters are not aware of?

### 5. Stage directions

Stage directions are comments which are not part of the dialogue in the play.
They reveal the intention of the dramatist or playwright so the audience knows more about the setting of the scene, the mood of the characters etc. When a playwright includes stage directions, they are usually important for interpretation. Shakespearean extracts do not have many stage directions.

The stage directions in some plays can be quite detailed and can give us an idea of how the playwright wants certain moments to look, sound and feel on stage. Examine carefully any stage directions included in the extract and ask yourself what they contribute to the scene.

(a) Do they help to advance the plot in some way? Look carefully at exits and entrances.

(b) Do they give us an insight into the personality or mood of a character? Look particularly at gestures and facial expressions.

(c)  Do they add to the atmosphere in any way?

(d)  Do they tell a part of the story, like a mime? (i.e. no words are spoken; the audience relies on an actor's movements or facial expressions to work out what is happening. For example, *John enters, tiptoes to the window, opens it and climbs out*.)

(e)  Do they help us to work out the relationships between characters?

## 6. Stagecraft

Stagecraft is not the same thing as setting or stage directions, although these may contribute. When you write about staging or stagecraft, you are writing about the play as it is performed on stage. The questions listed below are important ones to consider if you are answering a question on how you would produce a scene on stage. Comment on such things as:

(a)  **Props:** Do they help to move the action forward or reveal character or themes? Are they essential to understanding some part of the plot? Why has the director or playwright included them?

(b)  **Costume:** Is it used to show a particular period or time? Does it help show the social status of the characters? Is there anything unusual about the clothing worn by a character which may reveal their personality? Does it show their profession or trade?

(c)  **Lighting:** Is it used to create mood or a sense of time, such as day or night or if the scene takes place indoors or outdoors? Are spotlights used? Where? Why?

(d)  **Sound effects:** What sound effects are used and why? For example, how could you create a storm with sound effects or the sense of a battle raging in the background?

(e)  **Set:** Has any backdrop been created to suggest a setting? This could be like a painting in the background which would suggest the setting. How does this affect the visual impact on the audience? Is it a help or a distraction?

## Step-by-Step Approach
### How to Answer Questions on Unseen Drama

### Step One: Choose your Question

✿ Read the questions very carefully before you begin to read the extract. This will give you an indication of what you should be paying close attention to and will give your reading a sharp focus. You can only use information given in the extract in your answer. Even if you happen to have read the whole play before, you cannot use this knowledge in your answer.

✿ If given a choice to answer two out of the three questions asked on your chosen extract, decide which two you are going to answer.

✿ Underline/highlight the key word or words in the question. Your answer must be completely relevant to the question, so make sure that you understand the question. Do not leave out any part of the question if it has more than one part.

✿ At the beginning of Question One you will be given a short introduction to the extract which you should read very carefully. This introduction will help you to understand the background to the scene and it may also give you important information about the characters and their relationships. Underline/highlight any information which might be connected to the questions asked.

### Step Two: Planning and Writing your Answer

♦ Re-read the first question you have chosen to answer. Check the wording. Read carefully, bearing the exact question in mind. Tick, underline or highlight anything in the introduction and extract which is relevant to the question asked.

♦ Write your answer. Use the wording of the question when introducing your response. Write one paragraph for each point you wish to make. You can use the following approach:

> **State point:** Do this clearly and simply.
> Support your point with relevant **quotations** from the extract.
> **Explain** your point clearly.

This type of response is known as PQE: **P**oint - **Q**uotation - **E**xplanation. The quotations and explanations can be blended together. Depending on the question, three or four points are usually sufficient for a good answer. Length is not as important as quality, but you should attempt to develop your response adequately, without repeating points or summarising the extract.

### Step Three: Move on

∗ Re-read the second question you have chosen to answer. Check the wording.
∗ Repeat the same PQE procedure.

## Putting It Into Practice

Read this extract from a recent Junior Cert exam paper. This is Question One (A) **A Shakespearean Drama.**

The following extract (in edited form) is adapted from the opening scene of Shakespeare's play, *The Tempest*. Read the extract carefully and then answer the questions which follow.

*Introduction*

This scene is set on a ship at sea. A terrible storm is raging and a tempestuous noise of thunder and lightning is heard. The ship's master (the Captain) and the boatswain (the officer in charge of the ship's sails and rigging) are struggling in difficult circumstances to keep the ship afloat and to save the important passengers and the mariners (sailors) from drowning.

| Master: | Boatswain! |
|---|---|
| Boatswain: | Here, master. What cheer? |
| Master: | Good, speak to the mariners! |
| | Fall to't briskly, or we run ourselves aground. Bestir, bestir! [*Exit*] |
| | *Enter Mariners* |
| Boatswain: | Heigh, my hearts! Cheerly, cheerly, my hearts. Briskly, briskly! |
| | Take in the topsail! Tend to the master's orders! |
| | (*addressing the storm*) Blow till thou burst thy wind! |
| | *Enter passengers, Alonso (King of Naples), his brother Sebastian,* |
| | *a noble named Antonio, Gonzalo – an honest old counsellor, and others.* |
| Alonso: | Good boatswain, have care. Where's the master? |
| Boatswain: | I pray now keep below. |
| Antonio: | Where is the master, boatswain? |
| Boatswain: | Do you not hear him? You mar our labour. Keep to your cabins; |
| | You do assist the storm. |
| Gonzalo: | Nay, good fellow, be patient. |
| Boatswain: | When the sea is. Hence! What care these roarers*          (*stormy waves*) |
| | for the name of the King? To cabin! Silence! Trouble us not! |
| Gonzalo: | Good man, yet remember whom thou hast aboard. |
| Boatswain: | None that I love more than myself. You are a counsellor, if you can |
| | command these elements to silence and restore the present to peace, |
| | we will not handle a rope more. Use your authority. If you cannot, |
| | give thanks you have lived so long, and make yourself ready in your |
| | cabin for the mischance of the hour, if it so happen. |
| | Cheerly, good hearts! Out of our way, I say. |
| Gonzalo: | I have great comfort from this fellow: methinks he hath no |
| | drowning-mark upon him; his complexion is perfect gallows. If he be not |
| | born to be hanged, our case is miserable. [*Exit Gonzalo and nobles*] |
| Boatswain: | Down with the topmast! Briskly! Lower! Lower! |
| | Bring her to try with main-sail! (*A cry within*) |
| | A plague upon this howling! These passengers are louder than the weather. |
| | *Re-enter Sebastian, Antonio and Gonzalo* |
| Boatswain: | Yet again? What do you here? Shall we give o'er and drown? |
| | Have you a mind to sink? |
| Sebastian: | A pox on your throat, you bawling, blasphemous, incharitable dog. |
| Boatswain: | Work you then. |
| Antonio: | Hang cur! Hang, you insolent noisemaker! |
| | We are less afraid to drown than thou art. |
| Boatswain: | Lay her a-hold, a-hold! Set her two courses off to sea again! Lay her off! |
| | *Enter Mariners wet* |
| Mariners: | All lost! To prayers, to prayers! All lost! |
| Gonzalo: | Now would I give a thousand furlongs of sea for an acre of barren ground, |
| | long heath, broom, furze, anything. The wills above be done! But I would |
| | fain die a dry death. |

### Step One: Choose Your Question

◉ Read all three questions below carefully. You must answer **two** of these questions. Each question is worth 15 marks. Underline/highlight key words in each question. This has already been done for you in the questions below.

---

1.

What **impression of the boatswain** do you form from your reading of this extract? **Support your answer** with reference to the text.                              **(15 marks)**

2.

There are many elements that help to make the passage [on page 175] a powerful piece of drama. **Identify the elements in the passage** that, in your opinion, **contribute to the dramatic power** of the piece. **Explain** your answer.                              **(15 marks)**

3.

Staging a storm scene would prove challenging for any director. **Describe how you** think the above extract could be successfully staged.  In your answer you may wish to consider some of the following: lighting, special effects, sound, set design, props etc. **(15 marks)**

---

◉ Read the information given in the introduction: Here we are told where the scene is set, who the characters are, what they are doing and why they are doing it. This is essential information for answering each question.

◉ Decide which two questions you are going to answer. In the sample answer provided below, Questions 1 and 2 are answered.

### Step Two: Planning and Writing your Answer

Sample Answer to Question 1 using PQE approach

*I get the impression that the boatswain is an experienced and skilful sailor. He is courageous and refuses to be intimidated by either the storm or the importance of his royal passengers.* **[Points stated in opening]**

*His experience and skill are apparent in the way he calmly deals with the situation.* **[Point]** *He does not panic but gives orders firmly, 'Briskly, briskly! Take in the topsail!' He orders the mariners to lower the topmast, emphasising the importance of speed.  Although he is insulted by Antonio, who calls him a 'cur' and a 'noise-maker', he keeps his mind on the task of steadying the ship and maintains control in a confident way.* **[Quotations and support from text to explain point]**

*The impression is clearly given of a man who is courageous and outspoken.* **[Point stated]** *When most of the passengers and even the other mariners are panicking, the boatswain shows very little fear. He confronts the storm by telling it to 'Blow till thou burst thy wind!'  He will not allow the passengers, regardless of their importance, to 'assist the storm' by coming on deck and orders them to return to their cabins: 'To cabin! Silence! Trouble us not!'  He reminds the nobles that the 'roarers' have no respect for titles or 'the name of the King'.* **[Quotations and explanation of point]**

*Although the other characters seem to have little faith in the boatswain, I get the clear impression that he is a capable individual who takes his duties seriously and who will 'command' the elements and 'restore ... peace'.* **[Conclusion addresses question and offers further quotation as support]**

## Step Three: Move on to next question

Sample Answer to Question 2 using PQE approach:

*This passage has several elements which contribute to its dramatic power and intensity. These elements relate to the setting, the interaction of the characters and the use of dramatic language.*
**[Points stated]**

*The setting is powerfully dramatic in its depiction of a storm at sea, which threatens to sink the ship.* **[Point]** *The abrupt opening dialogue between the Master and the boatswain reflects urgency. The Master demands that actions are carried out 'briskly', a phrase which is repeated by the boatswain, 'Briskly, briskly!... Tend to the master's orders'. This urgency creates suspense from the outset. The dramatic tension is also increased by the terror of the passengers and the other mariners who believe they are doomed, 'All lost! To prayers, to prayers! All lost!'* **[Quote and explanation]**

*The interactions between the boatswain and the passengers create further conflict, mirroring the storm at sea.* **[Point]** *The boatswain refuses to be swayed by the passengers who are obstructing his work by refusing to stay below deck. He engages in an argument with Gonzalo, Sebastian and Antonio. These confrontations add to the drama of the situation and increase the sense that the ship will not withstand the storm. The boatswain urges Gonzalo to use his 'authority' or else 'make yourself ready in your cabin for the mischance of the hour'. He is enraged that the nobles 'mar our labour'. This conflict increases the suspense in a powerful way.* **[Quote and explanation]**

*The strong use of language also adds to the drama.* **[Point]** *Exclamations, questions and orders are used frequently. The boatswain tells the storm to 'Blow till thou burst thy wind!'. Vulgar name-calling and insults abound as the boatswain is called a 'blasphemous, incharitable dog', 'a cur', and an 'insolent noise-maker'. The audience feels the potential for violence to break out, especially when Antonio says that the boatswain should 'hang'.* **[Quote and explanation]**

*The 'cry within', which is cursed by the boatswain who says 'A plague upon this howling', adds to the dramatic atmosphere as we can imagine the noise of the storm competing with the howls of the terrified passengers and crew.* **[Point-Quote-Explanation]**

*Each of the above elements contributes to the dramatic power and intensity of this passage.*
**[Conclusion focuses on question]**

You should practise answering questions based on the PQE method. Make sure that the points you are making are relevant to the exact question asked and try to shape your answer nicely by having a short introduction and conclusion.

**Remember:** In the Unseen Drama section, you can choose **either** the Shakespearean Drama question **or** the Other Drama question. Do not answer **both** the Shakespearean Drama question **and** the Other Drama question.

Now read the extract below and see how the same steps and techniques are being followed for the Other Drama option. This is an example of Question One (B) **Other Drama**.

The following extract (in edited form) is adapted from the play *Alphabetical Order* by Michael Frayn. Read the extract carefully and answer the questions which follow.

# Introduction

Lucy works in the library of a provincial newspaper. It is her job to cut out and file extracts from a variety of newspapers for reference purposes. The other characters in this extract (Wally, John, Nora, Geoffrey and Lesley) are Lucy's colleagues. They also work for the newspaper. In this scene one of the journalists, Wally, has cut his hand and comes to Lucy for assistance.

| | |
|---|---|
| Lucy: | (*lack-lustre*) What do you want now, Wally? |
| | (*He whips away the handkerchief he is holding, and reveals that the hand is injured*) |
| Lucy: | Oh my God! What happened? |
| Wally: | Where do you want me to bleed? Over *The Times* or *The Guardian*? |
| Lucy: | Hold on. I'll get the first aid box. |
| John: | A miracle she hasn't lost the first aid box. |
| Lucy: | But ... the key ... |
| John: | And she's lost the key! |
| Nora: | Oh dear. Lucy. |
| | (*Lucy, Geoffrey, John and Nora all search urgently. Wally waits patiently. Lesley watches them all.*) |
| Lucy: | Everyone was helping themselves. |
| John: | She's locked the first aid box, and she's lost the key! |
| Lucy: | It was my one bit of efficiency. |
| Nora: | Oh dear, this could be rather serious. |
| Wally: | Would you like me to die in here, or shall I go outside? |
| John: | (*to the world at large*) We've got the box. But we can't open it. |
| Nora: | This really is one of our less appealing muddles. |
| Lucy: | Well you look after it! I don't want to do it! |
| Geoffrey: | Now let's all keep calm. |
| Lucy: | I always get landed with these rotten jobs that no one else wants! |
| John: | Hadn't we better discuss the injustice of the world later? |
| Lucy: | Do the collections for farewell presents. Run the Christmas raffle. Sell the tickets for the staff dance. Help with the children's treat. And I haven't got any children! I hate children! |
| Nora: | No, you don't ... |

| | |
|---|---|
| Lucy: | Yes, I do! I hate their parents, too! And I'm sick of being nice! Everyone takes it for granted I'm nice, and I'm not, and I'm fed up of pretending to be! I'm also fed up with the effort of thinking everyone else is nice! I'm worn out from the sheer hard labour of seeing any sense in anything! |
| John: | Sit down. |
| Geoffrey: | Take a deep breath. |
| Lucy: | I sit here all day keeping nothingness stuck together by sheer effort of will. And what happens? I lose the only thing that really matters! Now I have to watch Wally stand there and bleed to death! |
| John: | He's not bleeding to death. |
| Lucy: | I'm sorry, Wally! I'm sorry! I've come over all to pieces! I don't know what I'm doing! *(Lesley comes forward holding the leg of a chair that had broken earlier, and opens the first aid box with a single sharp blow. Silence)* |
| Geoffrey: | Well, that's one way of doing it. |
| Lesley: | Sorry. I thought probably we'd better not wait for the key. Sorry. *(Lucy dresses Wally's hand.)* |

Remember that you usually only have to answer **two** of the three questions in the Unseen Drama part of the Drama section.

**Question 1**
What **impression of Lucy** do you form from reading this extract? **Support** your answer with reference to the extract.

**Question 2**
There are many elements that help to make the above passage an entertaining piece of drama. In your opinion, **what are these elements?**

**Question 3**
You have decided to audition for a part in your school's production of *Alphabetical Order*. Based on your reading of the above extract, which part would you most like to play? **Explain** your answer.

**Note:** A sample answer for each of the three questions is provided here.

Sample Answer to Question 1 using PQE approach

*From reading this extract, I get the impression that Lucy is a bit of a scatterbrain who resents the fact that she is taken for granted by her colleagues. She seems to be completely overwhelmed by her many and varied duties.* **[Points]**

*I can tell that Lucy is disorganised* **[Point]** *because John sarcastically remarks that it is 'A miracle she hasn't lost the first-aid box' and also points out that Lucy has 'lost the key'. Lucy herself acknowledges she*

**179**

*is a bit disorganised and inefficient by admitting that looking after the box was her 'one bit of efficiency'.* **[Quote and explanation]**

   *It is clear from the extract that Lucy resents being taken for granted by others.* **[Point]** *She complains that she always gets 'landed' with the 'rotten jobs that no one else wants'. She becomes self-pitying and sulky when listing all the jobs she undertakes. This makes me wonder why she accepts these responsibilities in the first place. Perhaps she is just trying to be 'nice' and has now become 'sick of being nice'. Her resentment sounds slightly childish when she says 'Well you look after it! I don't want to do it!'* **[Quote and explanation]**

   *There is no doubt that Lucy feels overwhelmed.* **[Point]** *She appears to me to be having an hysterical fit when she uses phrases like 'I'm sick of ...' 'I'm fed up of ...', 'I'm worn out ...' and ends up by telling Wally that she has '... come over all to pieces! I don't know what I'm doing!' Her tendency to be melodramatic is obvious when she thinks she has to 'watch Wally bleed to death'* **[Quote and explanation]**

   *Overall, I get the impression that Lucy has taken on too many responsibilities for such an inefficient, highly-strung person.* **[Conclusion]**

## Over to You

**(a) In the sample answer below, mark where the points, quotes and explanations occur.**
**Sample Answer to Question 2 using PQE approach:**

*There are several elements which help to make this an entertaining piece of drama. In my opinion, comedy is created in the situation, in the dialogue and in the characterisation.*

   *The lost key results in an entertaining reaction from Lucy who blows the situation out of all proportion to its real importance. Wally is certainly not 'bleeding to death' and if he was, they would need much more than a 'first-aid box'! The situation has many elements of slapstick comedy. Wally's dramatic whipping away of the handkerchief to reveal his cut hand and the frantic search for the key are funny. The problem is resolved in typical slapstick fashion when the box is broken open with the leg of the chair. Stage directions helped me to visualise the scene and be amused by it.*

   *Comedy is also created in the use of dialogue. Wally asks Lucy if she wants him to bleed 'over The Times or The Guardian', while John keeps up a running commentary on Lucy's incompetence, 'She's lost the first-aid box and she's lost the key!' The one line spoken by Lesley at the end of the passage is very funny as he apologises for smashing open the box, 'I'm sorry. I thought probably we'd better not wait for the key. Sorry'. I enjoyed the dialogue immensely and was very entertained by it.*

   *All of the characters are entertaining in different ways: Lucy in her hysterical reaction and bubbling resentment, Wally in his dramatic gestures, John in his role as judge of Lucy's efficiency and his biting sarcasm. The other characters, Nora and Geoffrey, are more calm and balanced in their response. Nora keeps saying 'Oh dear', while Geoffrey appeals for calm, 'Now let's all keep calm' and advises Lucy to 'Take a deep breath'. This contrast between the characters serves to highlight the exaggeration of the pretended conflict in the situation. The silent, practical Lesley provides a very comic moment when, after a dramatic pause, he suddenly takes things into his own hands and, with apologies, smashes the box open.*

   *In my opinion, the writer of the above piece creates entertainment by blending characters, situation and dialogue in a very clever and amusing way.*

**(b) In the sample answer below, mark where the points, quotes and explanations occur.**

Sample Answer to Question 3 using PQE approach

*If I could audition for a part in 'Alphabetical Order', the part I would most like to play would be that of Lucy.*

*I find Lucy to be a funny, entertaining character. I would enjoy portraying her changes in attitude and control as she reacts to Wally's injury. She begins by speaking in a 'lack-lustre' way, but her tone quickly changes to concern, confusion about the key, defensiveness until, eventually, she has a full-blown, hysterical fit. The audience would enjoy watching these changes in Lucy, which I would exaggerate as much as possible for maximum comic effect.*

*Lucy is also a complex character which would make her an interesting part to play. She obviously wants people to think that she is 'nice' and allows herself to take on all the 'rotten jobs' until she becomes overwhelmed and resentful. I think there is something sad in the way she arranges the treats for the children although she hasn't got any children herself. I don't believe her when she says 'I hate children!' and 'I hate their parents too!' I think she is just overcome by a sense of frustration and failure. I would try to bring this aspect of the character across to the audience.*

*Her colleagues allow her to 'Do the collections for the farewell presents', and organise the 'Christmas raffle', but she is treated with insensitivity and even contempt by most of them, particularly by John. I would play her as a comic character, but I would enjoy trying to let the audience see the pathetic side of her situation also and would make some of her complaints seem genuine and not just melodramatic.*

*Needless to say, the part of Lucy is the main part in this particular scene and because I am a bit of a show-off, I would want the part with the most dramatic lines and the funniest actions to perform. I think the part of Lucy would suit me perfectly!*

## Advice

As you can see from the sample answers, the length of each response depends on the question. The answers do not have to be the same length.

It is worth bearing in mind that the Chief Examiner of Junior Certificate English has referred to the fact that many students do not develop their answers in sufficient detail. While you do not have to write very long answers, you need to make sure that what you write is relevant, supported and clearly expressed.

Practise as much as you can using past exam papers and you will find that it is not too difficult to write a short introduction, three developed and well-supported points and a short conclusion within the time limit of 15 minutes for each question.

If you find that you cannot write very much in 15 minutes, then just concentrate on ensuring that you have three points clearly expressed in three paragraphs and that you quote from or refer to the text as evidence. You can shorten the amount of support and explanation until you have had more practice in thinking and writing quickly. Plenty of practice and having a clear method to follow will ensure a good grade.

### Over to You (A)

**Question (A): Shakespearean Drama**

The following extract (in edited form) is taken from Act I, Scene II of Shakespeare's play *A Midsummer Night's Dream.* Read the extract carefully and answer the questions which follow it.

## *Introduction*

This scene is set in the house of Quince, a carpenter, who is directing a play which will be performed at the Duke of Athen's forthcoming wedding. All of the characters are uneducated, working men known as 'Mechanicals' who are keen to take part in the play. The scene depicts the first meeting of the cast.

| | |
|---|---|
| Quince: | Is all our company here? |
| Bottom: | You were best to call them generally, man by man, according to the scrip. |
| Quince: | Here is the scroll of every man's name, which is thought fit, through all Athens, to play in our interlude before the duke and the duchess, on his wedding-day at night. |
| Bottom: | First, good Peter Quince, say what the play treats on, then read the names of the actors, and so grow to a point. |
| Quince: | Marry, our play is, The most lamentable comedy, and most cruel death of Pyramus and Thisby. |
| Bottom: | A very good piece of work, I assure you, and a merry. Now, good Peter Quince, call forth your actors by the scroll. Masters, spread yourselves. |
| Quince: | Answer as I call you. Nick Bottom, the weaver? |
| Bottom: | Ready. Name what part I am for, and proceed. |
| Quince: | You, Nick Bottom, are set down for Pyramus. |
| Bottom: | What is Pyramus? a lover, or a tyrant? |
| Quince: | A lover, that kills himself most gallant for love. |
| Bottom: | That will ask some tears in the true performing of it: if I do it, let the audience look to their eyes; I will move storms, I will condole in some measure. |
| Quince: | Francis Flute, the bellows-mender? |
| Flute: | Here, Peter Quince. |
| Quince: | Flute, you must take Thisby on you. |
| Flute: | What is Thisby? a wandering knight? |
| Quince: | It is the lady that Pyramus must love. |

**Flute:** Nay, faith, let me not play a woman; I have a beard coming.

**Quince:** That's all one: you shall play it in a mask, and you may speak as small as you will.

**Bottom:** An I may hide my face, let me play Thisby too, I'll speak in a monstrous little voice: Thisne, Thisne;' - 'Ah, Pyramus, lover dear! thy Thisby dear, and lady dear!'

**Quince:** No, no; you must play Pyramus: and, Flute, you Thisby.

**Bottom:** Well, proceed.

**Quince:** Robin Starveling, the tailor?

**Starveling:** Here, Peter Quince.

**Quince:** Robin Starveling, you must play Thisby's mother. Tom Snout, the tinker.

**Snout:** Here, Peter Quince.

**Quince:** You, Pyramus' father: myself, Thisby's father: Snug, the joiner; you, the lion's part: and, I hope, here is a play fitted.

**Snug:** Have you the lion's part written? pray you, if it be, give it me, for I am slow of study.

**Quince:** You may do it *extempore, for it is nothing but roaring.

**Bottom:** Let me play the lion too: I will roar, that I will do any man's heart good to hear me; I will roar, that I will make the duke say 'Let him roar again, let him roar again.'

**Quince:** An you should do it too terribly, you would fright the duchess and the ladies, that they would shriek; and that were enough to hang us all.

**All:** That would hang us, every mother's son.

**Bottom:** I grant you, friends, if that you should fright the ladies out of their wits, they would have no more discretion but to hang us: but I will aggravate my voice so that I will roar you as gently as any sucking dove; I will roar you an 'twere any nightingale.

**Quince:** You can play no part but Pyramus; for Pyramus is a sweet-faced man; a proper man, as one shall see in a summer's day; a most lovely gentleman-like man: therefore you must needs play Pyramus.

**Bottom:** Well, I will undertake it.

* extempore = improvised or made up.

Answer **two** of the following questions. Each question is worth **15 marks**.

1. What impression of the character of Bottom do you form from your reading of this extract?

2. What evidence can you find in the above piece to show that the Mechanicals (working men) are not familiar with plays and are inexperienced as actors?

3. This scene is going to be staged and you are the Director. How would you direct this scene? You should refer to the following:

   (a) Gestures by the actors

   (b) Costume / dress to be worn by the actors

   (c) How the characters should speak their lines.

## Over To You (B)

**Question (B): Other Drama**

The following extract (slightly shortened) is taken from the play *The Granny Project* by Anne Fine.

**Background to the extract:** Ivan, a teenage boy, has written a project for school which he has named *The Granny Project*. In it, he describes very intimate details of his family life, particularly those concerning his grandmother, who is about to be sent into an old folks' home. His father, Henry, has just found and read *The Granny Project*.

*Henry is standing behind the kitchen table on which the Granny Project lies like a trial exhibit. Ivan is standing in front.*

| | |
|---|---|
| **Henry:** | This thing here. This - Granny Project. Well ...? |
| **Ivan:** | Yes? |
| **Henry:** | I'm asking you! |
| **Ivan:** | Well, I was going to hand it in on Monday. |
| **Henry:** | Is it a joke? |
| **Ivan:** | No. Not a joke. |
| **Henry:** | Who chose this topic? |
| **Ivan:** | It was Sophie's idea at the very start. |
| **Henry:** | I don't see Sophie's name on this. |
| **Ivan:** | Sophie dropped out. |
| **Henry:** | Thought better of it you mean? |
| **Ivan:** | Changed her mind, yes. |
| **Henry:** | And so it's all yours now. And what's it for? |
| **Ivan:** | Well, it's for Social Science homework, in one sense ... |
| **Henry:** | And in another ...? |
| **Ivan:** | I suppose, in another, you could say that it was blackmail. |
| **Henry:** | Blackmail? |
| **Ivan:** | Blackmail. To stop you putting Granny in to that Home. |

Henry: We keep your Granny here, or you hand this in at school.

Ivan: That's right.

Henry: I see. Tell me, this thing, this vicious and disloyal document, this hurtful and insensitive catalogue of eavesdroppings - you don't feel this to be dishonourable?

Ivan: I **feel** it is, yes. But I don't **think** it is. With Sophie, the feelings took over. That's why she dropped out in the end. I reconsidered then. Of course I did. But still I thought that I was right, so I kept going.

Henry: Ivan, it makes me ill to think a son of mine could act like this. That he could think this thing through in such a cold, inhuman fashion. You carry on this way and God knows what a barbarous mess you'll make of your life. You live in this house. You know what a strain it's been looking after my mother. Where's your sympathy, your understanding, your warmth? If you act this way in your own family, where do you think you will end up?

Ivan: Sophie thinks I'll be a revolutionary.

Henry: You're not a grown-up revolutionary yet, you know. And I'm still your father. I could just burn this folder.

Ivan: I'm not playing games, Dad, I have copies.

Henry: Ivan, I'm coming very close to hitting you - **hard**.

Ivan: That isn't going to help.

Henry: I would feel better.

Ivan: Feelings, again.

Henry: Get out! Get out of here! **Get out**!

Answer **two** of the following questions. Each question is worth **15 marks**.

1. What kind of relationship exists between Ivan and his father? Support your answer from the text.

2. You have been asked to write three stage directions into this script. What directions would you insert and where would you insert them? Give reasons for your choices.

3. Ivan says that Sophie, his sister, thinks that he will become a 'revolutionary'. Do you think that Ivan's behaviour justifies Sophie's opinion? Explain your response with reference to the text.

## (b) Studied Drama: Question Two

This question is worth **30 marks** in the Junior Cert exam. It is recommended that you spend approximately **30** minutes on the Studied Drama part of the Drama section. You will get a choice of two questions and you must answer one. Each question may be divided into two parts. Pay attention to the marks allocated to each part of the question as this will guide your length of answer. Read the question carefully as this arrangement may vary.

When you have decided which of the two questions to answer, you must give the name of the play that you studied and the name of the playwright at the very beginning of your answer.

If, by chance, the extract for Unseen Drama is taken from the play you are going to discuss in Studied Drama, then you will have to refer to other scenes and parts of the play in your response in order to show that you have read and studied the entire play. In this case, be very careful to keep your answers for the Unseen Drama section based only on what is in the extract provided and not from your full knowledge of the play.

## KEY SKILLS

The skills required to answer on Studied Drama are exactly the same as those required for Unseen Drama so it is worth revising the Key Skills provided on pages 171-173.

However, you will not have an extract from the drama in front of you and you will be expected to show a thorough knowledge and understanding of the entire play you have chosen.

The **KEY SKILLS** relate to CSEM:

**Content.**    You must answer the question asked and support your answer with relevant quotation.

**Structure.**    You must structure your answer in an intelligent way. Organise your responses into paragraphs. Develop one major point in each paragraph. Use varied sentence structures.

**Expression.**    You should be able to express yourself with clarity and fluency. Varied vocabulary is important, but you should avoid using language that is too 'flowery' or affected. Aim for **precision** and clear communication.

**Mechanics.**    Spelling, punctuation and grammar are important in everything that you write. Always check these areas for total accuracy.

The major differences between answering Studied Drama questions and answering Unseen Drama questions are:

### I. Setting

You will need to be familiar with the general setting of your studied play, e.g. Verona in *Romeo and Juliet*, Venice in *The Merchant of Venice*, a rural area of south-west Ireland in *The Field* etc. You also need to know the time period in which the play is set, e.g. Italy in the sixteenth century, England during the reign of Elizabeth I, Ireland in the early 1960s etc.

In addition to the general setting, you will also need to be aware of where specific scenes are set and when locations change. Remember, you are dealing with the entire play, as opposed to a short extract such as those given in Unseen Drama.

### 2. Characterisation

For Studied Drama, you will be expected to have studied the main characters in considerable depth. Ask yourself the same questions about the characters as you would for Unseen Drama and be very clear on how each character's actions influence the plot and themes of the play.

Be prepared to discuss the characters, showing an awareness of their personalities, strengths, weaknesses, motivations and roles in the plot. Decide what you admire or dislike about each of them. Have quotations prepared to support your points.

You should also be able to explore the conflicts between characters in the play you have studied. Know how and why these conflicts arise, how they develop in the course of the play and how they resolve. Have key scenes prepared in some detail so that you can illustrate major moments of conflict.

Be ready to discuss the way characters are contrasted throughout the play. Be able to show the effect of the contrasts and how they add to our understanding of the play.

Be prepared to discuss the use of language and dialogue in revealing characters.

## 3. Plot

Ensure that you know the full story of the play and the sequence of events.

Be able to show how certain major events create a change in the direction of the plot. For example, by killing Tybalt in revenge for Mercutio's death, Romeo in *Romeo and Juliet* becomes an exile in Mantua, something which contributes to the disastrous ending of that play. Similarly, the trial scene in *The Merchant of Venice* in which Portia manages to get the better of Shylock influences the outcome of the play and allows it to end on a generally positive note.

It can be very helpful to create a timeline of events for the play you have chosen to study. Clearly highlight the turning points or major events and be aware of how each one influences the plot. You should also be able to show your understanding of how the plot opens, develops, reaches a climax and resolves.

## 4. Mood or Atmosphere

Because you will be dealing with an entire play as opposed to a short extract, you will need to be aware of the changing moods in different scenes of your chosen play.

Be prepared to select specific scenes to illustrate how the playwright creates mood or atmosphere. Pinpoint scenes in which the mood changes gradually or abruptly and show how this is achieved. Characterisation, dialogue, actions and consequences of actions will all affect the mood of the play.

For each of the above areas for discussion, ensure that you can quote accurately and/or use close textual reference to support your points.

## 5. Stagecraft

Because plays are different to fiction texts, you must be able to discuss how they can be performed on stage. It is advisable to select at least three key scenes – the opening, climax and closing scenes are particularly important – and be able to write a reasonably detailed analysis of how they could be performed on stage successfully.

As in Unseen Drama, you could refer to such things as props, costume, lighting, sound, backdrops or any other technique which you think would bring the play alive for the audience and create a vivid, realistic impact.

If you are asked to comment on how you would direct the scene, you need to include stage directions, instructions to actors regarding facial expressions, gestures, movements, tone of voice etc. In other words, imagine the scene in your head and describe it in as much detail as you can. Be sure to explain why you would use certain techniques and the impact you would be attempting to achieve.

It is a good idea to prepare a short list of props for each of the three key scenes in the play and also a short list of appropriate lighting, sound effects and costumes. Be ready to explain why you have chosen each item on these lists.

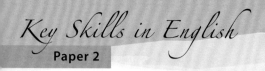
## Step-by-Step Approach
### How to Answer Questions on Studied Drama
### Step One
- Read both questions carefully, underlining/highlighting exactly what you are required to do. Each question is usually divided into two parts: (a) and (b). You must do both of these parts in the question you select.

### Step Two
- Decide which question you are going to do. Check the wording of both parts of this question again.

### Step Three
- Make a short plan for your answer using the brainstorming techniques described on page 174. Keep this plan short and focused on the question. For each point you intend to make, jot down a quotation or a reference which you can use for support.

- It is a good idea to plan both part (a) and part (b) answers together so that you avoid repeating points.

- Before you write your answer, ensure that you are not simply narrating the plot. A good plan will help you to avoid this common pitfall.

### Step Four
- Write your answer, using the **Point-Quotation-Explanation** technique which you used in Unseen Drama.

## Putting it Into Practice
These questions are taken from a recent Junior Cert exam paper.
Read them carefully.

1. (a) **Identify an important character** from a play you have studied and **outline** some of the **obstacles or challenges** faced by him or her in the course of the play. (15)

   (b) **What do you learn about this character** from **the way** in which he or she **deals with one or more** of these obstacles or challenges? Explain your answer. (15)

OR

2. (a) The opening scene or scenes of a play often convey information that is important to the audience. **What important information is conveyed in the opening scene or scenes** of the play that you have studied? (15)

   (b) In your opinion, **how successful** is the playwright in **capturing the attention** of the audience in the **opening scene or scenes** of the play? Support your answer with reference to your studied play.

**Step One:**
As you can see from the highlighted tasks in each question, there is a link between both parts (a) and (b). Make sure that you do not answer part (b) in your response to part (a).

**Step Two:**
- Decide which question you are going to do. The sample answer below is in response to **Question 1.**
- Before you begin writing, check the highlighted phrases and make sure that you know what is being asked.

**Step Three:**
- Jot down a brief plan for both parts of the question. Avoid overlapping or repetition of points.

### SAMPLE PLAN FOR QUESTION 1
### STUDIED PLAY: *ROMEO AND JULIET*

| (a) Identify character | (b) What do we learn? |
| --- | --- |
| Identify character: Juliet | Learns a lot from way she deals with challenges |
| Obstacle 1 = Loves enemy, has to keep it secret | Independent - can be secretive, even cunning, shows she is not all that innocent and biddable; Support: ballroom, balcony and later scenes |
| Obstacle 2 = Killing of cousin, divided feelings | Supports Romeo, shows love and faithfulness; Support: reaction to the news |
| Obstacle 3 = Father / marriage to Paris, she cannot obey | She tries to object, fails, determined not to commit bigamy, shows she is moral and true; Support: scene with Capulet, goes to friar |
| Challenge 4 = Will she trust Friar and drink potion? She does | Shows she is trusting and courageous; Support: scene just before she drinks potion |
| Obstacle 5 = Finds Romeo dead in tomb, kills herself | Shows depth of her love and desperation. Only sees death as an escape. Support: last scene |

As you can see from the above plan, both parts of the question are being planned alongside each other, making sure that the terms of the questions are being addressed and that there is no overlap. It is worth spending a few minutes jotting down ideas like this as it will make the answers easier and quicker to write.

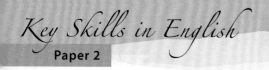

# Key Skills in English
## Paper 2

1. (a) **Identify an important character** from a play you have studied and **outline** some of the **obstacles or challenges** faced by him or her in the course of the play. (15)

**Sample Answer to 1. (a)**

*Juliet, from Shakespeare's 'Romeo and Juliet', is a character of tremendous importance in the play. She encounters many serious, even threatening, obstacles and challenges.* **[Identify character]** *The first major obstacle faced by Juliet is related to the fact that she falls in love with a member of the Montague family, the traditional enemies of her own family, the Capulets.* **[Point]** *Her 'only love' has 'sprung from ... a loathed enemy'. Knowing that her family would disapprove of the relationship, Juliet must keep her love and her marriage to Romeo a secret.* **[Quote and explanation]**

*When Romeo kills Juliet's cousin Tybalt in a fit of revengeful rage, Juliet is confronted with the challenge of divided loyalties* **[Point]**:*'Shall I speak ill of him that is my husband?' She loves her husband but she also loves her cousin,' But, wherefore, villain, didst thou kill my cousin?'*

*Her love for Romeo survives this challenge, but she is, nevertheless, placed in an awkward emotional position.* **[Quote and explanation]**

*To add to the obstacles which are created by Romeo being banished to Mantua, Juliet also has to deal with her father's insistence that she immediately marry the young nobleman Paris.* **[Point]** *'... fettle your fine joints 'gainst Thursday next' he commands or he will 'drag' her 'on a hurdle thither'. Juliet cannot commit bigamy and finds herself challenged to act against her conscience by the arguments of her Nurse, who recommends the immoral union of herself and Paris, 'I think it best you married with the county'.* **[Quote and explanation]**

*When she turns to the Friar for comfort, yet another challenge arises as Juliet questions the Friar's motive in giving her the potion.* **[Point]** *She wonders if it is 'a poison, which the friar /Subtly hath minister'd to have me dead.'* **[Quote and explanation]**

*Juliet's final and most dreadful obstacle occurs when she awakens in the tomb to find that Romeo has committed suicide.* **[Point]** *In a state of desperation and despair, she decides to join her lover in death. Grasping what she describes as a 'happy dagger' she stabs herself to death.* **[Quote and explanation]**

Notice that in this sample answer there are not too many 'Quotes and explanations' because the question asks you to 'outline' the obstacles. However you do need to show how they are obstacles.

(b) **What do you learn about this character** from the way in which he or she **deals with** one or more of these obstacles or challenges? Explain your answer. (15)

**Sample answer to 1. (b)**

*Much can be learnt about the character of Juliet by seeing the way she deals with these obstacles and challenges.*

*Her decision to marry Romeo and to keep it from her parents reveals an independent personality, capable of engaging in secrecy.* **[Point]** *It also shows her to be an impulsive young woman.* **[Point]** *It is she who suggests the marriage to Romeo: 'If that thy bent of love be honourable, / Thy purpose marriage, send me word to-morrow... / Where and what time thou wilt perform the rite; / And all my fortunes at thy foot I'll lay'. She uses the Nurse, 'one that I'll procure to come to thee', as a messenger and ally in maintaining her secret. These aspects of her character surprised me as I initially thought she was very innocent and childlike.* **[Quote and explanation]**

*When she is confronted with the demand that she marry Paris and her father's rage when she refuses, Juliet displays a degree of morality and loyalty which I found very impressive.* **[Point]** *Her statement that her 'husband is on earth', and her 'faith in heaven' acknowledges the enormity of the challenge facing her. She dispenses with the advice of the Nurse in a very determined way, 'Go, counsellor; / Thou and my bosom henceforth shall be twain' and accepts the challenge of trusting the Friar by drinking the potion.* **[Quote and explanation]**

*Although I was not surprised that Juliet committed suicide when she awoke in the tomb and found Romeo dead, nevertheless I was upset that she chose such a desperate remedy to end her grief. It seems out of character with the other moral decisions she made in the course of the play.* **[Point]** *However, I realise that she was in a state of enormous distress, had just awakened from a profound sleep, was shocked at the sight of death all around her and felt abandoned by everybody.* **[Quote and explanation]** *I don't think we can form any impression of her actual character from the way she dealt with this situation, as she was pre-destined to die and was pushed beyond her limits of endurance.* **[Point]**

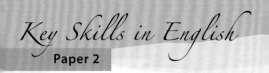
## Preparing for Studied Drama

In order to do well in this section of the paper, you need to:

◎ Be completely familiar with the plot of the play you have studied. Know what happens and when it happens. Be aware of incidents which change the course of events in the play. Prepare a timeline and highlight the key moments.

◎ Be able to discuss the characters in the play, their relationships with other characters, their motives and actions. Be clear in your opinions of them.

◎ Be aware of the major themes and issues explored in the play. Identify themes clearly and be able to trace them through the play.

◎ Analyse the atmosphere or mood in key scenes and be able to show how it is created. Be able to contrast the atmosphere of one scene with another which creates a different mood.

◎ Be able to discuss the role played by language and imagery in the play.

◎ Prepare three key scenes in great detail, using each of the above bullet points as guidance.

◎ For every one of the above points, make sure that you have learnt suitable quotations and can engage in close reference to support points.

◎ Be able to discuss how you would stage a scene from the play. Prepare three key scenes in advance, paying attention to the aspects listed under Stagecraft on page 173.

◎ Avoid any simple narration of the plot unless you are specifically asked to outline what happens in a particular scene. You may, of course explain or refer to what happens at a key moment in order to make a relevant point.

### Checklist

Use the following checklist to ensure that you have complied with the demands of the marking scheme:

Have I **read** the instructions on the exam paper properly and ensured that I am answering the **required number** of questions? ❏

Have I **underlined** the task or tasks in each question? ❏

Have I **planned** my response to address the exact question asked? ❏

Have I **paragraphed** correctly – **one** point in each paragraph? ❏

Have I **supported** and **explained** my responses? ❏

Have I used the **PQE** method or another logical method to ensure good structure? ❏

Have I checked that I am **not repeating** points? ❏

Have I **avoided** simply telling the story of the scene or play? ❏

Have I checked my **spelling, grammar** and **punctuation**? ❏

If you can tick all the above boxes and practise writing answers within the time limits allowed, you will do very well in the Drama Section of Paper Two.

# Glossary

**abound:** to occur/exist in large quantities

**abrupt:** brief, curt

**bigamy:** marrying someone while still legally married to someone else

**dispenses with:** gives up, does without, releases

**endurance:** the ability to handle strong pain (physical or mental)

**enraged:** furious

**hysterical:** loss of self-control, an emotional excess

**immoral:** to act in a way that is against the usual idea of what is right

**intensity:** to act with an extreme amount of force, concentration, effort or feeling

**lacklustre:** lacking enthusiasm

**melodramatic:** excessively dramatic

**morality:** knowing what is wrong and what is right

**obstructing:** preventing, getting in the way of

**pathetic:** causing pity, sympathy or compassion

**portraying:** showing in a certain way, depicting

**precision:** exactness, accuracy

**remedy:** a treatment or action to correct a mistake or wrongdoing

**slapstick comedy:** a physical type of comedy involving actions such as people crashing into each other, slipping on banana skins etc

# 6. Poetry

## Contents

---

## Key ^Exam Skills: *Fiction*

**Understanding and responding to:**

1. **Themes**
2. **Tone**
3. **Point of view**
4. **Imagery**
5. **Language**
6. **Sound**

#  Poetry

It is recommended that you spend approximately **45** minutes on this section. It is worth **60 marks:** 30 for Question One (Unseen Poetry) and 30 for Question Two (Studied Poetry). You must answer on both Unseen Poetry **and** Studied Poetry.

In Question One, you will be given a poem which you will probably never have seen before. There are usually three parts to Question One, and you must choose two parts to answer. Each part is worth 15 marks. Read the question carefully as this arrangement may vary.

In Question Two, you will get a choice of two questions. You must choose a poem which you have already studied and answer the question in relation to that poem. Each question is usually divided into two parts. Each part is worth 15 marks. Read the question carefully as this arrangement may vary.

The **KEY SKILLS** for answering poetry questions relate to:

**Content:** Ensure you are really answering the question asked. Support your answer with relevant quotation from the poem.

**Structure:** Organise your responses into paragraphs. Develop one major point in each paragraph. Use varied sentence structures.

**Expression:** Aim to be as clear as possible in your answer. Try to write with fluency.

**Mechanics:** Spelling, punctuation and grammar are important in everything that you write. Always check these areas for total accuracy.

## (a) Question One: Unseen Poetry

**KEY SKILLS** for Analysing a Poem (Unseen)

In responding to poetry questions you must display an ability to 'connect' with the poem and the poet. You are expected to make intelligent use of the text of the poem to support your **interpretation**.

**Note:** The poems mentioned in the following points are widely available to read in poetry anthologies or online.

The following **KEY SKILLS** need to be demonstrated in your responses:

### I. Theme

Be able to comment on the theme of the poem. Ask yourself what the poem is about and what is its purpose. Is there a message in the poem? For example, *Dulce et Decorum Est* by Wilfred Owen is a poem about the horrors endured by soldiers during World War I. Dreadful scenes of suffering are described. However, the poem was written for the purpose of showing that it is not a glorious or sweet thing to die in war. Owen is trying to **portray** the reality and show others that it is a 'Lie' to pretend that war is anything other than horrific and a waste of human life.

Ask yourself if the poem was written to entertain or amuse the reader, without making any serious point. Why would a poet write a poem just to make the reader laugh? Most of the poems by Spike Milligan, for example, are written simply to amuse the reader, but they also demonstrate wit and can be extremely clever in the use of sound and rhyme. Not every poem needs to have a serious message or theme although many do say something **insightful** and thought provoking.

**195**

## 2. Tone

Be able to comment on tone. The tone of a poem refers to the atmosphere created in the poem and the feelings of both the poet and the reader. Think of tone of voice and how it changes if someone is happy or sad, angry or calm, bitter or pleased about something. Poems are ideally meant to be read aloud, which helps establish tone. However, the words chosen and the images used in a poem can also convey powerful feelings and create atmosphere. Ask yourself the following questions: What is the atmosphere of this poem? How is it created? What is the poet feeling about his/her subject matter? What do I feel after reading the poem? Make sure that you can explain the answers to these questions and find evidence in the poem to back up your points.

## 3. Point of View

Be able to identify the speaker or voice in the poem. Poets do not always write from their own point of view. They often adopt a persona (a role or character) to express an attitude. For example, in the poem *Dress Sense* by David Kitchen, the poet creates a character to make a point about double standards. The poet himself is not the speaker in the poem. When you read a poem, ask yourself if the 'I' in the poem is really the poet speaking personally or if it is a persona, adopted to **mimic** somebody or mock an idea. Show why you believe that it is not the poet speaking in his own voice but rather that of a created persona.

## 4. Imagery

It is important that you know how to to comment on the use of imagery in a poem. Imagery refers to the pictures that can form in the imagination as one reads a poem. Poets usually try to make their images original in order to **convey** their meaning. Most images relate to familiar things so that the reader can draw on their own experience or memory and make the necessary connections.

Always look for images or words which involve the senses and make you see, hear, touch, taste or smell. These images appeal to our senses and create a very powerful impact on the reader.

A **simile** is a stated likeness of one thing to another, using **like** or **as**. In *Dulce et Decorum Est*, Wilfred Owen uses powerful similes to describe the plight of the weary soldiers. He describes them as being *'like old beggars under sacks ... coughing like hags'*. These similes are based on familiar things, so we can visualise the men, but the images are original and striking because we do not associate heroic men fighting a war with old beggars hauling sacks.

A **metaphor** compares two things without using **like** or **as**. For example, we could describe a man as being *'like a lion in battle'* (**simile**) or we could say that *'He was a lion in battle'* (**metaphor**). The metaphor makes a stronger impact here, as it suggests that the man almost became a lion in his strength and **ferocity**.

A **symbol** is an image which represents or stands for something else. For example, in the poem *Nettles* by Vernon Scannell, the nettles symbolise all those things in life which can cause a person pain. In particular, the nettles have become the symbol for the various hurts and injuries that life will **inflict** on his son. When you are discussing images say why they are appropriate and how effective they are in communicating the theme and tone of the poem.

## 5. Language

You should be prepared to comment on the word choices made by the poet. A word can have a literal meaning, which is known as its **denotation**. The denotation of a word can be found in a dictionary. However, poets are more interested in the **connotations** of words. This refers to the associations which words can have. Take for example the word **fire**: What associations can be made with this word? Heat, comfort, life, energy, rage, temper, burning, destruction etc. Clever choices and combinations of words create layers of meaning in a poem. Be on the lookout for unusual or striking use of language when you read a poem and be able to discuss the associations of certain words.

## 6. Sound

Be aware of the impact of sound techniques. The sound of a poem, its verbal music, can often indicate its main theme or purpose. Poems are best read aloud. In the Junior Cert exam, read the poem aloud in your head and identify any techniques which add to the quality of the poem.

**Alliteration:** This is where words begin with the same consonant, creating a certain type of music and linking ideas, e.g. *I hear lake water lapping with low sounds by the shore.* The alliteration on the **l** sound creates a gentle flowing motion in the line. The sound of the lapping lake water is low and gentle. Compare this to *Over the cobbles he clattered and clashed*, where the alliteration on a hard **c** consonant imitates the harsh noise made by a horse's hooves on an uneven surface. Watch out for alliteration in all your studied poems and also in the unseen poem. Be ready to comment on its effect. It is not enough to just say it is there!

**Assonance:** This refers to the patterns made by vowel sounds. The main vowels are **a, e, i, o** and **u**, but **w** and **y** can also sometimes act as vowel sounds. Vowels can be long or short. Compare the **a** sound in the word *cage* with the **a** sound in the word *cat*. Long vowels slow down the pace of a poem and can be used to show sadness or grief. *Alone, alone, all, all alone, / Alone on a wide wide sea!* However, if a poet wants a lively, brisk pace, he/she will use assonance on short vowels, '... *the tedding and the spreading / Of the straw for a bedding'*.

**Onomatopoeia:** This is where a word imitates a sound, e.g. *buzzing of the bees, the ting, tong, tang of the guitar, cuckoo, splash, crack* etc. Onomatopoeia can add tremendous music to the sound quality of a poem.

**Rhyme:** Rhyme refers to words which sound almost the same, e.g. *hair, lair* or *spare, dare*. It helps to emphasise words and make them memorable. It also adds to the music of a poem. The pattern of rhymes in a poem is known as its rhyming scheme. In the past, poems were recited and passed from one generation to another orally. Rhyme helped people to remember the poems so that they could pass them on to the next generation. Modern poets often choose to **dispense with** rhyme completely. Look at poems which rhyme and ask yourself if the rhymes make the poem more musical and appealing. If there is no rhyme, the poem may come close to ordinary speech which could add to a sense of realism. A poem does not have to rhyme to be a good poem, but be aware of the contribution rhyme can make to the sound of a poem and its skilful craftsmanship.

## You Try It

Read the following extracts from poems and answer the questions which follow.

1.  *The trees are in their autumn **beauty**,*
    *The woodland paths are dry,*
    *Under the October **twilight** the water*
    *Mirrors a **still** sky;*
    *Upon the brimming water among the stones*
    *Are nine-and-fifty swans.*

    Extract from
    'The Wild Swans at Coole' by WB Yeats

**(a)** How would you describe the atmosphere or tone in the above verse? How is it created?

**(b)** Look at the highlighted words and comment on how each of them contributes to the overall atmosphere.

**(c)** Is there any use of alliteration or assonance in the above verse? Select an example of each and comment on how it adds to the atmosphere or tone.

2.  *If I were fierce, and bald, and short of breath,*
    *I'd live with scarlet majors at the Base,*
    *And speed glum heroes up the line to death.*

    Extract from
    'Base Details' by Siegfried Sassoon

**(a)** Do you think that the poet, who fought in the trenches of World War One, is writing from his own point of view in this extract or has he created a 'voice' for someone else? Explain your response.

**(b)** What image of the the major and of the ordinary soldiers emerge from these lines? Comment on the role played by word choice in creating these images.

**(c)** How would you describe the poet's tone in these lines? Explain your answer.

3.  *And the Hip! Hop! Hap!*
    *Of the clap*
    *Of the hands to the twirl and the swirl*
    *Of the girl gone chancing,*
    *Glancing,*
    *Dancing,*
    *Backing and advancing,*
    *Snapping of a clapper to the spin*
    *Out and in –*
    *And the Ting, Tong, Tang, of the Guitar.*

    Extract from
    'Tarantella' by Hilaire Belloc

**(a)** What sound techniques are being used in this extract from 'Tarantella'? How does this use of sound affect the atmosphere of the lines?

**(b)** How does the poet create the image of the dancing girl? Comment on his choice of words and say why you think they are effective.

**(c)** What atmosphere or tone is being created here? Explain your response.

# Step-by-Step Approach: Unseen Poetry

## Step One

☐ Check the number of questions you are required to answer on the unseen poem. There are usually three parts to Question One, from which you choose two parts to answer. Each part will be worth 15 or 10 marks each.

☐ Read the poem carefully. This will give you a general idea of its subject matter. Do not worry if you do not understand every word or line of the poem. You will not be asked to write the whole poem out in your own words!

Now read the three parts of the question again very carefully. Highlight/underline the important words in each part and make sure that you answer two parts.

## Step Two

Beginning with the first part of the question you have chosen to answer, read over the poem again marking any words or phrases which you think will be useful as support for your response. Keep asking yourself questions. For example, if you are asked what impression you got of a person or scene, ask yourself why you got that impression, what words created it, why did the poet pick certain words etc. This will help to give your response a sharp focus.

## Step Three

Write your answer. Answers do not need to be very long, but they must be relevant to the question asked. If you find yourself telling the story of the poem: **stop**! You are probably moving away from the question. Check again to see what the question asked you to do. Now continue your answer, keeping an eye on exactly what you have been asked.

Make sure that you support your points with quotation from, or reference to, the poem. There is no need to write out chunks of the poem. This will not get you marks and is a waste of precious time. Choose quotations carefully. It may be that one word or a short phrase will illustrate the point you are making.

Try to insert personal comments into your response. You will be rewarded for showing that you understand what the poet is saying and that you can connect to the poem. Ask yourself how the poem made you feel. Why did you feel like that? Then ask yourself if there is anything in the poem that is relevant to your life. What is it? How is it relevant? Is there anything you learnt from the poem?

## You may be asked to:

**Respond to Language.** Look carefully at the poet's use of language. Are there any words or phrases that you thought were particularly effective or clever? Ask yourself why you thought this.

**Respond to Imagery.** Examine the poem carefully, checking for any use of **simile** or metaphor. If you can identify a good image, comment on its effectiveness. Say why you thought it was a good image and how it contributes to the poem's message.

**Respond to Sound.** Examine the poet's use of sound. Does the poem rhyme? Is there any use of **alliteration**, assonance or **onomatopoeia**?

**Say whether you liked or did not like the poem.** You must explain your answer here. It is not enough to just state that you did or didn't like the poem. When answering, you should consider all of the **KEY SKILLS** discussed earlier for answering a question on a poem.

Take care with spelling and punctuation, especially when you quote from the poem. Conclude each answer with a reference back to the question asked.

## Putting It Into Practice

Read the following poem, *Mrs. Reece Laughs*, by Martin Armstrong and answer the questions which follow.

# Mrs. Reece Laughs

Laughter, with us, is no great undertaking,
A sudden wave that breaks and dies in breaking.
Laughter with Mrs. Reece is much less simple:
It germinates, it spreads, dimple by dimple,
From small beginnings, things of easy girth,
To formidable redundancies of mirth.
Clusters of subterranean chuckles rise
And presently the circles of her eyes
Close into slits and all the woman heaves
As a great elm with all its mounds of leaves
Wallows before the storm. From hidden sources
A mustering of blind volcanic forces
Takes her and shakes her till she sobs and gapes.
Then all that load of bottled mirth escapes
In one wild crow, a lifting of huge hands,
And creaking stays, a visage that expands
In scarlet ridge and furrow. Thence collapse,
A hanging head, a feeble hand that flaps
An apron-end to stir an air and waft
A steaming face. And Mrs. Reece has laughed.

### Questions
1. **What is the difference** between Mrs. Reece's laughter and other people's laughter according to the poet, Martin Armstrong?
2. **What impression of Mrs. Reece do you form** from reading this poem? Support your answer with reference to the poem.
3. **How does the poet,** Martin Armstrong, **capture the extraordinary nature** of Mrs. Reece's laughter in this poem? Explain with reference to the poem.

**Sample answer to Question 1:**

According to the poet, Martin Armstrong, Mrs. Reece's laughter is quite different to that of other people. Most people's laughter is like 'a sudden wave that breaks' and then dies away. It is 'simple', a small 'undertaking'. However, Mrs. Reece's laughter is far more extreme and dramatic in nature. It builds up slowly, then 'spreads, dimple by dimple', until it reaches a climax. Her whole body responds to her laughter as 'all the woman heaves' and she is left quite exhausted physically, even in a state of 'collapse' by the 'blind volcanic forces' which overpower her. Mrs. Reece's laughter is undoubtedly unique.

**Sample answer to Question 2:**

From reading this poem, I have formed the impression that Mrs. Reece is a very large woman, good-humoured and possessing an almost overwhelming personality.

The poet describes her as being like a 'great elm with all its mounds of leaves'.

Phrases like 'volcanic forces', 'huge hands' and 'creaking stays' all contribute to the impression that she is a very large woman.

She certainly has a great sense of humour which expresses itself in this wonderful laughter. It 'Takes her and shakes her till she sobs and shakes'. This description conveys the strong impression that she is a woman who can see the fun in situations. Her laughter is 'bottled up' until it explodes in 'redundancies of mirth'.

I think Mrs. Reece could be an overwhelming personality. She does not seem to be able to control her laughter and it could be quite intimidating, although funny, when she lets out 'one wild crow' that turns her face 'scarlet.' I can just imagine how she might react if something made her angry! In general, I get the impression that Mrs. Reece is a larger-than-life character in every sense of the phrase.

**Sample answer to Question 3:**

Martin Armstrong captures the extraordinary nature of Mrs. Reece's laughter by using very graphic, detailed imagery.

A series of images appeals to our senses of sight and hearing. We are able to see her smile spreading 'dimple by dimple', her eyes closing into 'slits' and her whole body heaving with laughter. We can hear the 'chuckles', the 'sobs' and the 'loud crow' as the laughter escapes. By using such details in the description, the poet makes the readers feel as though they have actually witnessed the extraordinary event themselves.

Armstrong also uses splendid metaphors and similes, drawn from nature, to bring out the dramatic quality of the laughter. 'Clusters of subterranean chuckles rise' to the surface and she 'heaves / As a great elm with all its mound of leaves'. The reference to a 'storm' and 'blind volcanic forces' are very powerful in capturing the extraordinary, powerful nature of her laughter.

By describing the draining effect which the laughter has had on Mrs Reece, Armstrong captures the exhaustion which results from such a unique explosion of mirth. She is left with 'a hanging head' and feebly tries to cool her 'steaming face' with the end of her apron.

Armstrong certainly succeeded in capturing the unusual laughter of his subject. I found myself laughing as I read, which was quite an extraordinary experience for me!

**OVER TO YOU**

Read the following poem, *The Heron*, by Colm O'Shea and answer the questions which follow.

# THE HERON

Every lunch, I long to sit alone by the river,
but they keep mesh fence around our schoolyard
to save wayward students from drowning.

Amid the shouting, spitting, jeering, fighting,
bouncing tennis balls off heads, and crafty smokes,
I peer, penned behind net, at a lone heron.

Coolly balanced out on the waters,
he stares through raging currents
as mad schools of fish speed by.

My angler never even glances at me
while I enviously gaze at him: aloof,
sovereign, serene as a god.

No one worries about our drowning in a
screeching yard, sinking deeper day by day
into the endless grey of concrete.

Answer **two** of the following three questions. Each question is worth **15 marks**.

1. Do you think the poet captures the scene well in this poem? Support your answer with reference to the poem. (15 marks)

2. What points about school life do you think are being made in this poem? Explain your answer. (15 marks)

3. Why, in your opinion, is the speaker envious of the heron? Base your answer on evidence from the poem. (15 marks)

# (b) Question Two: Studied Poetry
**KEY SKILLS** for Analysing a Poem (Studied)

The questions in this section will allow you to show your knowledge of and response to poems you have already studied for your Junior Certificate.

There are usually two questions to choose from. Each question may be divided into two parts. Each part is usually worth 15 marks. Read questions carefully, as this format could change.

- Revise the **KEY SKILLS** on pages 195-198.

- Make sure that you are clear on the theme, tone, point of view, imagery, language and sound of each poem studied. Be able to demonstrate the part played by each of these elements of poetry.

# Step-by-Step Approach: Studied Poetry

## Step One
Read both questions carefully, underlining the exact task or tasks. Make sure that you do not forget any part of any question. Highlight/underline key words.

Select the question you wish to answer.

## Step Two
Think of the poems you have prepared for the exam and select a suitable one to use in your answer. You may have to refer to more than one poem if the question demands it. You may not use the unseen poem from Question One, even if it is one you have previously studied.

## Step Three
Plan your answer. Brainstorm relevant points for each part of the question. Think of suitable quotations from your studied poem to support these points.

Organise your points into a logical order. Make sure that you are not repeating yourself if there are parts (a) and (b) to the question. Each part will require a different response.

## Step Four
Write your answer. Name the poem and the poet at the beginning of your response.

Briefly introduce your response using the wording of the question.

Make roughly three relevant points using the Point-Quote-Explanation method, i.e. one point per paragraph.

Briefly conclude your response. Refer to the wording of the question in your conclusion.

# Putting It Into Practice

### Sample Question

N.B. In answering you may **NOT** use the poem already given in Question One. You must give the title of any poem and the name of any poet you refer to in your answer.

Answer **EITHER 1 OR 2** which follow.

**1.** From the poetry you have studied, **choose one poem** in which the poet uses interesting language to convey powerful thoughts and feelings.

**(a) What powerful thoughts and feelings** are conveyed by the poet in your chosen poem? **Support** your answer with reference to the poem. (15)

**(b) Explain** what you find **interesting about the language** used by the poet in the poem you have chosen. **Support** your answer with reference to the poem. (15)

### OR

**2.** From the poetry you have studied **choose a poet** whose work impressed you.

**(a)** What **topics or themes** does the poet deal with in the poetry that you have studied? Support your answer with reference to the work of your chosen poet. (15)

**(b) Explain why you find the work of your chosen poet impressive.** Give **reasons** for your answer with reference to his or her poetry. (15)

## Sample Answer

Sample answers to 1(a) and 1(b):

**Step 1:** Underline/highlight tasks in each part, (a) and (b).
**Step 2:** Select poem (*Dulce et Decorum Est* by Wilfred Owen) and plan your answer.

**Plan:** Decide your three points for part (a) and your three points for part (b). Plan both parts together to avoid overlap or repetition.

| (a)  Powerful thoughts and feelings | (b) Interesting language |
|---|---|
| Opens with a feeling of weariness and despair<br>Thought: war breaks people | Description of soldiers, similes, opposite of heroic |
| Thought: no soldier ever escapes memory<br>Feelings of fear and grief | The dreams, powerful description |
| Wants to present the truth about war, feels angry | Graphic imagery brings out the horror and the lie |

**Step 3:** Write answer using quotes and references from poem.

**Sample answer to part 1(a)**

*I have chosen the poem 'Dulce et Decorum Est' by Wilfred Owen to demonstrate how a poet can convey powerful thoughts and feelings through the use of interesting language.*

*The powerful opening of the poem makes one think of how war breaks the spirits of soldiers.* **[Point]** *Instead of the glorious future promised by war propaganda, they are reduced to the level of a pitiful procession of broken men, more like old 'hags' than heroes. Feelings of pity are evoked in the reader as they imagine the suffering, weariness and despair as the soldiers 'cursed through sludge', 'marched asleep' and 'limped' back to their base.* **[Quote and explanation]**

*Following on from this image, the poet explores the thought that no soldier who has experienced the horror of seeing others die ever really escapes from the memory.* **[Point]** *The poet cannot forget that he saw a comrade 'floundering like a man in fire or lime', 'drowning ' in the 'green sea' of a gas attack. Feelings of the same helplessness which he experienced at the time come back to haunt him. The fear as the soldier 'plunges' at him, 'guttering and choking', never leaves his memory.* **[Quote and explanation]**

*The powerful ending of the poem presents the major theme or thought to the readers.* **[Point]** *The poet is disgusted by the 'old Lie', which is told with 'high zest' to innocent school children. He declares that it is neither noble nor sweet to die for your country on the battlefield. The poem ends on this note of anger and disgust for the masking of truth.* **[Quote and explanation]**

*This poem, powerful in both thoughts and feelings, had a strong impact on me.*

**Sample answer to part 1(b)**

*I thought that the poet used extremely interesting language techniques in this poem.*

*Superb images are employed to graphically describe the procession of weary men.* **[Point]** *Owen compares them to 'old beggars under sacks' and 'hags'. These images are interesting because they create a stark contrast to the expectations of 'glory', which the soldiers once cherished. The language chosen emphasises their degradation in war.* **[Quote and explanation]**

*The use of verbs such as 'coughing', 'cursed', 'began to trudge', all conjure up the atmosphere of despair and fatigue.* **[Point]** *The pace of the poem is slow and tedious. Sentences are varied in length and broken up by punctuation marks. This gives the impression of the uneven steps taken by men who are 'drunk with fatigue'. The sudden change of pace as the gas attack occurs is also reflected in the skilful and interesting choice of verbs: 'fumbling', 'yelling out', 'stumbling', 'floundering'. This use of contrast powerfully creates the panic and horror and leaves a permanent impression on the mind of the reader.* **[Quote and explanation]**

The most interesting example of dramatic use of language occurs in the description of the gas attack. **[Point]**. The panic of the men is captured in the order 'Gas! Gas! Quick, boys!' The use of the word 'ecstasy' to describe the 'fumbling' to fit the masks in time is both interesting and terrifying. We don't usually associate ecstasy with such horror. The language engages the senses in a powerful way. We see the unfortunate man's 'hanging face, like a devil's sick of sin'. We hear his howls of pain and the 'gargling' of blood in his throat as he chokes to death. We almost feel the jolting of the wagon and the violence of his body being 'flung' into it. **[Quote and explanation]**

The use of language throughout this poem is not only interesting, it is memorable and disturbing. it forces us to confront the reality that war is far from being sweet and honourable.

---

 **OVER TO YOU**

Answer **EITHER 1 OR 2** which follow.

N.B. In answering you may NOT use the poem given on this paper. You must give the title of the poem you choose and the name of the poet.

1. Choose a poem you have studied in which the poet deals with an important issue.

    **(a)** Explain what the poet had to say about the important issue in the poem.     (15)

    **(b)** What insights into the issue did you get from studying this poem?     (15)
       Explain your answer with reference to the poem.

OR

2. Imagine you have to recommend one poem that you have studied for a new
    publication entitled, *A Book of Favourite Poems for Young People of the 21st Century*.

    **(a)** Name the poem you would choose and explain why this particular poem would
       be suitable for inclusion in this collection.     (15)

    **(b)** In your answer you may wish to consider some of the following; the poem's theme,
       the way the poet uses language, the use of imagery, tone and/or mood, the structure
       of the poem etc.     (15)

# (c) Commentaries on Three Poems

## Ozymandias
by *Percy B. Shelley*

I met a traveller from an antique land
Who said: Two vast and trunkless legs of stone
Stand in the desert. Near them, on the sand,
Half sunk, a shattered visage lies, whose frown
And wrinkled lip, and sneer of cold command
Tell that its sculptor well those passions read
Which yet survive, stamped on these lifeless things,
The hand that mocked them and the heart that fed.
And on the pedestal these words appear:
"My name is Ozymandias, king of kings:
Look on my works, ye Mighty, and despair!"
Nothing beside remains. Round the decay
Of that colossal wreck, boundless and bare
The lone and level sands stretch far away.

## Commentary

**Theme:** This poem teaches us a very important lesson about life and the foolishness of believing that power or fame will last forever.

Ozymandias was once a powerful ruler who imagined that his great 'works' and statue would be an everlasting monument to his greatness as the 'king of kings'. He thought that the 'colossal' statue on its stately **pedestal** would be a permanent reminder not only to his own people but to the 'mighty' rulers of every generation, making them 'despair' of ever reaching such heights of splendour or power.

**Tone:** The poet clearly mocks the empty pride and arrogance of Ozymandias when he describes what became of his statue and his kingdom. His head has fallen into the sand and is 'Half sunk'. His face is no more than 'a shattered visage'. Interestingly, enough of the face remains for us to glimpse the 'frown / And wrinkled lip and sneer of cold command'. This is all that remains – the ugly face of an arrogant **tyrant**. The sculptor has captured the character of Ozymandias very well. He mocked others and treated them **contemptuously**; now his own monument is a mockery of himself. It is a reminder of empty, hollow **vanity**. This point is emphasised by the fact that all around the statue 'the lone and level sands stretch far away'. Even the mighty 'works' of Ozymandias have become 'nothing' – just like himself.

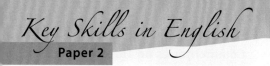

**Point of view:** Although the poem is given a speaker, the 'traveller from an antique land', the attitude of the poet himself is extremely clear. He relates the traveller's story in a detached, factual way, but the sarcasm is obvious. We also hear the imagined voice of Ozymandias in the words engraved on the pedestal. Shelley is showing that what remains, if anything, is captured in art and in words. Everybody who knew Ozymandias is dead. Those who didn't know him, but who discover the shattered statue by chance while crossing a lonely desert, can laugh at the writing on the pedestal, dictated by a man with a 'colossal' ego. They can also think about the fact that even the most powerful 'king of kings' cannot escape the reality of death and decay.

**Imagery:** The imagery in this poem is very powerful. The detailed description of the remains of the statue brings the image to life for the reader. We can just imagine 'Two vast and trunkless legs of stone' standing in the midst of desert, while the head of the statue, the most important part, is sinking into the sand. Not only is the face of the tyrant 'shattered' but so is his power and sway. The image is symbolic in this sense.

The images of the 'wrinkled lip' and the 'sneer of cold command' help the reader to form an impression of the character of Ozymandias. It is not a flattering portrait! The arrogance of the ruler is captured superbly, not only by the sculptor who carved the likeness, but also by the speaker who is able to interpret the 'passions' which remain 'stamped on these lifeless things'.

The final image of the 'colossal wreck', which is all that remains, is made even more forceful by the description of the 'lone and level sands' which stretch far away into the distance. The reader is left in no doubt that not only is the statue decaying but very few people will even see it as it is so removed from public life and view.

**Language:** The poet's word choice in this poem emphasises the theme and tone of the poem. Words like 'vast' and 'colossal', used to describe the statue, could also be used to describe the arrogance and power of Ozymandias. The use of the word 'antique' emphasises the passing of time and the great changes which can take place. What was once a great statue of a ruler, surrounded by his mighty 'works' or creations, is now no more than a crumbling 'wreck' in a vast desert.

Words like 'frown', 'wrinkle' and 'sneer' are very well chosen to suggest the character of Ozymandias, while 'shattered' and 'half-sunk' stress the vanity of human pride and ambition.

**Sound:** Shelley makes use of many sound techniques in this poem. **Alliteration** is used both for sound effect and also to join ideas. Phrases like 'cold command', 'hand ... heart', 'boundless and bare', 'lone and level' all create verbal music (music created by words) and are also used to link ideas. We connect the 'command' or power of Ozymandias with coldness of emotion. He ruled his people with an iron hand and a cruel heart. The fact that the desert is 'boundless' only serves to highlight the limited rule of the 'king of kings' and the 'bare' remains of his tyranny. Not alone are the desert sands 'lone and level', Ozymandias's image is isolated and levelled also.

The use of the sibilant (hissing) 's' sound is also very effective in the poem. Note how many words either begin with 's' or have an 's' in them. This sibilance serves to bring out the hushed silence of the desert place. It also creates a tone of hissing contempt for the self-centred Ozymandias. Rhyme and **assonance** also add to the musical quality of the poem.

# Base Details

by *Siegfried Sassoon*

If I were fierce, and bald, and short of breath,

I'd live with scarlet Majors at the Base,

And speed glum heroes up the line to death.

You'd see me with my puffy petulant face,

Guzzling and gulping in the best hotel,

Reading the Roll of Honour. "Poor young chap,"

I'd say - " I used to know his father well;

Yes, we've lost heavily in this last scrap."

And when the war is done and youth stone dead,

I'd toddle safely home and die – in bed.

## Commentary

**Theme:** This poem is an anti-war poem. Siegfried Sassoon is attacking the attitudes of the 'scarlet Majors' who keep well away from the front lines of battle while ordering young recruits to fight to the death. The poet is also attempting to raise public awareness of the futility (pointlessness) of war.

The poet, who fought in the trenches during World War I, imagines how easy his life would be if he was one of the Majors, living in the army base. He refers to the greedy, **self-indulgent** life he would have, 'guzzling and gulping in the best hotel', while young men are dying in the latest 'scrap' ordered by those in authority.

**Tone:** Sassoon is bitingly sarcastic in his description of the lives led by the majors. He describes them in contemptuous language as being 'fierce, and bald, and short of breath'. These words suggest old age, but the majors are **depicted** as being more like children in their attitudes to war. They see the fierce battles which are fought as a 'scrap', which is a word usually used to describe a childish fight in a playground. The words 'toddle' and 'petulant' (sulky) are also associated with very young children. The poet's use of such words cleverly reveal his anger at the authorities, who seem to be playing war games while young, heroic men die in a real war.

A tone of disgust is evident as the poet describes the majors indulging themselves, 'Guzzling and gulping in the best hotel,' after they have hurried young men 'up the line to death'.

**Point of view:** Although the poet states that 'If' he was a Major, he would live the life described, there is no doubt that he **despises** such a life and is fiercely attacking it. He would never wish to be in such a position of authority and responsibility for the deaths of young men. The point of view is extremely negative towards war and towards those who profit at the expense of others. The final rhyming couplet expresses the key viewpoint in the poem – those with the power will survive and eventually die a natural death in their beds, while the 'youth' of the country will be 'stone dead', having died horrific deaths in war. The injustice and inequality of that situation inspires the poet to express his point of view through his use of verse.

**Imagery:** Sassoon uses several powerful images in the poem. The first image is that of the 'scarlet Majors'. These men are shown as being almost like animals in their greed, 'guzzling' their food and 'gulping' their drink. One gets the impression that they feed themselves with the same energetic 'speed' as they use to hurry young soldiers to the front battle lines. The 'puffy, petulant' faces add to the almost cartoon-like image of men who are 'fierce, and bald, and short of breath'. These images **ridicule** the majors.

By contrast, the young soldiers are 'glum heroes', who may make it to the Roll of Honour but only by losing their lives in battle.

The final image again uses effective contrast as the 'stone dead' youths are compared to the majors, toddling 'safely home' to die natural deaths in their own comfortable beds.

**Language:** Sassoon's word choice emphasises theme and tone. 'Scarlet' was the colour of the uniforms worn by officers of this rank, but it is also the colour associated with shame. Sassoon clearly sees the conduct of these men as being shameful. The word can also suggest the red, puffy faces of the majors which comes from over-eating and drinking too much alcohol.

The verb 'speed' effectively captures the arrogant attitude of the majors as they hurry the soldiers to the front line. The use of the word 'scrap' to describe the battles where lives are 'lost heavily' just goes to show how removed from reality these officers are. We are not surprised at the use of the word 'glum' to describe the feelings of the young 'heroes' who knew only too well what lay before them.

The use of effective dialogue serves to emphasise the self-centred nature of the major speaking. He refers to one young man as a 'Poor young chap', only worth remarking on because the major 'used to know his father well'.

Effective wordplay or use of puns can be seen in the choice of the word 'Base'. Here, it refers to the military base from where the majors control operations. Something which is 'base' however can also mean the lowest part of something. Sassoon is using the word deliberately to pour contempt on those officers as being the most base compared to the young, heroic soldiers. The word 'Details' of the title shows a similar use of puns. The scarlet uniforms of the majors would have detailed embroidery, showing the importance of their ranks. Another meaning of 'Base Details' is connected to the words inscribed on the base of war monuments, which were erected to honour those who died in war. Each of the young soldiers is a 'Base Detail' in this sense.

**Sound:** This short poem is organised around an alternating **ababcdcdee** rhyme scheme. The rhyming couplet at the end is typically used to express key ideas, in this case, Sassoon's own contempt for the majors living at the base.

Alliteration is used to enhance the sound and to link ideas. Notice the way the letter 'p' explodes from the lips, almost imitating the breathless, pompous nature of the majors in the phrase 'puffy petulant face'. Likewise, the hard 'g' in 'guzzling and gulping' brings out their hardness of hearts, while also highlighting the characteristics Sassoon dislikes most in the officers – they are like greedy pigs with their snouts in feeding troughs.

The assonance in most of the rhymes is on short vowels, e.g. 'breath ... death', 'hotel ... well', 'chap ... scrap', 'dead ... bed'. This assonance helps draw attention to the short, curt manner of the majors as they carry out their duty of speeding the heroic soldiers to the front lines of battle.

# Nest

by Colm O'Shea

That's the branch, slighter than I recall.
The tyre still hangs, a black O in space,
its rope little more than thread –
hard to discern at dusk.

I remember the boy, mud-stained,
spinning, squealing for height.
He retains little of deeds done here,
of treasures found, lost in long grass.
No, that small person has mostly
blown away, stolen hair by hair by
the tiny summer whirlwinds he once
stood inside, clutching
at their hay-lined walls.

Above the tyre branch
twig lines pretend a rampart,
the barest shelter possible.
Mostly space, feathered space:
to near-weightless creatures,
home. Cosy as a cot.

Who is more peaceful than the sleeper
cupped in a shell? Unless
it's the mother herself,
receding from threats below,
swaying beneath stars
in a mostly-empty sky,
half-dozing on the smooth, perfect
oval of her child.

## Commentary

**Theme:** The theme of this poem is not as immediately obvious as the themes in the previous two poems. Modern poetry often requires a little more thought to arrive at an understanding of the theme.

As the poet looks up at a tyre hanging from a rope tied to the branch of a tree, he remembers his childhood and how quickly time has stolen that precious period of life away – 'that small

person has mostly / blown a way, stolen hair by hair'. While he remembers himself as a child playing happily with the tyre, he sees a nest which seems to be protected by the twigs and branches of the tree. He reflects on the mother bird who protects her unhatched chicks in the nest. She has removed herself from the 'threats below', to sway peacefully 'beneath stars in a mostly-empty sky'.

The poem is a reflection on the passing of time, the protective instinct of motherhood and how life constantly changes and renews itself.

**Tone:** The tone of this poem is mainly reflective (thoughtful). There is a slight hint of **nostalgia** as the poet thinks of the child he once was – 'mud-stained, / spinning, squealing for height'. The innocence and joy of childhood passes and now 'He retains little of deeds done here, / of treasures found, lost in long grass'. There is a sense of remembered joy which emphasises his present sense of loss.

The tone changes as he catches a glimpse of the nest, where the mother bird is 'half-dozing on the smooth, perfect / oval of her child.' The atmosphere is one of serenity (calm) and peace. Only the unhatched chick 'the sleeper / cupped in a shell' is more 'peaceful' than the mother bird herself.

The calm, peaceful ending against a background of 'stars / in a mostly empty sky' shows how the poet's sense of loss is beautifully balanced with his realisation that all things in nature are engaged with the same process of life. The baby birds will hatch, they will be cared for by the mother bird, they will grow to maturity and they will fly away from their nest. Life is constantly being renewed. The night sky will change to the light of a new day.

**Point of view:** The point of view in this poem is that of the poet himself as he **contemplates** change. He is the speaker or the 'I' of the poem, who is reflecting on how time changes the way we look at things and see them. The 'rope' he remembered now seems to be 'little more than thread', the branch is actually 'slighter' than he has remembered it. His present view of life is connected to his memories of how he once was and how he now is. This place is his 'home' in the same way as the 'near-weightless creatures' consider the nest their home – 'Cosy as a cot'. He has changed, he 'retains little of deeds done here'. The eggs will change in time and will hatch out the new birds. The role of the mother will change also, as will the changing face of the sky. This view of life as being a process of constant change is central to the way the poet makes sense of his experiences.

**Imagery:** The poet uses several images which help to clarify the theme of the poem and to establish the atmosphere. The first image is one we can easily visualise, a tyre hanging from the branch of a tree to provide a simple swing for a child. In the 'dusk' it appears as a 'black O in space'. Not only does the shape of the letter 'O' correspond to the shape of the tyre but it also sounds like a sigh of regret, an 'oh' of sadness. The image of the day's light fading, 'dusk', also creates a sense of something fading into darkness, of being at an end.

The happy image of the child 'mud-stained/spinning, squealing for height' is contrasted with the image of him being 'Blown away, stolen hair by hair...clutching at their hay-lined walls,' as though reluctant to leave his childhood world.

Images of childhood then move to images of the nest which appears to be almost floating in space, barely supported by a 'rampart' or fortress of twigs. We get a sense of the fragile nature of the nest as the 'barest shelter possible / Mostly space, feathered space' and 'cosy as a cot'. The image of the cot recalls the earlier image of childhood and home.

The description of the unhatched bird as a 'sleeper / cupped in a shell' is beautiful in its simplicity, as is the image of the mother bird 'half-dozing on the smooth, perfect / oval of her child'. The shape of the egg recalls the shape of the tyre as it hangs from the tree in the first verse. Symbolically, a circle or oval suggests continuity (a continuous line, with no beginning or end). The poet is using this symbol to show the circles of life – the movement from birth to maturity, from morning to dusk to night, from the egg to the new life which will hatch forth and become independent.

**Language:** The word choice in this poem is essentially simple, in keeping with the subject matter. **Adjectives** are well chosen to bring out the fragile nature of the nest and its occupants: 'feathered space', 'near-weightless creatures'. The description of the mother bird protecting her egg 'swaying beneath stars / in a mostly-empty sky' captures the mood perfectly. The use of a question to focus the attention on the bird and nest is very effective.

**Sound:** The poem is written in free verse, which does not use any particular rhyme scheme or rhythm. Instead, the content of the poem decides the pace. Absence of rhyme brings the poem closer to ordinary speech and creates communication between the speaker and the reader.

Alliteration is used to create music and to link ideas, e.g. 'discern at dusk', 'spinning, squealing ...', 'deeds done', 'cosy as a cot'.

Sibilance (repetition of 's' sound) creates the mood of hushed silence: peaceful ... sleeper ... shell ... swaying ... stars ... sky' etc.

Repetition gives emphasis to ideas also. Notice the repetition of 'hair' and 'space'. The assonance here is on broad vowels, which slows down the poem, in keeping with its subject matter and reflective mood.

**Note:** Commentaries on more poems are available to read on www.mentorbooks.ie

## (d) Advice

Prepare at least ten poems on different themes using the **Key Skills** for analysing poetry given on pages 195-197. This will put you in a strong position to answer well in the exam.

Practise writing answers following the PQE method. At first, your answers may be quite short as you attempt to write them within the time limit. However, as you improve with practice, you will find that you can think, plan and write quickly.

Aim to develop your answers a little more each time you write answers to questions on a poem. Eventually, you will find that you can write a detailed and developed response.

Keep strictly within the time limits. You have less than half an hour to do the studied poetry section. You must not steal time from the final section on Fiction. If you find that you simply cannot write at length in these samples, shorten your quotes and explanations. But do try to make three valid points and offer some support and explanation from the text.

## CHECKLIST

Use the following checklist to ensure that you have complied with the demands of the marking scheme:

Have I **practised writing** both unseen and studied poetry questions? ☐

Have I prepared **at least ten poems** following the guidelines for analysing poems? ☐

Have I **read the questions very carefully** and ensured that I am addressing all parts of the questions? ☐

Have I **underlined/highlighted** the key words in all questions before choosing a question to answer? ☐

Have I **made a short plan**, ensuring that I am addressing the question? ☐

Have I made **relevant points** and supported them with **quotation** from the poem/s? ☐

Have I offered some **explanation** of my points? ☐

Have I made some **personal comments** in the course of my answer? ☐

Have I used **paragraphs** properly, developing one point in each paragraph? ☐

Have I checked my **spelling, punctuation and grammar**? ☐

If you can tick each of these boxes, you will do very well in the Poetry Section of Paper Two.

# Glossary

**adjectives:** words that describe nouns, e.g. a **pink** hat, a **beautiful** day

**alliteration:** repeating the same sound in a series of words

**assonance:** repeating the same vowel sounds in a series of words

**cherished:** to protect/care for something or someone very lovingly

**conjure up:** to call or bring something into existence as if by magic

**contemplates:** thinks about, considers, reflects

**contemptuously:** showing or expressing scorn/lack of respect

**convey:** make known

**degradation:** decline in quality

**depicted:** shown, portrayed

**despises:** detests, dislikes intensely

**dispense with:** do without, release

**evoked:** brought to mind, recollected

**ferocity:** being ferocious; being very fierce

**inflict:** force something unpleasant/painful on someone

**insightful:** able to understand something/someone at a deeper level

**interpretation:** explanation

**masking:** hiding, concealing

**mimic:** imitate, copy

**mirth:** amusement, joy

**nostalgia:** longing for the past

**pedestal:** support, base for a column or statue

**portray:** show, depict

**propaganda:** information, often inaccurate, which an organisation distributes in order to influence people

**ridicule:** mock, make fun of

**self-indulgent:** doing exactly what you want, particularly if it is pleasant

**tedious:** slow, tiresome

**tyrant:** ruler who uses power unjustly

**unique:** being the only one

**vanity:** having too much pride in yourself

# 7. Fiction

## Contents

## Key Exam Skills: Fiction

**Understanding and responding to:**

1. **Characters**
2. **Setting**
3. **Plot**
4. **Theme**
5. **Style**

#  Fiction

It is recommended that you spend approximately **45 minutes** on this section. It is worth **60 marks**: 30 for Question One (Unseen Fiction) and 30 for Question Two (Studied Fiction). You must answer a question on Unseen Fiction **and** a question on Studied Fiction.

In Question One, you will be given a passage to read which you will probably not have seen before. There are usually three parts to Question One, and you must choose two parts to answer. Each part is worth 15 marks. Read the question carefully as this arrangement may vary.

In Question Two, you will get a choice of two questions. You must answer one. Each question is usually divided into two parts. Each part is worth 15 marks. Read the question carefully as this arrangement may vary.

## (a) Question One: Unseen Fiction
**KEY SKILLS** for Analysing a Passage (Extract)

The **KEY SKILLS** for answering questions on a piece of fiction relate to:

**Content:** Ensure you are really answering the question asked. Support your answer with relevant quotation from the passage.

**Structure:** Organise your responses into paragraphs. Develop one major point in each paragraph. Use varied sentence structures.

**Expression:** Aim to be as clear as possible in your answer. Try to write with fluency.

**Mechanics:** Spelling, punctuation and grammar are important in everything that you write. Always check these areas for total accuracy.

When you respond to fiction texts, you must display an ability to understand and **interpret** what you have read. In your response you are expected to make relevant points, which you can support with reference to the text.

You need to understand each of the key areas which follow:
### I. Characters
Characters must be credible and interesting in order to engage the reader. Remember that characters in fiction are not real people. They have been created by the writer. Your task is to explain how the writer has done this.

Writers use different methods when creating fictitious characters:
(a) The reader may be given explicit information about the character, e.g. **Mrs O'Connor was a mean-minded, irritable woman, who revelled in causing trouble for the children of the neighbourhood.** Here, we are told what we should think of Mrs O'Connor. There is no room for any doubt due to the use of specific adjectives and the use of the word **revelled**.

217

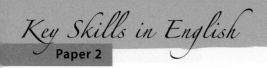

**(b) Implicit** information can be given through the character's actions. In this case, the writer does not tell us directly, but allows us to form our own opinion on a character based on how they act and/or react in situations. This is the most reliable indication of what a character is like. Look at the following description from *Great Expectations* by Charles Dickens. The characters of both Estella and Pip are suggested rather than told:

> *She came back, with some bread and meat and a little mug of beer. She put the mug down on the stones of the yard, and gave me the bread and meat without looking at me, as insolently as if I were a dog in disgrace. I was so humiliated, hurt, spurned, offended, angry, sorry – I cannot hit upon the right name for the smart – God knows what its name was – that tears started to my eyes. The moment they sprang there, the girl looked at me with a quick delight in having been the cause of them. This gave me power to keep them back and to look at her: so, she gave a contemptuous toss – but with a sense, I thought, of having made too sure that I was so wounded – and left me.*

The highlighted words and phrases suggest that Estella is a cruel and **haughty** individual who enjoys humiliating another child. Pip's reaction to this treatment shows his sensitivity and passionate nature. Although he is deeply offended by Estella's actions and attitude, he maintains his dignity by refusing to cry and by looking straight at his **tormentor**.

**(c)** Dialogue assists greatly in the creation of character. What characters say and the way that they say it can reveal their attitudes and certain aspects of their personalities. Take for example this piece of dialogue from the novel *To Kill a Mockingbird* by Harper Lee. Atticus Finch, one of the main characters in the book, is speaking to his young daughter, Scout:

> *'First of all', he said, 'if you can learn a simple trick, Scout, you'll get along better with all kinds of folks. You never really understand a person until you consider things from his point of view … until you climb into his skin and walk around in it'.*

This small excerpt from the dialogue of Atticus is very revealing of his attitude to other people and shows him to be both just and wise.

We can also learn about characters from what others say about them and from how they relate to other characters. Ask yourself if characters are liked by others and try to explain the reasons why or why not. Are they sincere, friendly, open, cunning, nasty, devious etc.?

What characters say about themselves and their feelings can give us an insight into their personalities, attitudes and motives. Be careful, however, because a character may not be speaking the truth about themselves or about somebody else.

## 2. Setting
The time and location in which a story takes place is called the setting.
An author can bring the setting alive by using descriptive details. You need to ask yourself the following questions about setting:
- Where is this story taking place?
- What is the importance of the setting to the story?
- How does the writer use language to create the setting?

It is usually quite easy to establish the time and place of the setting. Sometimes writers give neutral, factual details which **convey objective** information.

> *The town of Ballymore has a population of three thousand people. Many of the present inhabitants have lived in the town for most of their lives and can trace their roots back several centuries. Very few outsiders come to live in Ballymore, as it does not have much to offer as regards employment or opportunity. The old square, where people once congregated on fair days, is now home to a few small shops, a couple of pubs and a small filling station.*

However, it can be more challenging to create a setting which contributes to the narrative. When commenting on setting, it is a good idea to ask yourself the following question: What can I see, hear, taste, feel, smell? All writers appeal to the senses to create a vivid sense of reality and invite the reader into the imagined world. Take for example the introduction to Maycomb in Harper Lee's *To Kill a Mockingbird:*

> *Maycomb was an old town, but it was a tired old town when I first knew it. In rainy weather the streets turned to red slop; grass grew on the sidewalks, the courthouse sagged in the square. Somehow, it was hotter then; a black dog suffered on a summer's day; bony mules hitched to Hoover carts flicked flies in the sweltering shade of the live oaks on the square. Men's stiff collars wilted by nine in the morning. Ladies bathed before noon, after their three o'clock naps, and by nightfall were like soft tea-cakes with frostings of sweat and sweet talcum.*
>
> *People moved slowly then. They ambled across the square, shuffled in and out of the stores around it, took their time about everything. A day was twenty-four hours long but seemed longer. There was no hurry, for there was nowhere to go, nothing to buy and no money to buy it with.*

Here the writer appeals to several of the reader's senses and captures the slow pace of life in an American small town in the 1930s. The description enables the reader to experience the world of the narrative which later helps in understanding the thoughts, actions and feelings of different characters.

Word choice can help establish setting and mood. In the above extract we can see some excellent examples of well-chosen words. Notice how the courthouse **sagged**, how men's collars **wilted**, how people **ambled**. These verbs help to create the atmosphere of a place which could be unpleasant in both rainy and in **sweltering** weather. The town is captured as being **old** and **tired**; the people behave in a predictable manner and are set in their ways. All of these aspects become crucially important as events unfold because they influence the behaviour of the characters.

### 3. Plot
The plot refers to the sequence of events or the shape that a story takes. One could imagine it as a sort of map for a journey which the reader takes during the course of the narrative.

When planning the plot of a narrative, the writer has to make certain decisions. You should examine the following in any extract, short story or novel:

How is the **time sequence** handled? Is there a chronological order, where the writer works progressively through the events as they occur, or is there a flashback or a series of flashbacks which shape the narrative?

How and when are **new characters** introduced? What complications and obstacles arise for the main characters that make us want to read on to find out what is going to happen?

How are conflict and tension created? **Suspense** is a prime ingredient of any story and is necessary to maintain the reader's interest. Suspense comes from the building up of tension, keeping the reader in a state of heightened anxiety or uncertainty. It may rely on conflicts or tensions between the characters themselves, conflicts/tensions surrounding events or tensions relating to the setting, e.g. a battlefield or a haunted house. The important ingredient is that the reader is left uncertain as to what will happen and wants to read on to find out.

**Climax** may be described as the point at which after a series of events increasing in tension, a critical moment is reached. It is usually the turning point in a story and leads to the conclusion. Where does the story come to a climax? Is there more than one climax? Ask yourself where the story has been going, i.e. follow the 'map'. Take for example the climax in John Steinbeck's novel *Of Mice and Men*. George is about to kill his close friend Lennie to spare him from a **lynch mob**. The two friends share a dialogue about the dream they had to own their own home. As Lennie looks across the river, George brings the novel to its climax:

> *'... George raised the gun and steadied it, and he brought the muzzle of it close to the back of Lennie's head. The hand shook violently, but his face set and his hand steadied. He pulled the trigger. The crash of the shot rolled up the hills and rolled down again. Lennie jarred, and then settled slowly forward to the sand, and he lay without quivering.*

How does the **pace** vary? It is important to have changes in the speed at which events happen. Too much dialogue slows the action down, but enough must be given to make the characters seem real. Likewise, too many events happening in quick succession or the plot lurching from one crisis to another creates a sense of unreality.

How does the conflict **resolve**? Remember, there may be more than one conflict in a novel. What happens as a result of the resolution of the conflict? How does the story end?

## 4. Theme

A theme is a central idea that provides the inspiration for a plot. A short story normally develops one theme, whereas a novel may have several themes. Themes may focus on such things as prejudice, war, love, loyalty, ambition etc. Most aspects of human life can provide the writer with a theme on which to base a plot. Themes provide a springboard for the plot and give meaning to the lives and relationships of the characters.

You should be able to answer the following questions about themes:

◉ How does the theme emerge from the actions and dialogue of the characters? Be able to trace a theme or themes from beginning to end.

◉ How does the setting contribute to the theme? After you have identified the theme, examine the setting carefully. Ask yourself if the setting has an important role to play in bringing out the theme.

◉ How does the language and imagery contribute to the theme? Descriptive details and specific word choice can indicate or highlight the theme. Watch out for language which appeals to the senses and examine any symbols or other images to see how they influence the theme.

Read the extract below as an example of how a theme can be traced through a narrative extract:

The following letter is taken from the novel *Remembrance* by Theresa Breslin. Francis, a soldier, is writing to his friend Maggie. In this letter he shares with her his experiences of the trenches of World War I.

*My dear Maggie,*
*We came up from our rest billet the other night to relieve the troops in the front lines. I swear the times of our movements must be known to our enemies for they shelled the road as soon as we began, and stopped immediately we reached the communications trenches. We left the road at once and crawled through an orchard and some pigpens to reach our destination by another route. It seems incredible, but among this devastation the trees here are beginning to bud – after a bitter Winter, Spring now struggles to break through. As the thaw sets in it is the most punishing work to keep the trenches free of water. The pumps are poor excuses, and barely work. Our engineers have designed crude constructions which they call "duckboards" – long square poles of wood with thick crossbars set at intervals. These are made from whatever can be requisitioned, stolen or scavenged. Wood from shelled and bombed buildings, empty ration crates, wattle fencing, anything and everything is used.*

*My "hotel" view at the moment is out across the stretch of earth they call No Man's Land and the very phrase sums up the waste of war – there is a solitary tree stripped of life and colour, spent ammunition, shrapnel and shell and . . . the unburied dead.*

*I am strangely unafraid of death; there is a trance-like quality to life under these circumstances. What frightens me more is the death of spirit, that I have so quickly become accustomed to the sights and sounds of war . . . such an ache in my head and in my heart.*

*Francis*

The theme of war, its suffering and waste, is very carefully traced throughout the extract. The speaker in the extract recounts the actions of the soldiers in some detail as they make their way to the trenches. The highlighted sentences illustrate the use that can be made of action, setting, language and imagery to bring out the dominant theme that war is a waste of life, which can also kill the human spirit.

## 5. Style

The style of a narrative refers to the way it is written. It includes how characters, setting and atmosphere are created. It also includes the way in which the writer uses dialogue, language and imagery. These are covered in the headings 1-4 on pages 217-221. However, you also need to examine and be aware of:

✿ How the writer uses verbs to provide **insight** into character and assist atmosphere. For example, let us take the extract from *Of Mice and Men* referred to on page 220:

'... George **raised** the gun and **steadied** it, and he brought the muzzle of it close to the back of Lennie's head. The hand **shook violently**, but his face **set** and his hand **steadied**. He **pulled** the trigger. The crash of the shot **rolled** up the hills and **rolled** down again. Lennie **jarred**, and then **settled** slowly forward to the sand, and he **lay** without quivering.

The verbs highlighted in green are carefully selected and are crucial in showing us that George does not want to shoot Lennie. He has difficulty in carrying out the act. This shows his love and loyalty to his friend and his conflict at that moment. The atmosphere is tense and dramatic as George steadies the gun, shakes and steadies himself again before pulling the trigger. The repetition of the verb **rolled** creates an atmosphere of the exploding, **reverberating** sound of the gunshot. Lennie's body did not just 'fall'. It **jarred** and **settled**. Always examine how a writer uses verbs in a passage and be able to comment on their effect.

✿ Note the point of view of the narrative. Ask yourself if it is written in the first person (I, we) or the third person (he, she, they). The use of the first person makes the narrative more immediate to the reader and allows them to view characters and events from the narrator's **subjective** perspective. The use of the third person or the 'omniscient' (all-knowing) viewpoint allows for greater insight into the minds and thoughts of other characters and creates a more objective viewpoint.

✿ Narratives are usually written in the past tense, but the present tense is also used effectively in some stories. Examine the tense in the passage you are given in the exam and note if the writer suddenly changes tense. This usually indicates that something important or noteworthy is happening.

✿ Note how the writer carefully chooses **adjectives** and **adverbs**. These must be used **judiciously** to bring the story alive, accurately **portray** the action and provide description and information for the reader.

✿ Pay particular attention to how the writer uses images which appeal to the senses. We have seen an example of this in the extract from *To Kill a Mockingbird*, but every narrative will provide plenty of examples of such images.

✿ It is important to recognise and be able to comment on any use of **simile**, **metaphor** or symbol used in the text. Be also on the lookout for **personification**, which can create dramatic effects.

✿ Look carefully at the details in descriptions. Ask yourself why the writer is describing someone or something in such detail. Pay attention to specific words and ask yourself why they have been selected by the writer.

✿ Examine how the writer varies sentence structure. Check the paragraphs to get a sense of how many sentences are short or **abrupt**, how many are long and complex and how many are questions or exclamations. Good writers always vary their sentence structure.

## You may be specifically asked to:

Comment on characters. Be able to form impressions about the characters, their relationships and their motives from reading what is said about them, what they say about themselves or others and what they do. Pay special attention to any dialogue.

Comment on setting. You might be asked how the setting affects the passage given in the unseen extract or how it affects the novel or short stories you have prepared.

Comment on theme. From your reading of the narrative, what main idea or ideas are driving the plot? Be prepared to give evidence to support your views.

Comment on atmosphere and how it is created. This is a style question.

Comment on a key moment. This could be any event leading up to the climax or it could be the actual climax of the narrative.

Comment on the opening or the closing sections in studied fiction. You will be expected to have opinions about these sections or chapters and be able to discuss the effect they had on you as a reader.

Imagine that you are one of the characters and write a diary entry or a letter. You might be asked to recount events from the point of view of a particular character.

## Step-by-Step Approach: Unseen Fiction

### Step One

✳ Read the number of questions you are required to answer on the unseen fiction extract. You are usually given three questions from which you choose two. Each part of the question will be worth 15 marks. However, this can change, so read the instructions carefully.

✳ Read the introduction to the extract carefully. This will give you a general idea of the setting.

✳ Now read the questions very carefully. Highlight/underline the important words in each question and make sure that you do not leave out any part of the questions.

### Step Two

✳ Select the questions which you are going to answer.

✳ Beginning with the first question, read the extract again marking any words or phrases that you think will be useful as support for your response. Keep asking yourself questions. For example, if you are asked what impression you got of a person or a relationship, ask yourself why you got that impression, what words created it, why did the writer pick certain words etc. This will help to give your response a sharp focus.

### Step Three

✳ Write your answer. Answers need not be very long but they must be relevant to the question asked. If you find yourself telling the story to the reader, **stop**! You are probably moving away from the question. Check again to see what the question asked you to do. Now continue your answer, keeping an eye on exactly what you have been asked.

Make sure that you support your points with quotation from or reference to the extract/passage. Choose your quotations carefully. You may only need to use a few words or a short phrase to illustrate your point.

If you are asked for your opinion or to form an impression, make sure that you respond personally when answering and that you explain your reasons for your opinion or impression.

## Putting It Into Practice

Read the following edited extract from the novel *Slam* by award-winning writer Nick Hornby and then answer the questions that follow.

[**Background to the extract:** In this edited extract, from the opening of the book, we are introduced to Sam, a skateboard loving teenager. Sam tells us about himself in his own words. He reveals that he holds imaginary conversations with his skateboarding hero, Tony Hawk.]

*So things were ticking along quite nicely. In fact, I'd say that good stuff had been happening pretty solidly for about six months.*

*   *For example: Mrs Gillett, my art and design teacher took me to one side after a lesson and asked whether I'd thought of doing art at college.*
*   *For example: I'd learned two new skating tricks, suddenly, after weeks of making an idiot of myself in public. (I'm guessing that not all of you are skaters, so I should say something straight away, just so that there are no terrible misunderstandings. Skating = skateboarding.)*

*All that and I'd met Alicia too.*

*If you knew something about me, you might actually care about some of those things. But then, looking at what I just wrote, you know quite a lot already, or at least you could have guessed a lot of it. You could have guessed that I skate, and you could have guessed that my best subject at school was art and design, unless you thought I might be the sort of person who's always being taken to one side and told to apply for college by all the teachers in every subject. You know, and the teachers actually fight over me. 'No, Sam! Forget art! Do physics!' 'Forget physics! It would be a tragedy for the human race if you gave up French!' And then they all start punching each other.*

*Yeah, well. That sort of thing really, really doesn't happen to me. I can promise you, I have never ever caused a fight between teachers.*

*If I'm going to tell this story properly, without trying to hide anything, then there's something I should own up to, because it's important. Here's the thing. I know it sounds stupid, and I'm not this sort of person usually, honest. I mean, I don't believe in, you know, ghosts or reincarnation or any weird stuff at all. Anyway. I'll just say it and you can think what you want.*

*I talk to Tony Hawk, and Tony Hawk talks back.*

*Some of you probably won't have heard of Tony Hawk. Well, I'll tell you, but I'll have to say that you should know already. Not knowing Tony Hawk is like not knowing Robbie Williams, or maybe even Tony Blair. It's worse than that, if you think about it, because there are loads of politicians and loads of singers. But there is only one skater, really, and his name's Tony Hawk.*

*Well, there is not only one. But he's definitely the Big One. He's the J.K. Rowling of skaters, the Big Mac, the iPod, the Xbox. The only excuse I'll accept for not knowing Tony Hawk is that you're not interested in skating.*

*When I got into skating, my mum bought me a Tony Hawk poster off the Internet. It's the coolest present I've ever had, and it wasn't even the most expensive. And it went straight up onto my bedroom wall, and I just got into the habit of telling it things. At first I only told Tony about skating – I would talk about the problems I was having or the tricks I'd pulled off. I pretty much ran to my room to tell him about the first rock 'n' roll\* I'd managed, because I knew it would mean much more to a picture of Tony Hawk than it would to a real-life Mum. I'm not dissing\* my mum, but she hasn't got a clue, really. So when I told her about things like that, she'd try to look all enthusiastic, but there was nothing really going on in her eyes. She was all, 'Oh, that's great'. But if I'd asked her what a rock 'n' roll was, she wouldn't have been able to tell me. So what was the point? Tony knew, though. Maybe that was why my mum bought me the poster, so that I'd have someone else to talk to.*

**Glossary**
**rock 'n' roll:** skateboarding term     **dissing:** disrespecting

## QUESTION ONE                                                              (30)

Answer **two** of the following questions. Each question is worth 15 marks.

(1) From your reading of the passage, **what do you learn about the character of Sam? Support** your answer with reference to the passage.

(2) Nick Hornby, the author of *Slam*, has described the novel as being 'about and hopefully **for teenagers'.** From what you have read of this extract, **do you think he has achieved his aim?**

(3) In the passage Sam tells us that he sometimes holds imaginary conversations with his skateboarding hero, Tony Hawk. **Based on information from the extract,** write out the **conversation** that might take place **between Sam and Tony.**

**Sample Answer to Question One: Parts (1) and (3)**

**Step 1:** Underline/highlight key tasks in each part of the question.
**Step 2:** Select the parts of the question you are going to answer. The sample answers on pages 226 and 227 deal with parts 1 and 3.

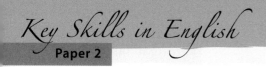

Read the passage and highlight/underline anything which you can use to support your points. This has been done in red for part (1). Look at the red highlighted words in the passage. Now jot down a few words to describe the character of Sam. Remember that you have been asked what you 'learnt' about Sam – keep that as the central focus. Don't just summarise the passage.

*Positive attitude; upbeat about his life, loves skating; honest about his skills; artistic and imaginative.*

**Sample answer to part (1):**

> *From reading this passage, I learnt quite a few things about Sam.*
>
> *It is obvious from the opening that he is a very positive, upbeat kind of person. He says that 'things were ticking along quite nicely' in his life and that 'good stuff had been happening pretty solidly for about six months.' He is also very pleased that he has learned some 'new skateboarding tricks' and that he is beginning a relationship with a girl called Alicia. There is no doubt that he loves skating and takes great pleasure and pride in this activity. He actually cannot understand how anybody would not have heard about Tony Hawk, as he is such an important influence in Sam's life: 'The only excuse I'll accept for not knowing Tony Hawk is that you're not interested in skating'. I also learnt that Sam has a positive, respectful relationship with his mother, although she doesn't have 'a clue' about his beloved hobby.*
>
> *Sam is an honest person. He is modest about his skills and doesn't mind admitting that he spent weeks 'making an idiot' of himself in public, while trying to learn 'new skating tricks'. He also admits to having 'problems', which he discusses with Tony Hawk. His honesty is further evident in the fact that he wants to 'tell this story properly, without trying to hide anything', and owns up to his habit of talking to a poster. These details showed me his open, truthful nature.*
>
> *I also learnt from the passage that Sam is a very artistic and imaginative kind of person. This is evident from the fact that his art teacher thinks that he should study art at college and he believes that his 'best subject at school was art and design'. I liked his sense of humour when he imagined all the teachers having a 'fight' about his talents. This artistic, imaginative quality makes him place great value on a poster, which he treasures above any other present he has ever received and with which he has conversations.*
>
> *I learnt quite a lot about Sam from reading this passage and found him a very appealing, unusual kind of person.*

**Sample answer to part (3):**

**N.B.** Before you write the imaginary conversation, underline/highlight in the passage the essential information we are given about Tony Hawk and about Sam's relationship with him. This has been done in green on pages 224-225. Remember that you must use 'information from the extract'.

| | |
|---|---|
| Sam: | Tony! Tony! Wake up man! I did it at last! |
| Tony: | Ah Sam, you know this is my nap time. I've asked you before not to interrupt nap time. What's the big deal this time? |
| Sam: | I did it! I got my first rock 'n' roll - perfect at last! |
| Tony: | So what? It's about time you got that right after making such an idiot of yourself for the last few weeks. It only took me one week to perfect that trick when I was your age. |
| Sam: | Yeah, well. I'm not you, am I? No posters of me yet on the internet but there will be one day Tony. Our names will be up there together as the all-time greats of the skating world. You and me Tony, just imagine it. |
| Tony: | It's a bit hard for me to imagine anything when I'm only half-awake. |
| Sam: | Sorry Tony. I just thought ... just thought you'd be ... really interested. I forgot about your nap time. I'll go now if you like. |
| Tony: | Sit down Sam. Of course I'm interested. Tell me again what happened and how it came right. |
| Sam: | Well, the usual crowd were there, making a laugh out of me and calling me a 'loser'. They told me that I looked like a clown who had slipped on a banana skin. One of the Smith boys sang out: 'Look at the gawk, who thinks he's Hawk' and the others joined in. Something about the jeering, and Alicia's face, made me determined and I concentrated on getting it right. Just once! |
| Tony: | Good man Sam. The whole trick really is to relax and focus your mind on your balance, not on what those mockers are saying. They wouldn't know a skate-board from a banana skin anyway. |
| Sam: | I dragged the board up to the top of the roll, just like you told me to, kept my head at the right angle and pushed off for the millionth time. I couldn't believe it! I stayed on and made the right swing and turn. It just worked. I did it at last. I can't believe it! |
| Tony: | Did you try to do another? |
| Sam: | No way! The smile on Alicia's face stretched from ear-to-ear and the lads were just dumbfounded. There was no way I was going to show-off and probably mess up again. You know me Tony. I like to wallow in the glory and satisfaction for a while. |
| Tony: | Well, you've had your moment in the sun. So take my advice. Do your practice in the evening, around tea-time, when the others are not around. Keep getting that move right every time and don't give up if you land on your behind. Practice is the key, but you don't need an audience. |
| Sam: | Not even Alicia? |
| Tony: | Especially not Alicia. Girls can be distracting. It's bad enough that your art teacher is trying to move you away from becoming the next Tony Hawk, without the distraction of the lovely Alicia. |
| Sam: | Hmmm! I'll think about that one Tony. |
| Tony: | There's nothing to think about. Remember what I said. Focus. Focus. Focus. |
| Sam: | Cool down! I get it. I'd better get down to tea, Mum's been calling for ages. |

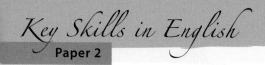

You would not need to write at quite this length in the exam. If pressed for time, the last six comments could be omitted. Remember that you need to use the information in the passage as the basis of the conversation. Look again at the words and phrases marked in green and see if you can spot how they have been used to inspire the dialogue in this answer.

 **OVER TO YOU**

**Read the following extract, adapted from the short story *No Place Like* by Gene Kemp and answer the questions which follow.**

*Background to the extract: In this extract, Pete, an accident-prone 16 year old, discovers that he has forgotten toast which he placed under the grill.*

I must have fallen asleep for I came to suddenly woken by the sound not of the universe but loud banging and roaring going on somewhere. I heaved myself off the bed in time to see Dad filling the doorway. Speaking.

'I come home early,' he was saying in a voice loud even for him, 'having spent my lunch-time beavering away on your behalf ...'

'You needn't have bothered ...' I began and then sniffed the air.

'Dad, what's that terrible smell?'

My father did a dance up and down in the doorway. For a big man he's light on his feet.

'Aha, so you noticed, did you? You're quick, I'll say that for you. In fact you amaze me. I never fail to be amazed at you through life, but today you have surpassed even yourself "What's that smell?" you ask, standing there like a great goop. That smell, my boy, is the smell of the house burning.'

'The house burning?'

'You heard me. That's what I said. And you understood did you? Clever boy.'

I managed to peer past him to a blue and smoke-filled landing. A strong pong of grilled grill was floating up the stairs.

'Hadn't we better do something?' I tried to push past him.

'Don't worry,' he said soothingly. 'It's all under control. But only because,' his voice started to get louder until it beat into my skull like hammer blows, 'I arrived home early full of peace and goodwill towards men, to find what? What indeed?' he bellowed, lowering his face close to mine. 'You might well ask. Half a dozen people crowding round the front door, its bell out of action, telephone engineers trampling all over the garden because the line's been reported out of order, and a fire engine screeching to a halt outside the house. Didn't you even hear that?'

I shook my head.

'The kitchen full of smoke and about to burst into flames!'

I tried to speak and couldn't.

'But don't worry about it. Don't give it a thought. It was just someone who shall be nameless, had left the grill on with toast under it, or what had been toast in earlier times ...'

Answer **two** of the following questions. Each question is worth **15 marks**.

**(1)** What impression of Pete's father do you get from reading this extract. Support your answer with reference to the extract. (15)

**(2)** Do you think the author meant this to be a serious or a funny incident? Explain your response. (15)

**(3)** Imagine that you are Pete. Write a diary entry, based on the above incident. (15)

## (b) Question Two: Studied Fiction
### KEY SKILLS

The questions in this section will allow you to show your knowledge of and response to fiction you have already studied for your Junior Certificate.

There are usually two questions to choose from. One of the questions may be divided into two parts, (a) and (b), while the other may be worth the full 30 marks. Read questions carefully, as this format could change.

Revise the **KEY SKILLS** on pages 217-223.

Make sure that you can discuss the characters, setting, plot, themes and style of your chosen text. Be able to demonstrate the part played by each of these elements in the narrative.

## Step by Step Approach
### Step One
◉ Read both questions carefully, highlighting/underlining exact task or tasks. Make sure that you do not forget any part of any question. Highlight/underline key words.
◉ Select the question you wish to answer.

### Step Two
◉ Plan your answer. Brainstorm relevant points for each part of the question. Think of suitable quotations to support these points.
◉ Organise your points into a logical order. Make sure that you are not repeating yourself if there are parts (a) and (b) to the question. Each question will require a different response.

### Step Three
◉ Write your answer. Name the novel/short story and the author at the beginning of your response.
◉ Briefly introduce your response using the wording of the question.
◉ Follow the **P**oint, **Q**uotation, **E**xplanation: PQE method. Make one point per paragraph.
◉ Briefly conclude your response. Refer to the wording of the question in your conclusion.

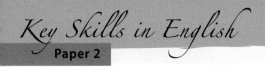

## Putting It Into Practice

**N.B.** When answering Question Two, you **cannot** base your answer on the extract provided in Question One (Unseen Fiction). You must give the title of the text you choose and the name of the author.

Question Two:

Answer either 1 OR 2:

**(1)** Select a novel or short story you have studied which has **an interesting theme**.

    (i) **Outline the theme** of the text you have chosen. (15)

    (ii) As the theme develops **why does it interest you?** (15)
        **Support** your answer with reference to your chosen novel or short story.

OR

**(2)** From a novel OR short story you have studied, **choose a character who learns something important about themselves or others. Discuss** what the **character learns,** supporting your answer with reference to the text. (30)

**Step 1:** Read each question carefully, highlighting/underlining the tasks in each. This has been done in the questions above.

Then decide which question you will answer.

**Note:** Sample answers to both (1) **and** (2) have been provided on pages 232-234, but in the Junior Cert exam, you must choose either (1) **OR** (2) to answer.

**Step 2:** Brainstorm relevant points. Make a short plan for your answer to both parts of the question. Think of relevant quotations or incidents to use as support.

In planning your answer, you may use a spider diagram, flow chart, a mind map or a Question & Answer type of plan. The type of question you have chosen to answer will suit some plans more than others.

  You can use two separate columns to jot down ideas if a question has two parts. This will help you to avoid repeating the same points in your answer.

  Answer each part of the question separately. You can see this method demonstrated on page 231.

Short story chosen: *The Majesty of the Law* by Frank O'Connor

**Note:** To fully grasp the points made in this sample answer, it is worth reading *The Majesty of the Law.*

**Short plan:**

| (a) Outline theme | (b) Why is it interesting? |
|---|---|
| A strange version of legal justice. | We are not told reason for Sergeant's visit |
| Sergeant drinking poitín, which is illegal | Sergeant doesn't seem to care about laws |
| Dan ready, tea and bread: 'a sure sign that he had been expecting a visitor' | Very friendly atmosphere, 'there was never a good job done in a hurry'. |
| Sergeant leaves, but then comes back to ask Dan about fine he owes. | Sergeant a bit embarrassed |
| Dan refuses to pay fine, explain why | Strange that Dan would prefer jail |
| Offers to go to prison, but allowed to choose time | Strange that Dan can choose |
| Motive becomes clear, wants to embarrass the other man. | 'unneighbourly document'– knows he'll get support |
| Neighbours support Dan, old man hides indoors. | The victim is ashamed! Has set law on 'one of his own', we only learn reason at the very end |

These ideas do not need to be fully written out. They can be jotted down quickly using a few words or abbreviations which you understand yourself. But it is important to make a plan!

**Step 3:** Write answer. This answer asks for an outline, so you will not be using the PQE method for part (a) of the question.

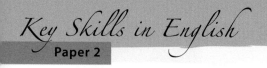

**1.** Select a novel or short story you have studied which has **an interesting theme**.

(i)  **Outline the theme** of the text you have chosen.                    (15)

---

**(i)** *A short story which I have read and which has an interesting theme is 'The Majesty of the Law'*
*by Frank O'Connor. The theme of legal justice develops in an unusual way in this story.*

*The theme is introduced when Dan Bride, who lives alone in a cottage, has a visit from a*
*sergeant. Dan has prepared whiskey, tea and bread to offer his guest, 'a sure sign that he had*
*been expecting a visitor'. The sergeant is supposed to uphold law and order but has no problem*
*in drinking the illegally-made whiskey, even going so far as to say that he does not agree with the*
*law which bans the practice.*

*Later, the sergeant asks Dan if he is willing to pay a fine which he owes. Dan refuses as he does*
*not want to give 'that fellow' the satisfaction. The sergeant then produces a warrant for his arrest.*
*This entire exchange takes place in a polite and respectful manner. The sergeant suggests that*
*others are willing to pay Dan's fine if he cannot afford to pay it himself. Rather than grasping*
*at the opportunity to escape imprisonment, Dan refers to the warrant as an 'unneighbourly*
*document' and chooses to go to prison.*

*It is not until the end of the story that we discover what offence Dan has been accused of: he*
*'had the grave misfortune to open the head of another old man', who had to be hospitalised.*
*There is no doubt that Dan wants to go to jail in order to embarrass his victim, not because it*
*is legally and morally just that he pays for his crime. He knows that his neighbours will support*
*him, which they do, and that the old man will be punished for seeking justice.*

*The story ends with the 'victim' having to scurry indoors to hide from the group of Dan's friends*
*who are openly shaking his hand and offering him support.*

---

**(ii)**  As the theme develops **why does it interest you?**                    (15)
    **Support** your answer with reference to your chosen novel or short story.

You can use the P-Q-E technique for this answer.

---

*This theme developed in a way which held my interest right up to the final sentence. The fact that I did*
*not know the reason for the sergeant's visit but guessed from the title that it had something to do with*
*the law made me want to read on.*

*It came as a bit of a shock to discover that a man suffering from arthritis and as old as Dan Bride*
*could be capable of splitting open the head of another old man in the course of a row.* **[Point]** *This*
*was not a 'grave misfortune', it was an assault which left the victim 'hospitalised'. I found it very*
*interesting to observe the attitude of the sergeant. I would have expected a more abrupt and official*
*manner, not bread and tea and plenty of small talk!* **[Quote and explanation]**

*There is also something very interesting in the fact that Dan is allowed to choose the day he will*
*go to jail.* **[Point]** *That is not usual for somebody who has committed a serious, violent crime. The*
*fact that the sergeant is treating Dan so politely is nothing short of astonishing. He even tells Dan*

*that he will ensure that he is made 'as comfortable as if you were at home' while he is in prison. This sergeant, who drinks illegally-made alcohol with Dan, certainly has an extraordinary attitude to law and order! I began to wonder about the majesty of the law, which seems to condone violence.* **[Quote and explanation]**

*Of most interest, however, is the reaction of Dan's neighbours.* **[Point]** *Not only are they willing to pay his fine but they shake his hand before he is taken away. This sympathy shows an interesting attitude to the law and how the people view justice. Although I sympathised with Dan - he was not a wealthy man and had been cheated by the other individual - I still found it interesting that the community would condone his violent behaviour. In the end, the old man who was assaulted is left feeling ashamed that he set the law on 'one of his own'.* **[Quote and explanation]**

*I found it very interesting that Dan's assault on a man who cheated him was seen as a lesser crime than that committed by his victim. The whole story questions the notion of what constitutes legal, impartial justice.*

2. From a novel OR short story you have studied, choose a character who learns something important about themselves or others. Discuss what the character learns, supporting your answer with reference to the text.

**Step 1:** Read the question carefully, highlighting/underlining the tasks.

**Step 2:** Brainstorm relevant points. Make a short plan for your answer. Think of relevant quotations or incidents to use as support.

**Novel chosen:** *To Kill a Mocking Bird* by Harper Lee

## Question & Answer Plan

Which character do I feel changes and learns? *Scout*

How does she change?

*Begins by being very innocent and naive.*

*Learns from Calpurnia and from Atticus, refer to incident with Walter Cunningham, acceptance of difference*

*Learns from advice Atticus gives her, self-control and meaning of courage*

*Learns about racism and prejudice in Maycomb, refer to trial scene and Boo Radley.*

**Step 3:** Write answer. Follow PQE technique.

*The novel which I have studied is 'To Kill a Mockingbird' by Harper Lee. Scout Finch, who is the narrator and one of the main characters, undergoes a journey of discovery about herself and her society in the course of the plot. At the start of the novel, Scout is only six years of age and has a naive and childish view of life. However, throughout the next three years of her life, she learns many important lessons which help her to grow up and become more mature.*

*One of these lessons is that people should be accepted for who they are and not treated with disrespect because they do things differently.* **[Point]** *Calpurnia, the family housekeeper, insists on Scout treating her schoolmate Walter Cunningham with respect, even when he eats differently to the Finch family. She tells Scout crossly that she 'aint called on to contradict 'em ... if he wants to eat*

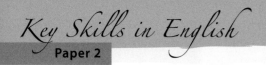

up the table-cloth, you let him, you hear?'. Calpurnia will not tolerate Scout acting as if she were 'high and mighty' and accuses her of disgracing the family by commenting on Walter's request to pour molasses on his vegetables. This is an important lesson for Scout and one from which she learns. **[Quote and explanation]**

   Atticus, Scout's father,  also teaches Scout important lessons which bring about a change in her outlook on life and which make her change and grow up. **[Point]** He encourages her to remain calm in heated situations and to avoid fighting as a means of venting her anger.  He encourages her to try to see things from the point of view of others, telling her that she will 'never really understand a person' until she climbs 'into his skin' and 'walks around in it'. Although Scout has many problems heeding the advice of her father, she does learn these lessons and matures as the story progresses. **[Quote and explanation]**

   One of the most important lessons which Scout learns is that her society has the 'disease' of prejudice. **[Point]**  Scout learns that this prejudice  is 'as much Maycomb as missionary teas' and comes to realise  'the simple hell people give other people.'  She is not as insightful as her brother Jem, who is older than her, during the trial of Tom Robinson. She naively believes that Tom must have been treated fairly in court. However, we see her growing maturity in the way that she understands that  Boo Radley, a recluse who lives opposite her, is not the monster that local ignorance and superstition have made him out to be. She learns that it would be 'sort of like shootin' a mockingbird' not to allow Boo the right to his privacy, although the local people would treat him like a hero for saving the lives of herself and Jem. **[Quote and explanation]**

   Throughout the novel, Scout learns many important lessons that help her to become more of a 'lady' and to behave with true courage and dignity. She still has a long way to go though and I found it very amusing when she remarked, at the end,  that there wasn't much left for herself and Jem to learn,' except, possibly, algebra'.

## Over to You

**Answer either 1 OR 2:**

1. From the short stories and novels you have studied, choose either a character you like OR a character you dislike. Identify one or more incidents from the text that particularly influenced your feelings towards this character and explain why your chosen incident(s) influenced you to either like or dislike him or her.

### OR

2. Write the text of a talk that you would give to your class in which you explore the relevance of a novel or a short story that you have studied to the lives of young people today. Support your answer with detailed reference to your studied text.

# (c) Advice

Prepare your novel or short stories well in advance. Pay particular attention to key chapters or sections of the narratives. This will put you in a strong position to answer well in the exam.

Practise writing answers following the P-Q-E method where suitable. At first, your answers may be quite short as you attempt to get them written within the time limit. However, as you improve with practice, you will find that you can think, plan and write quickly.

Aim to develop your answers a little more each time you write an answer. Eventually, you will find that you can write a detailed and developed response.

Keep strictly within the time limits. You have less than half an hour to answer the Studied Fiction section. If you find that you simply cannot write at the same length as the samples provided in this section, shorten your quotes and explanation. But you must make at least three valid points and offer some textual support and explanation.

## CHECKLIST

Use the following checklist to ensure that you have complied with the demands of the marking scheme:

- Have I **practised writing** both unseen and studied questions on fiction? ❏
- Have I **prepared my texts** carefully following the guidelines for analysing fiction? ❏
- Have I **read the questions** very carefully and ensured that I am addressing all parts of the questions? ❏
- Have I **underlined/highlighted** the key words in all questions before choosing a question to answer? ❏
- Have I made a short plan, ensuring that I am addressing the question? ❏
- Have I made **relevant, supported** points? ❏
- Have I offered some **explanation** of my points? ❏
- Have I made some **personal comments** in the course of my answer? ❏
- Have I **used paragraphs** properly, developing one point in each paragraph? ❏
- Have I checked my **spelling, punctuation and grammar**? ❏

If you can tick each of these boxes, you will do very well in the Fiction Section of Paper Two.

# Glossary

**abrupt:** curt, brief

**adjectives:** words that describe nouns, eg a pink hat, a beautiful day

**adverbs:** words that describe verbs, he ran quickly, she talked ceaselessly

**condone:** approve, accept with reluctance

**convey:** make known

**evident:** easily seen, obvious

**haughty:** arrogant, acting in a superior way

**impartial:** neutral, unbiased

**implicit:** understood although not directly stated

**insight:** being able to understand something in a deeper way

**interpret:** understand and explain the meaning of

**judiciously:** showing good judgement

**lynch mob:** a group of people determined to hang someone

**metaphor:** an image which compares two things without using 'like' or 'as'

**modest:** free from vanity or ego, unassuming

**molasses:** a thick brown syrup made from raw sugar

**objective:** not influenced by personal opinions or bias

**personification:** giving personality traits to an object

**portray:** show, depict

**prejudice:** bias, taking sides

**recluse:** someone who withdraws from the world and lives in isolation from others

**reverberating:** echoing

**simile:** an image which compares two things using 'like' or 'as'

**subjective:** influenced by personal feelings or opinions

**tormentor:** a person who torments/tortures another

# Common Mistakes

## (a) Commonly Confused Words

Read the meaning and example of the word in the Word 1 column and then read the meaning and example of the word in the Word 2 column.

| Word 1 | Meaning and example | Word 2 | Meaning and example |
|---|---|---|---|
| accept | to agree, to receive: I accept your offer. | except | not including: Everybody is going except John. |
| advice | suggestions about what to do (noun): Take my advice. | advise | to recommend a course of action (verb): I advise you to work hard. |
| affect | to change or make a difference to something: If it rains, it will affect the match. | effect | a result; to bring about a result (in this case, noun): Smoking has a bad effect on your health. |
| aisle | a passage between rows of seats: The bride walked up the aisle. | isle | an island: I like the poem 'The Lake Isle of Innisfree'. |
| all together | all in one place, all at once: The visitors arrived all together. | altogether | completely, in total: He bought three books altogether. |
| aloud | out loud: I read my essay aloud in class. | allowed | permitted: You are not allowed to go to the party. |
| altar | a sacred table in a church: They brought the gifts to the altar. | alter | to change: Please do not alter the seating arrangements. |
| bare | naked, to uncover: It is not a good idea to bare your skin to the rays of the sun without protection. | bear | 1. (verb) to put up with: I cannot bear the pain. 2. (noun) an animal: The bear came out of the forest. |
| born | having started life: The baby was born yesterday. | borne | carried or endured (suffer patiently): The illness was borne courageously. |
| bough | a branch of a tree: When the bough breaks the cradle will fall. | bow | 1. to bend the head (verb): People bow to the king. 2. a decorative ribbon (noun): The girl had her hair tied back with a bow. |

**237**

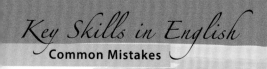

*Key Skills in English*
**Common Mistakes**

| Word 1 | Meaning and example | Word 2 | Meaning and example |
|---|---|---|---|
| brake | 1. a pedal for stopping a vehicle (noun): He hit the brakes. 2. to stop a vehicle (verb): She had to brake hard to avoid an accident. | break | 1. to separate into pieces (verb): Sticks and stones may break my bones. 2. a pause (noun): I need a break from school. |
| cereal | a breakfast food made from grains: I eat a bowl of cereal every morning. | serial | Story that happens in regular instalments: My mum hates missing any episode from her favourite serial on TV. |
| chord | a group of musical notes: Mike taught me a new chord on the guitar. | cord | a piece of string: The parcel was tied with cord. |
| coarse | rough, rude: The drunk man spoke in a coarse manner to the police. | course | 1. a direction: Follow the course of the river. 2. a series of lessons: We are beginning a new course in maths. |
| council | a group of people who manage or advise: Amy is on the student council. | counsel | advice (noun), to advise (verb): I was given good counsel regarding my choice of subjects. |
| curb | to keep something under control: You need to curb the money spent on sweets. | kerb | the stone edge of a pavement: The little boy tripped over the kerb. |
| currant | a dried grape: I love eating a currant bun. | current | happening now; a flow of water, air or electricity: He swam with the current. |
| desert | 1. a waterless, empty area (noun), 2. to abandon someone (verb): I'd hate to be deserted in a desert. | dessert | the sweet course of a meal: The meal finished with a delicious dessert. |
| draught | a flow of air: There is a cold draught from under that door. | draft | an unfinished version of a piece of writing: You need to draft your essay a few times. |
| dual | having two parts: There is a new dual carriageway in my area. | duel | a fight or contest between two people: The men fought a duel to the death. |

| Word 1 | Meaning and example | Word 2 | Meaning and example |
|---|---|---|---|
| ensure | to make certain that something will happen: Please ensure that the room is left tidy. | insure | to arrange compensation against a risk: John insured his life for a large sum of money. It is necessary to insure your house against flood damage. |
| exercise | physical activity, to do physical activity: Everybody needs to exercise to maintain good health. | exorcise | to drive out an evil spirit: Not many priests are called on to exorcise evil spirits. |
| loose | wobbly or unstable (noun): I have a loose tooth. | lose | to be unable to find (verb): Did you lose your wallet? |
| our | belonging to us: This is our house. | are | from the verb 'to be': We are good friends. |
| pedal | 1. a foot-operated lever (noun): Her leg was too short to reach the pedal. 2. to move a bike or car (verb): I like to pedal through the autumn leaves on my bike. | peddle | to sell goods: Many goods can be peddled in garage sales. |
| pour | to flow or cause to flow (verb): Pour some milk into the cat's dish. | pore | 1. to study something closely (verb): Darren had to pore over the details of his contract carefully. 2. a tiny opening (noun): The pores on my nose are blocked. |
| practice | 1. repeated exercise of a skill (noun): Practice makes perfect. 2. Exercise of a profession: Dr. Murphy has a large dental practice. | practise | to do something regularly to gain skill (verb): I am going to practise playing the piano every day because my music exams are next week. |
| principal | most important, the head of a school: Mr. Jones was appointed as school principal. | principle | a rule or belief: It is important to follow your principles in life. |
| quiet | making little or no noise: Be quiet! | quite | absolutely: are you quite sure about that? |
| sight | the ability to see: I could hardly believe the sight of my own eyes! | site | a location: That is a good site to build your house. |

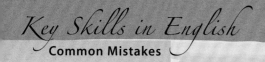
| Word 1 | Meaning and example | Word 2 | Meaning and example |
| --- | --- | --- | --- |
| stationary | not moving: The van was stationary outside the shop. | stationery | writing materials: I must buy more stationery because I have letters to write. |
| storey | a level of a building: The house is three storeys high. | story | a tale or account: Children love to hear a story. |
| threw | past tense of the verb 'to throw': he threw the stone at the pig. | through | a preposition meaning in one side and out the other: The sun shone through the window. |

**Correct the mistakes in the following sentences:**

1. The boy kicked a ball threw the bedroom window.
2. If you take my advise, you will practice your spelling every day.
3. We are not aloud to go out tonight.
4. Did you loose your wallet?
5. The traffic accident had a terrible affect on the children.
6. Everyone is invited to the party accept Kevin, who is not aloud to come.
7. Who through that stone?
8. We had a tasty desert after the main meal.
9. What can we do about that draft from the back porch?
10. The principle of our school is a man of principal.

## (b) More Commonly Confused Words

**1. There, Their** and **They're**
**There, Their** and **They're** are homophones (words that are spelt differently but pronounced the same).

(a) **There** always refers to a place or an action.

*Does anyone live **there**? **There** will be a day off tomorrow. Put it over **there**.*

(b) **Their** shows belonging or possession.

*They put **their** books in their lockers. **Their** house is in the city. I think they spend **their** money wisely.*

(c) **They're** is a contraction of the words 'they' and 'are'.

*They're on their way to the party. I will tell you if they're coming. They're almost there now.*

TIP: Replace the word **there** with either 'here' or 'was it/is it/will it'.
    Replace the word **their** with 'our'.
    Replace the word **they're** with 'they are'.
If the sentence still makes sense, you've got it right.

(a) *I will see you **there**.*    *I will see you **here**.* (It makes sense so you've got it right!)

    ***There** will be a day*    ***Will** it be a day off tomorrow?* (It makes sense so you've got it right!)
    *off tomorrow.*

(b) ***Their** marks are good.*    ***Our** marks are good.* (It makes sense so you've got it right!)

(c) ***They're** going away.*    ***They are** going away.* (It makes sense so you've got it right!)

**2. Your and You're**
(a) **Your** is a possessive adjective. It is used to describe something as belonging to you. It is usually followed by a noun. For example:
    *Is this **your** bag?*
    ***Your** party really was a great success.*
    *Did **your** exams go well?*

(b) **You're** is the contraction of two words 'you' and ' are'. It is often followed by a verb ending in 'ing'. For example:
    ***You're** looking very well today.*
    ***You're** going to be glad that you did your revision for the test.*
    *I will go if **you're** going too.*

**3. Its and It's**
**Its** and **it's** are often incorrectly used.

(a) **Its** shows possession, e.g. *The dog buried **its** bone in the garden.*

(b) **It's** is a contraction of the words 'it is' or 'it has', e.g. *It's all his fault.*

**Re-write the sentences correctly.**
1. Tracy and her sister are not allowed to have there friends visit they're house on weekdays.
2. There my friends over their.
3. Your not supposed to put those books their.
4. Its not fair to the rest of the team if your allowed to skip football practice.
5. Their is great excitement in Alan's house; its his graduation day.
6. The cat got it's paws wet in the garden pond.
7. You're dog is burying a bone in they're garden.
8. Its a pity you and you're friends don't take part in sports.
9. When your supposed to be working, you're friends are not supposed to ring your mobile.
10. Their not going for a picnic because its raining heavily.

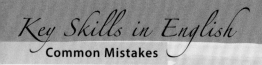
**4. Where** and **Wear**

**(a)** The word **where** is used when asking a question about a location.

*Where are you going?*

*Where is the cash kept?*

*Where did you stay when you went away?*

**(b) Wear** has a couple of meanings.

It can refer to an article of clothing that a person is 'wearing'.

*I wouldn't wear that to a dog-fight!*

*What will you wear today?*

*Wear something special today.*

**Wear** can also mean to make tired or exhausted.

*She would wear you out!*

*The wear and tear of life can be seen in the old man's face.*

**5. We're** and **Were**

**(a)** The word **we're** is a contraction of the two words 'we' and 'are'.

*We are coming tomorrow.* → *We're coming tomorrow.*

*We are playing together.* → *We're playing together.*

*We are best friends.* → *We're best friends.*

**(b) Were** refers to something that happened in the past.

*Where were you going?*

*Were you lost?*

*We were on the beach when it started to rain.*

**6. To, Too, Two**

**(a) To** can be used in the following ways:

(i) A preposition, in which case it always goes before a noun, e.g. *I am going to school;*
*She is on her way to the house.*

(ii) An infinitive, in which case it always goes before a verb, e.g. *I am going to work during
the summer holidays from school; He thought he was going to have the day off.*

**(b) Too** can be used in the following ways:

(i) Another word for 'also', e.g. *Mark would like to come to the party too. Jane worked in
the supermarket too.*

(ii) Another word for 'excessively', e.g. *I am too tired to go for a walk. This soup is too salty.*

**(c) Two** is the number that follows one. It has no other meaning.

**7. Of and Off**

(a) The words **of** and **off** are commonly confused.

> The word **of** has several uses, but it is usually a preposition which expresses a link between a part **of** something and the whole, e.g. *The sleeve of his coat is torn; I put it in the back of the car.*

> It is often used to point out what something is made of or what it contains, e.g. *I ate a bag of crisps; She loves her cup of tea.*

TIP: You will know that you should only use one f if the f sounds like a v.

(b) **Off** is frequently used as an adverb or a preposition.

> As an adverb, it is used usually to describe a state of finishing something:
> *Turn off the light.*

> As a preposition, it is used to show the physical separation or distance from two positions: *Take those things off the table; The shop is just off the main street.*

TIP: You will know that you should use **off** if the f sounds like an f.

> **Re-write each of these sentences correctly:**
> 1. Wear is you're school uniform?
> 2. Too of the team could not attend the meeting because they where sick.
> 3. Take of your coat when you come into the house.
> 4. Do you we're warm clothes in the winter?
> 5. Its two late too apply for the summer job.
> 6. Your going to be very happy when you get the day of school.
> 7. I love a cup off tea with my too biscuits.
> 8. I forgot were I put my books.
> 9. Jack would like to go too the disco to.
> 10. My mother doesn't think those shoes will where well.

**8. Either and Neither**

Both words can be used as pronouns, conjunctions and adjectives; however, the use of **either** is positive, while **neither** is negative.

(a) As an adjective:

> **Either** indicates one or the other, or both. For example:
> *You may choose either the white or the pink dress.* = You may choose the white or the pink dress – not both.
> *There were trees growing on either side of the river.* = There were trees growing on both sides of the river.

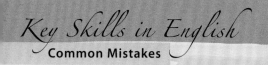

**Neither** indicates not one or the other; none of the two. For example:
*Neither of the children was willing to share the toys.* = None of the children was willing to share the toys.

(b) As a pronoun:

Either indicates one or the other. For example:
*Both planes are flying to London, you can get on either.* = Both planes are flying to London, you can get on one or the other.

**Neither** indicates **not** one or the other. For example:
*Both of the boys were shocked, but neither let it be seen.* = Both of the boys were shocked, but not one nor the other let it be seen.

(c) As a conjunction:

Either is used with or to imply a choice of alternatives. For example:
*You can either come with me to the shops or stay at home and study.* = You can do one of two things: come with me to the shops or stay at home and study.

**Neither** is used with **nor** to make both parts of a statement negative. For example:
*I can neither sleep nor eat.* = I cannot sleep or eat.

TIP: Remember this sentence: Either goes with or, **neither** goes with **nor.**

**9.** Double negatives

You should avoid using two negatives in a sentence, e.g. *I never do nothing right.*
This should be: *I never do anything right.*

*We aren't going nowhere.*
This should be: *We are going nowhere* or *We aren't going anywhere.*

*I didn't do nothing.*
This should be: *I didn't do anything* or *I did nothing.*

Check your sentences to make sure that you only use one negative.

**10. Would, Should and Could**

**Would, should** and **could** are auxiliary verbs. This means that they help or assist main verbs. For example, in the sentence, *I would like to go to the beach* 'like' is the main verb assisted by **would.**

These three words are the past tenses of will (**would**), shall (**should**) and can (**could**).

Be very careful to use the past tense correctly: **would** have…**should** have… **could** have.
(Do not fall into the trap of using 'of' with these verbs instead of 'have'. It is never right to use 'of' with these verbs.)

**11. Can and May**
The key difference between **can** and **may** is that **can** is about ability and **may** is about permission.

**(a) Can** has two uses:

(i) It refers to ability. For example:
*I can play the guitar.*
*Can you come to the city with me today?*

(ii) To ask or give permission informally. For example:
*Can I borrow your book?*
*You can use my pen.*
**May** is used to ask or give permission formally. For example:
*May I leave the room please?*
*Yes, you may.*

**Re-write each sentence correctly.**
1. He should of put his books in his locker.
2. Can I eat some cake before the visitors arrive?
3. Paul thinks he never did nothing wrong in his whole life.
4. If I'd had a choice, I would of liked to learn music.
5. Neither Mike or Joe have revised for the exams.
6. You could of won a car in the local raffle. You should of bought a ticket.
7. You can neither come with me or stay in the house alone.
8. I would of taken a taxi if I'd known the bus was so slow.
9. Neither of the two men could of known where I kept my money hidden.
10. Never say nothing to nobody about the fight in the yard.

## (c) Spelling Lists
**1. Words that you might use in the Junior Cert English exam:**

| | | | |
|---|---|---|---|
| advertise | cliché | figurative | onomatopoeia |
| advertisement | comma | genre | pamphlet |
| alliteration | comparison | grammar | paragraph |
| apostrophe | conjunction | image | personification |
| assonance | consonant | imagery | playwright |
| atmosphere | dialogue | metaphor | plural |
| chorus | exclamation | myth | prefix |
| clause | expression | narrative/narrator | preposition |

| | | | |
|---|---|---|---|
| resolution | scene | subordinate | tabloid |
| rhyme | simile | suffix | vocabulary |
| rhythm | soliloquy | synonym | vowel |

## 2. General Spelling List

| | | | |
|---|---|---|---|
| accommodation | development | lovely | receive |
| actually | diamond | marriage | reference |
| alcohol | diary | material | relief |
| although | disappear | meanwhile | remember |
| analyse/analysis | disappoint | miscellaneous | research |
| argument | embarrass | mischief | resources |
| assessment | energy | modern | safety |
| atmosphere | engagement | moreover | Saturday |
| audible | enquire | murmur | secondary |
| audience | environment | necessary | separate |
| autumn | evaluation | nervous | sequence |
| beautiful | evidence | original | shoulder |
| beginning | explanation | outrageous | sincerely |
| believe | February | parallel | skilful |
| beneath | fierce | participation | soldier |
| buried | forty | pattern | stomach |
| business | fulfil | peaceful | straight |
| caught | furthermore | people | strategy |
| chocolate | guard | performance | strength |
| climb | happened | permanent | success |
| column | health | persuade/persuasion | surely |
| concentration | height | physical | surprise |
| conclusion | imaginary | possession | survey |
| conscience | improvise | potential | technique |
| conscious | industrial | preparation | technology |
| consequence | interesting | prioritise | texture |
| continuous | interrupt | process | tomorrow |
| creation | issue | proportion | unfortunately |
| daughter | jealous | proposition | Wednesday |
| decide/decision | knowledge | questionnaire | weight |
| definite | listening | queue | weird |
| design | lonely | reaction | women |

# Junior Certificate ENGLISH

# Indigo 1 & 2

Andrea Costello
John Moriarty

**Indigo 1** is the first in a two-volume series covering Junior Certificate English. It is suitable for First Year students.

- It provides a complete and carefully structured First Year English Ordinary Level course with the emphasis on Literacy Skills in line with the objectives of the new DES National Literacy Strategy.
- Key Feature: double page Contents spread showing the entire contents at a glance.
- A range of extracts in Reading (non-fiction), Fiction, Poetry, Drama/Film and Media, all followed by a wide selection of assignments with attainable targets, to suit a range of levels.
- Guidelines and assignments in Personal and Functional Writing.
- Texts selected feature a mix of traditional favourites, including *The Listeners* (Walter de la Mare) and *Sive* (J B Keane) as well as more modern material, for example *Skulduggery Pleasant* (Derek Landy).
- Packed with literacy building activities. Throughout, the text is interspersed with TASKS designed to develop literacy skills – spelling, proofreading, writing, cloze tests, vocabulary, e.g. 43 Literacy Workouts, 15 Spelling Challenges and 17 Word Scrambles. These interesting exercises are designed to develop student language and literacy skills.

€14.⁹⁵

**Indigo 2** is the second in a two-volume series covering the Junior Certificate English course and is suitable for second- and third-year students.

- Features a wide range of content which supports the implementation of the principles and objectives of the new DES National Literacy Strategy.
- Provides the flexibility to teach across a range of abilities, since the texts have sufficient depth to offer teaching opportunities at more than one level.
- All extracts are followed by an extensive range of questions and assignments covering all levels of comprehension skills.
- The fiction, drama and poetry sections feature a comprehensive mix of accessible material as well as classics such as 'Christmas Morning' (Frank O'Connor), 'The Secret Life of Walter Mitty' (James Thurber), 'The Road Not Taken' (Robert Frost) and 'Mid-Term Break' (Seamus Heaney).
- Packed with resources and exercises which support the teaching and assessment of key literacy skills and strategies.

€19.⁹⁵

**Online Teachers' Resources include:**
- Online textbook available to Teachers choosing it as their class textbook.
- Answers to selected exercises.

**Mentor ebooks**
These textbooks are also available to purchase as eBooks.